PAUL HARVARD

MW00782170

Paul Harvard has enjoy~~~~~~~~~~~~~~~~~, director,
musical director and composer. His work includes award-
winning productions in the West End and for the National
Theatre.

He is a hugely experienced trainer of actors. Currently he is
the Course Leader for the BA Acting at the London College
of Music. Prior to working at LCM he lectured at many of the
other leading drama schools in the UK – notably the Urdang
Academy where he was Head of Musical Theatre for four
years and Rose Bruford where he was Head of Third Year. He
has also taught at Arts Educational, the Drama Centre,
Guildford School of Acting, Trinity Laban, Italia Conti and
Webber Douglas.

Paul is the author of *Acting Through Song: Techniques and
Exercises for Musical-Theatre Actors*, also published by Nick
Hern Books. Paul's approaches to acting through song are
now recognised internationally and he regularly travels abroad
to deliver masterclasses and lectures based on his book.

Vocal range Feb.4.2022

High - D#5   TENOR

low - C2

THE GOOD AUDITION GUIDES

AUDITION SONGS
by Paul Harvard

CONTEMPORARY DUOLOGUES
edited by Trilby James

CLASSICAL MONOLOGUES
edited by Marina Caldarone

CONTEMPORARY MONOLOGUES
edited by Trilby James

CONTEMPORARY MONOLOGUES FOR TEENAGERS
edited by Trilby James

SHAKESPEARE MONOLOGUES
edited by Luke Dixon

SHAKESPEARE MONOLOGUES FOR YOUNG PEOPLE
edited by Luke Dixon

The Good Audition Guides

AUDITION SONGS
FOR MEN

PAUL HARVARD

NICK HERN BOOKS
London
www.nickhernbooks.co.uk

A NICK HERN BOOK

The Good Audition Guides:
Audition Songs for Men
First published in Great Britain in 2020
by Nick Hern Books Limited
The Glasshouse, 49a Goldhawk Road, London W12 8QP

Designed and typeset by Nick Hern Books, London
Printed and bound by Ashford Colour Press, Gosport,
Hampshire

A CIP catalogue record for this book
is available from the British Library

ISBN 978 1 84842 456 2

MIX
Paper from
responsible sources
FSC
www.fsc.org   FSC® C011748

Contents

6

Baritone/Bass

CLASSICAL MUSICAL THEATRE (1925–65)

CONTEMPORARY MUSICAL-THEATRE BALLADS (Post-1965)

PART ONE:
THE KNOWLEDGE

About This Book

If you need to sing in an audition, then this book is for you. It is an easy-to-use, accessible resource that will help you discover the perfect song choice – no matter what your audition needs. You might be applying for a vocational musical-theatre course, or a place on a performing-arts degree. If so, this book will help you find a first-rate, distinctive song that shows off your voice and reveals your full potential. Or you might have an audition for an acting programme. If singing is not your first skill, you will want to find a song that sits comfortably in your range ¯ *that you feel confident with* – but that also highlights your strengths as an actor. The songs you need are identified inside. The book can assist you if you are auditioning for a school production, or for a youth drama group – enabling you to find the song you need to land the role you want. Finally, this book is an invaluable tool if you are already in vocational training, or are a professional actor. It will help you broaden your understanding of the musical-theatre repertoire so you can continuously develop your portfolio of songs, and is a great resource when you need to find the right material for a last-minute casting.

WHAT IS INSIDE?

The book explores fifty songs that have been carefully selected because they work particularly well in audition. For each song there is a detailed, bespoke self-rehearsal guide. These guides contain the sort of information you would receive from sessions with a vocal coach and a director – providing you with the professional expertise and technical advice you need to deliver a high-quality performance. Each guide is like a singing lesson and an acting class rolled into one.

The self-rehearsal guides begin by describing what are commonly known as the given circumstances of the song (see p. 25). They outline how it fits into the narrative arc of the musical, summarise what has happened previously, and provide key information about character and setting. The lyric of the song is then analysed as a piece of dramatic text, helping you develop a clear understanding of the writer's intentions. Potential objectives and actions (see pp. 26–28) are discussed to open up possibilities for the sort of acting choices you might play. The pivotal dramatic moments of the song, called events, are pinpointed where appropriate – and acting tips are provided to help you shape your overall performance.

Alongside the investigation of the acting content, the self-rehearsal guides explore how to tackle the songs from both a musical and vocal perspective. A recommended recording of the song is suggested for you to listen to that can help you learn the music accurately and understand the correct vocal style. This is particularly useful if you don't have access to a singing teacher who can help you learn the music. The vocal range and original key signature of the song are identified, and your choice of accent is discussed. At times, cuts are also suggested, as you will need to shorten some songs for audition. Finally, the guides offer advice on how to deliver the songs vocally and musically. For those looking to deliver a more advanced-level performance, perhaps for a drama-school audition or a professional casting, the technical set-ups and vocal delivery required for the song are examined. These provide an overview of the musculature you should use to ensure your vocal performance is healthy, repeatable, dynamic and stylistically accurate. The technical language in this book is heavily reliant on the work of Jo Estill, the American voice specialist, who died in 2010. The Estill method is a very useful system because it is anatomically specific. It allows you to understand, feel and recreate the precise muscular patterning needed to achieve the different sounds used in musical theatre. In particular, this book frequently references Estill's work on voice qualities (see pp. 30–33), such as Twang and Belt. Advice is also given on musical decisions, such as dynamics and phrasing.

At the end of each guide you will find directions to a suggested website where you can purchase the correct sheet music for the song, as, for copyright reasons, the music and lyrics can't be included in this book.

ADDITIONAL SUPPORT

To support the specific detail of the self-rehearsal guides, at the beginning of the book there are three extended chapters that contain overarching advice that will help you to prepare, rehearse and perform any of the songs. The first chapter provides definitions for the acting, singing and musical terminology you will encounter in the book. The second contains a series of easy-to-follow acting and singing exercises that will help you to improve your vocal delivery, and to produce a truthful and spontaneous performance of the lyric. The final chapter provides advice about audition technique. It deals with issues like making a good impression when entering the room, communicating musical instructions to the pianist, singing to a panel, and responding to redirection.

CHOOSING A SONG THAT SUITS YOUR VOCAL RANGE

The first factor you need to consider when choosing a song for any audition is: 'Does it suit my vocal range?' The song material in this book is divided into two sections: Tenor/High Baritone and Baritone/Bass. The first section is generally for men with higher voices, the second for those who mainly have a deeper sound. These terms – Tenor, Baritone and Bass – categorise a singer not only by their pitch range, but also reflect where their voice has the best timbre, where it sits most comfortably and resonantly. Modern vocal training allows all singers to expand their upper ranges through exercise. So as a baritone, for example, you may find you are able to sing higher than some tenors – but are still classed as a baritone because your voice sounds best in a lower register.

Because of these anomalies, you may find that, if you are a baritone, some of the songs on the Tenor/High Baritone list may also work for you. Equally, if you usually sing tenor, you might find songs on the Baritone/Bass list that you can use. Therefore, to aid you with your decision-making, each song has its precise vocal range outlined in the self-rehearsal guide. If you don't know your own vocal range, it is worth asking a friend or teacher who plays the piano to check this with you. Typical vocal ranges for the four voice types are as follows:

Tenor: C3 to C5
(one octave below middle C to one octave above middle C)

High Baritone (sometimes called 'Baritenor'): A2 to C5
(the second A below middle C to one octave above middle C)

Baritone: A2 to G4
(the second A below middle C to the G above middle C)

Bass: E2 to E4
(second E below middle C to the E above middle C)

TRANSPOSING SONGS

Sometimes actors consider transposing a song into a lower key if it is too high for them. Whilst many sheet-music websites – which sell the music you will need for your audition – offer this facility, it is not something to be recommended. An experienced audition panel – who will know the repertoire well – are able to tell if you are not singing your song in its usual key. If you change the key signature of a song so you don't have to sing the high G, they will assume it is because you can't. You may as well enter the audition with a placard saying: 'I can't sing above an F♯!' Therefore you are well-advised to choose a song you can deliver in the original key – which is indicated in the self-rehearsal guides – in the vast majority of circumstances.

A final point to consider when thinking about range is ensuring that your chosen piece doesn't stretch you to breaking point. For a song to be advisable you need to be able hit the top note when you are nervous, feeling a bit off-colour, and at nine o'clock in the morning. Don't select a song if you can only deliver the big belt when you are feeling on top form, have your fingers crossed, and the wind is blowing from the south-west!

CHOOSING A SONG THAT SUITS YOUR CASTING TYPE

Whilst it is essential to choose a song that sits within your vocal range, it is also highly advantageous to pick material that reflects your 'casting type'. This term refers to the type of characters that you would most likely be cast as professionally – because they are of a similar age, physicality, personality and life experience to yourself. Traditionally your casting type would also have been defined by ethnicity, but with the advent of 'colour-blind' or 'non-traditional' casting, many contemporary productions commendably choose to ignore the ethnicity of the actors in stories in which race is not germane. An increasing number of productions are also casting 'gender-blind'. Although this is to be much encouraged in other circumstances, songs written for women have not been included in this book due to the technical difficulties presented by differences in the male/female vocal range. However, if you are particularly interested in singing a song originally written for the female voice, you can find some great material in the companion book *Audition Songs for Women*.

Reflecting your casting type in your song choice is particularly important in professional castings, as it allows the audition panel to sense whether you might be suitable for a particular role. If you are auditioning for *Les Misérables*, do they see you as a Marius or an Enjolras? If you have a casting for *Grease*, are you right for Danny Zuko or for Kenickie? Of course, if you are applying for a place at a drama school, you will not be auditioning for a specific role, but these questions are still valid. If you choose a song that suits your casting type it will give you the best opportunity to show the tutors your potential, and reveal that you have an understanding of yourself as a developing actor.

To help you decide which of the songs in this book might suit you best, look at the 'Choose this song if' section at the top of each self-rehearsal guide, which provides an overview of the character and helps you to understand quickly if it may work for you.

UNDERSTANDING YOUR CASTING

When I teach in drama schools, I often lead Professional Development classes for students who are preparing to enter the industry. A question I am regularly asked by final-year students is: 'What is my casting?' In helping them to answer this query I encourage them to look at the roles they have performed before, particularly those they felt they did well in, and to try and identify any commonalities they notice about those characters. If you have played parts before then try this task for yourself: you may find it gives you a clearer comprehension of your casting type.

If you have not had much previous performance experience, another way to gain an insight into your likely casting is to consider how you relate to some of the archetypes we see in plays and films. Are you the romantic lead, the villain, or the sidekick? Would you play the soldier or the solicitor? The chimney sweep or the aristocrat? You should also consider whether you look your age, or could be cast as someone younger or older. Decide if you have a modern, contemporary appearance that would work for musicals like *Spring Awakening* or *Hamilton*, or whether your style and demeanour is more suitable for period pieces like *Carousel* or *My Fair Lady*. You may be right for both – depending on how you choose to behave, dress and style your hair. These are all factors in understanding what type of material may suit you.

But perhaps the best way to understand your casting type is to ask some close friends, whose opinions you trust, how you come across in day-to-day life. Choose people who you think will not only be honest, but also sensitive. It can be challenging to hear how you come across to others, particularly if the answers are not entirely flattering and were not what you were expecting. Get them to answer the following questions about you, and encourage them to be as frank as possible:

- How old do you look? (Get them to express this in range of five years, for example: 15 to 20, or 33 to 38.)

- If they were to choose five adjectives to describe the way you come across, what would they be? (For example: inquisitive, shy, flirtatious, flamboyant, confrontational.)

- If they were to name three professions you could convincingly play, what would they be? (For example: a coal miner, an estate agent, a doctor.)

After this exercise you should have a much clearer understanding of your casting type – or what is sometimes called your 'unique selling point' (USP) – and therefore a better sense of what songs might work for you.

CHOOSING A SONG THAT IS THE APPROPRIATE MUSICAL STYLE

If you are auditioning for a particular production, it is beneficial to select material that has a similar style to the show you are trying out for. This helps the panel determine whether you can sing and act in an appropriate manner for that particular score. To aid your understanding of which composers and lyricists wrote in a similar stylistic vein, outlined below are some of the major sub-genres of musical theatre featured in this book, their characteristics, and the composers and lyricists who wrote in that particular style. To aid you, the sub-genre of musical theatre that each song belongs to is indicated in the self-rehearsal guides.

Note: If you are auditioning for a drama school, rather than for a production, you will not normally need to restrict yourself to a particular style of musical theatre – unless this is specified in the school's audition requirements. In auditions for vocational courses, you are normally best advised to choose any musical-theatre song that most suits your voice and personality.

MUSICAL COMEDY

When: The era of musical comedy was between approximately 1925 and 1943.

Key Composers/Lyricists: Cole Porter, Irving Berlin, Richard Rodgers and Lorenz Hart, Jerome Kern and Oscar Hammerstein II, Harry Warren, Kurt Weill, and the Gershwin brothers.

Acting Style: Musical comedy had its roots in the bawdy world of vaudeville and burlesque and, as a result, these first American musicals were often little more than a series of popular songs, comic sketches and dances strung together by a tenuous storyline. The frothy, light-hearted writing of this period was symptomatic of the prevailing social circumstances of the time, as it offered audiences of the 1920s and '30s some escape from their memories of the First World War and the harsh realities of the Great Depression. Because it is generally upbeat, to act this material well you need to find real pleasure in the linguistic ingenuity of lyricists like Cole Porter and Lorenz Hart. You should really taste the rhythms and rhymes in your mouth, so the panel can share in the wit and brilliance of the lyrics. Your performance usually needs to be positive, uplifting, and laced with a sense of cheek and fun.

Musical Style: The songs of this period tended to be heavily influenced by jazz, and many of them have gone on to become famous 'standards'. They therefore lend themselves to a jazz singer's interpretative skills, such as the ability to back-phrase, to 'bend' the pitch of notes, and to sing quartertones (a note that lies between two notes on a piano). In the terminology of singing teacher Jo Estill (see pp. 30–33), musical comedy requires a generous usage of the Speech and Twang voice qualities, with some Belt at the end of the big show-stopping numbers. The use of Sob and Cry qualities tends to be limited to the romantic ballads.

BOOK MUSICALS: THE 'GOLDEN AGE'

When: The 'Golden Age' of musical theatre can be defined as being between approximately 1943 and 1965. Some landmark 'book musicals', such as *Show Boat* and *Porgy and Bess*, came before this period, but the landscape of musical theatre is commonly perceived to have been revolutionised with the opening of *Oklahoma!* in 1943.

Key Composers/Lyricists: Richard Rodgers and Oscar Hammerstein II, Alan Jay Lerner and Frederick Loewe, Jerry Bock and Sheldon Harnick, Leonard Bernstein, Jule Styne and Frank Loesser.

Acting Style: Book musicals, which were initially pioneered by lyricist Oscar Hammerstein II, tackled more serious dramatic material than was the case in musical comedy. The songs in book musicals were written to emerge organically out of the scene and to further the plot. In some senses the book musical is the genre's equivalent of psychological realism – Stanislavsky's term for the believable representation of life on the stage. Although you could argue that musicals are not a realistic style of performance – because the characters are singing when they wouldn't do so in life – a key to the dramaturgy of a book musical is that the characters are not *aware* they are singing. In their heads, they are engaging in an ordinary conversation, or are voicing aloud their internal thoughts. The audience just hears these words as sung text, rather than a spoken scene or soliloquy. So when you act this type of song, your aim is to be as truthful and believable as possible, and to perform a series of actions that are psychologically coherent for the character. The acting style is what we might call 'musical realism'.

Musical Style: The vocal set-up required for the work of Rodgers and Hammerstein, Lerner and Loewe, and Bock and

Harnick is known as 'legit' singing. Legit singing is similar to a classical set-up; it can require you to be able to sing long phrases with a legato line and a lowered larynx. In Estill terms, a legit set-up makes considerable use of Cry and Sob qualities. In the book musicals penned by these writing teams, Speech quality is usually confined to the verses and pre-choruses at the beginning of songs. On the contrary, the musical style of Bernstein, Styne and Loesser had a strong connection with jazz and big-band music, so a legit style is less relevant. Speech, Twang and Belt qualities are more appropriate for these jazz-based composers, and in the specific case of Bernstein, Opera quality as well.

CONCEPT MUSICALS

When: Concept musicals were most prevalent in American and British musical theatre from roughly 1960 to 1990.

Key Composers/Lyricists: John Kander and Fred Ebb, Stephen Sondheim, and Andrew Lloyd Webber.

Acting Style: From the beginning of the 1960s, musical-theatre writers began to deconstruct the formula of the integrated musical play established by Hammerstein – in which the songs and dances emerged organically out of the plot and furthered the action. In musicals like Stephen Sondheim's *Company* and the film version of Kander and Ebb's *Cabaret*, the use of song was akin to the ideas of German playwright and director Bertolt Brecht. The songs, rather than moving the story forward, cut across it and commented upon it. To act songs from concept musicals, you therefore not only need to understand and be able to play the character's objectives, you must have the skills to interpret and communicate the themes and/or politics of the writing. To do this successfully, concept musicals often require the use of 'Epic' acting techniques, such as direct address (see p. 30), narration and the use of a heightened vocal and physical transformation.

Musical Style: Concept musicals varied greatly in their compositional styles during that thirty-year period, to an extent that it is nearly impossible to define a universal vocal style that would be appropriate. What can be agreed is that Speech quality became ever more vital, as the ability to communicate the themes articulated in the lyric often became more important than the beauty of the singing voice – particularly with the work of Sondheim.

CONTEMPORARY MUSICAL THEATRE

When: From 1965 to the present day.

Key Composers/Lyricists: Andrew Lloyd Webber, Alain Boublil and Claude-Michel Schönberg, Lin-Manuel Miranda, Jason Robert Brown, Andrew Lippa, Jeanine Tesori, Stephen Flaherty and Lynn Ahrens, Stephen Schwartz, Richard Maltby Jr. and David Shire, Alan Menken, Benj Pasek and Justin Paul, William Finn, Elton John, Cy Coleman, and Howard Goodall.

Acting Style: The performance style of contemporary musicals is now very broad. In the 1980s and 1990s there was a trend for productions that became known as 'mega-musicals', shows that were largely sung-through with minimal or no dialogue – and that had lavish production values. But in the last twenty years you will also find shows that are written in traditional book-musical format, like *Wicked* and *In the Heights*, and concept musicals, like *The Last Five Years* and *Spring Awakening*. As such, it is impossible to define a single acting style that is appropriate for contemporary musical theatre – the approach required can only be defined by looking at the form of a particular musical.

Musical Style: From the late 1960s there has been a gradual shift in the musical DNA of Broadway and West End musicals, in that the majority of scores are now influenced by pop or rock music – rather than jazz. (Shows written after 1980 that still use jazz music as their basis, such as Lippa's

The Wild Party and Flaherty and Ahrens's *Ragtime*, tend to be period pieces.) When working on contemporary, pop-based musical-theatre songs, Speech and Twang qualities are the staple set-ups, with Belt used for moments of passion. Cry is also used, though less frequently. Alongside scores where the pop idiom is clear are other musicals that require a different vocal set-up – musicals that have sometimes been classed, a little unkindly perhaps, as 'poperetta'. In musicals like *Les Misérables* and *The Phantom of the Opera*, the musical structures are those of pop songs, but in performance they are often delivered with a vocal set-up that sounds something like classical singing (though rarely what Estill would define as an Opera quality). As a contemporary version of legit singing, this set-up is based around a Speech quality, but is modified to include a lowered larynx, which makes it sound more classical.

The Terminology

ACTING TERMINOLOGY

In order to take best advantage of the advice and exercises in this book, you will need to understand some of the key concepts and terminology relating to performance that are used. Below is a glossary of the most important, beginning with those related to acting.

Given Circumstances

This term, from Russian practitioner Konstantin Stanislavsky, refers to the environmental and societal conditions of a song or scene that influence the actions and behaviour of the character. The given circumstances are derived by answering fundamental questions from the character's perspective, such as: Who am I? Where am I? When is it? What has happened previously?

When working on a full-length production, the answers to these questions are usually ascertained by deriving information through an analysis of the entire script, from historical and social research, and by informed, imaginative choices where no definite answer is possible from the first two approaches. In this book, the elements of the given circumstances that are most important to the delivery of the song are those outlined. On occasion, when the given circumstances of the song as they exist in the musical are unhelpful – or there are none, because the song is from a revue show without a through-narrative – then a set of given circumstances have been invented to make the song easier for you to perform in an audition context.

Objectives

An objective is what the character wants. For example, during 'Soliloquy' from *Carousel*, Billy's objective, what he wants, is: to decide what to do now that he is going to become a father. In 'Why, God, Why?' from *Miss Saigon*, Chris, an American GI, is feeling conflicted because he has just fallen in love with Kim, who is Vietnamese, when he was so close to finishing his tour of Vietnam. His objective in this song is: to get God to explain why he brought Kim into his life in this untimely manner.

Units

A unit is a section of dramatic text. Different practitioners divide a text into units in different ways. In my own practice, particularly with song lyrics, I have always found it most useful to start a fresh unit each time the character has a new objective. Here is an example of uniting from the song 'Hello, Little Girl' from *Into the Woods* by Stephen Sondheim:

UNIT 1

Look at that flesh,
Pink and plump.
Hello, little girl…
Tender and fresh,
Not one lump,
Hello, little girl,
This one's especially lush,
Delicious…

Mmmh…

UNIT 2

Hello, little girl,
What's your rush?
You're missing all the flowers.
The sun won't set for hours,
Take your time.

This song is sung by the hungry Wolf as he stalks Little Red Riding Hood. In the first unit he is talking to himself, and she can't hear him. His objective here is: to get himself salivating at the prospect of a tasty meal. During the second unit he talks directly to Little Red Riding Hood. His new objective, starting at the word 'hello', is: to convince her not to run away.

Trying to act a lyric in its entirety can sometimes be a daunting challenge, but dividing a song into units in this way – and by knowing what the character is trying to achieve in each section – makes it much easier to perform. As Stanislavsky famously suggested, it is like breaking a cooked turkey into pieces to allow you to consume it piece by piece, rather than trying to eat the whole thing at once.

Actioning

If an objective is what the character wants, then an action is the means they use to get what they want. An action always takes the form of a transitive verb. In the process known as actioning, which was first developed by the American acting teacher Stella Adler, you assign a different transitive verb to each sentence of the text. This system can help you find variety and specificity in your performance, making it more engaging to watch. An action should always help you achieve your objective and should fit into the following format:

I [action] you.

For example, in the song 'Willkommen' from *Cabaret*, the objective of the Emcee is: to welcome the audience to the Kit Kat Klub. If you were playing the Emcee, actions you could play on the clientele of the club might include: I greet you, I entertain you, I intrigue you, I amuse you, I provoke you.

When the character is singing onstage alone, the format of actions becomes as follows; if they are singing to themselves:

I [action] myself.

Or if they are singing to a higher power such as Fate:

I [action] Fate.

During the song 'Gethsemane' from *Jesus Christ Superstar*, Jesus is talking to God, his father. His objective is: to get God to change his mind about sending Jesus to his impending crucifixion. An actor performing this song might use actions such as: I challenge God, I implore God, I urge God, I hurry God, I defy God.

Circles of Attention

Your primary function as an actor is as a storyteller. Making good use of what are called 'circles of attention' can help clarify the narrative of your song and ensure your choices make logical sense to the audience or audition panel. This term was originated by Stanislavsky, and refers to the outer limit of where your focus and awareness is placed at any one time. There are three circles of attention. In the first circle, you focus very tightly on yourself. So if you are working in this circle of attention you might be looking at part of your own body, such as your hands, or something extremely close to you, like the floor beneath your feet. When we are remembering something, or dissecting a problem, we often look in the first circle, as our eyes tend to focus on points very close to us. When you are working in the second circle, you are looking at something within the playing space – or in this case, the audition room. If you are looking at the panel, for example, you would be working in the second circle. You are using the third circle when you are looking at something imaginary outside of the space, like the stars or the sky. When using the third circle, you should always see something in your imagination. Human beings often see memories, or picture a future event, in this circle.

Circles of attention are important, in that they enable those watching to infer meaning into what you are doing. When you are on an audition panel, it can be off-putting to watch a singer staring into the middle distance for no particular reason, or whose focus is flitting around nonsensically. Where appropriate, advice on this aspect of performance is given in the self-rehearsal guides.

Acting is Reacting

'Acting is reacting' is one of the most commonly used phrases in contemporary actor-training. As it is central to some of the advice given in this book with regards to acting through song, it merits explanation here.

This idea is centred around the conceit that, in order to perform truthfully, you must act upon genuine internal impulses. These impulses occur when you respond spontaneously to an external stimulus in the moment of acting the song, rather than making a predetermined choice. In many acting methodologies, notably the work of American acting teacher Sanford Meisner, the stimuli for these impulses are usually your fellow actors. When following this key principle of his training, you simply pay attention to their performance and respond. This approach can lead to very truthful, organic work – but must be adapted for audition, where there are rarely other actors to respond to.

Instead, in the audition room, you must generate what director and acting theorist Declan Donnellan calls a 'target'. To describe it somewhat simplistically, a target is a picture that you see in your imagination, and falls into one of four categories. It can be an object that is in the character's field of vision. For example, in 'Oh, What a Beautiful Mornin'' from *Oklahoma!*, Curly sings about the beauty of his surroundings, so the actor playing Curly's targets should include the meadow, the cattle, the willow tree. In the real world, Curly would actually be able to see what's around him; as an actor you must imagine them. The second kind of target is an image that relates to the character's memory. If I ask you to remember the last film you saw, after a second or two, you will see an image from that film. That is how human memory works – it is always preceded by an image. So when a character remembers something, if you want to act truthfully, you must emulate this process. In 'Empty Chairs at Empty Tables' from *Les Misérables*, the actor playing Marius, like the actor playing Curly, needs to imagine his surroundings – in this case the ABC Café. But he also needs to see targets from the character's memory, such as the bodies of his dead friends at the barricade. The third kind of target is an image that is prompted by the character thinking about the future. Again this reflects life. If I ask you to envision what you will do next weekend, an image will pop into your head. You might see the face of the friend you plan to meet, or the place you intend to visit. The fourth kind of target involves imagining the behaviour of another character. You might see them light a cigarette, begin to cry, or shrug their shoulders. Identifying what you need to see will be crucial when preparing the acting performance of your song, as when you begin to see detailed, well-chosen targets, it will provide you with the stimulus you need to respond organically in the moment.

Direct Address

Direct address is a technique that involves you talking straight to the audience or, in this scenario, the audition panel. Rather than pretending that the audience doesn't exist and hiding behind an imaginary 'fourth wall', in direct address the actor makes eye contact with those watching and seeks to change them – by playing their objectives and actions on the spectator. The use of direct address is incredibly useful when delivering certain audition songs – such as comedy numbers, narrative pieces, or a lyric in which the character is seeking answers to a problem – as it can be engaging to watch and can help the panel feel included in the performance.

ESTILL'S SINGING TERMINOLOGY: THE VOICE QUALITIES

The methodology of the late American vocal expert Jo Estill is now predominant in contemporary singing training in the United Kingdom. The methodology she developed has become invaluable because of its specificity – it is a system that allows you to understand, feel and recreate the precise muscular patterning needed to achieve certain identifiable sounds. One of the central tenets of her work is the six 'voice qualities'. A voice quality is a vocal set-up created by manipulating the movable structures of the vocal mechanism into a particular configuration in order to produce a desired, repeatable sound. Although most singing teachers would acknowledge that there are more than six voice qualities, in this book, the six that Estill documented are used as a means to recommend appropriate vocal choices for the songs. A brief outline of some of the main features of the six qualities are given below, along with a recommended example of each that you can listen to. The recordings are all from original cast recordings. In the next chapter there are some exercises that explore the practical application of Estill's ideas if you are interested in utilising some of the more complex technical details in your work.

Note: A detailed analysis of the vocal anatomy is beyond the remit of this book. However, if you want to discover more about the movable structures of the vocal apparatus, and the muscular set-ups of the voice qualities, then these are discussed in detail in *Singing and the Actor* by Gillyanne Kayes.

Cry Quality

Cry quality is a quiet, pure sound, useful for conveying character choices such as innocence, tenderness and thoughtfulness. A clear example of this quality is Mandy Patinkin singing George's section of the duet 'Beautiful' from *Sunday in the Park with George*. The key components of the set-up are a tilted thyroid cartilage (see p. 39), a raised larynx and thin vocal folds (the two small bands of muscle inside the larynx that vibrate and make contact in order to make sound).

Sob Quality

This quality is very similar to Cry quality in its muscular set-up, the only difference being that, in Sob quality, you have a lowered laryngeal position – which makes the sound darker and more intense. It can be used to communicate moments of sadness, grief and longing. A good example of Sob is Michael Crawford singing the opening verses of 'The Music of the Night' from *The Phantom of the Opera*.

Speech Quality

Speech quality is a fundamental sound of contemporary musical theatre. It is particularly useful when you want to focus the listener on the lyric, rather than the beauty of the voice, as it helps make your singing sound conversational. A clear example of this sound is Jonathan Pryce singing 'The American Dream' from *Miss Saigon*. As its name suggests, Speech is similar, in the way it sounds and is produced, to the manner in which many people talk. Its main features are a neutral laryngeal position, thick vocal folds, and a neutral tongue position.

Twang Quality

Twang quality is a very prevalent sound amongst singers working on contemporary musical theatre, particularly if it is an American show. Often mistakenly classed as purely a nasal sound, Twang can be either nasal or oral, depending on whether the soft palate is in a mid-position or is raised. (The soft palate controls whether sound is directed through your mouth, or through your nose, or through both; see p. 43.) A good example of Twang quality is Ty Taylor singing 'King of the World' from *Songs for a New World*. Some of the key features of the set-up include thin vocal folds, a raised larynx and a high back of the tongue. What differentiates it from Cry quality is that you narrow a fold of mucous membrane inside the pharynx called the aryepiglottic sphincter (or the AES for short). This creates an additional resonator, which gives your sound more edge so that it carries easily across large spaces.

Belt Quality

Described by Estill herself as 'happy yelling', Belt quality is the sung form of a shout. You would rarely belt more than one or two notes in a song, as the quality is normally used to highlight the most passionate and dramatic musical moments. A good example of belt is Terrence Mann singing the last note of 'If I Can't Love Her' from the stage version of Disney's *Beauty and the Beast*. The defining features of the quality include thick vocal folds, a high larynx, a tilted cricoid cartilage (which allows you to safely sing high in the voice with thick folds) and an anchored torso (see p. 51).

Opera Quality

A good example of Opera quality being used in a musical is Howard Keel singing 'Bless your Beautiful Hide' from the film version of *Seven Brides for Seven Brothers*. Commonplace in the opera house, the quality is less frequently used in musicals and would only be used for scores where it is stylistically appropriate, such as parts of *Sweeney Todd*, and in some productions, *West Side Story*. Opera is a mixed quality, comprising Speech and Twang qualities, but with thyroid tilt added to sweeten the sound, a lowered larynx to 'cover' the twang resonance, and a strong voice/body connection.

Falsetto Quality

Falsetto quality is very useful for displaying moments of vulnerability, fragility and reflection. A good example of this quality is Michael Crawford singing the Phantom's quiet section in 'All I Ask of You' from *The Phantom of the Opera*. Falsetto, as defined by Estill, uses an aspirate onset (where some of the breath escapes before the vocal folds vibrate) and vocal folds that are stiff – so they vibrate, but don't meet fully.

MUSICAL TERMINOLOGY

Musical instructions are traditionally written in Italian. The key terms used in the book are translated for you below. If you wish to understand others that may appear on sheet music you purchase, then these can easily and quickly be defined using Google.

- *Colla voce*: literally means 'follow the solo voice'. Wherever this is indicated on your music, it means that you are able to sing in a free manner, and the pianist will follow you.

- *Crescendo*: a gradual increase in volume.

- *Decrescendo*: a gradual decrease in volume.

- *Key signature*: a combination of flats ($\flat$) or sharps ($\sharp$) written at the beginning of each stave to indicate the key of a song.

- *Legato*: smooth and connected, without a break between notes.

- *Più mosso*: more quickly (in terms of tempo).

- *Rubato*: literally means 'robbed or stolen' time. At points where this is marked you have freedom to speed up and slow down the tempo at your artistic discretion.

- *Staccato*: short and detached, a note separated from that which follows. Staccato notes are indicated by placing a dot above or below the notehead.

- *Time signature*: an indication of rhythm recorded as two numbers, one on top of the other. The top number denotes the number of beats per bar, with the bottom number defining the note-length of each beat.

The Exercises

SINGING EXERCISES

In the first chapter, we discussed the various factors you must take into consideration when choosing a song. Once you have made a choice, if you are to do yourself justice in the audition, you must then prepare and rehearse that material thoroughly. In order to do this, it is advisable that you spend some time practising with a pianist. However, as this is not always possible, outlined in this chapter are a series of fundamental exercises that you can do on your own, and apply to any number, in order to develop your vocal delivery and improve your acting through song.

For some of the exercises you should work with a backing track to ensure you are working in the correct key. You can access backing tracks for many of these songs online, or you can ask a friend or teacher who plays the piano to record the accompaniment for you.

The technical singing exercises are divided into two categories: Fundamental Exercises, which are suitable for any singer, and Further Exercises, for more advanced material and the more experienced vocalist.

Your Working Copy

To undertake the work in this chapter you will need two copies of the music. The first will be eventually be marked up for the audition pianist (see p. 73). The second will be your own personal working copy – on which you can make notes as you undertake the following exercises.

FUNDAMENTAL EXERCISES

The following exercises are suitable for all singers.

Marking Your Breath

Your first rehearsal task when you start work on a song should be to decide at which points in the lyric you are going to breathe. You should record these breath-points on your working copy by marking them with small ticks in pencil above the stave. (You shouldn't put breath-marks on the pianist's copy.) It is helpful and important to make these choices *before* you begin any practical work, because, as soon as you start to rehearse a song, your body forms habits. If you make informed choices about where to breathe before you begin practising – and then repeat those choices each time you work on the song – your intended breath-patterns will become part of your muscle memory. This approach will prove to be invaluable, as the last thing the panel want to see in the audition room is you thinking about your breathing. They want to see you acting through song. If you fail to make these decisions before you begin practising, you may find you form bad habits during your early rehearsals – such as breathing in the middle of words or phrases – that can be problematic to rectify and lead to a poor interpretation of the song.

But how do you decide where to breathe? Phrasing your song effectively – and artistically – is an important part of your craft as a singer. In theatre songs, the primary consideration when making choices about phrasing is that the sense of the lyric is communicated – so you should begin by looking at the punctuation. To help make the thought process clear, you should breathe in at the beginning of a new sentence, as it indicates the start of a new thought. Work through your music, marking a breath after each full stop, exclamation mark or question mark. Sometimes, sentences may be too long to sing in one breath and you will need to mark in additional breaths. The composer and lyricist will indicate where these might be necessary in one of the following ways:

1. By using a comma or semicolon.

2. By adding a musical rest in the middle of the sentence.

3. By using a capital letter in the middle of a sentence.

At times you will also need to breathe at these points, at other points it will not be necessary. It is about applying common sense.

Abdominal Release

Once you have marked all of the breath-points, you want to imbed your chosen phrasing into your muscle memory. Before you can do this, it is important to understand a process known as abdominal release. Try the following awareness exercise, which is a technique advocated by singing teacher Janice Chapman called Accent Method breathing:

1. Place your right hand on your abdomen, with your thumb on your navel and the rest of the hand below.

2. Make three short 'z' sounds with an accent on the first sound (i.e. ZZ, zz, zz). With each sound, draw the navel towards the spine till the abdominal wall is pulled in. *Note:* You shouldn't relax the abdominals in between sounds; the abdominal wall should be moving further towards the spine with each sound.

3. After the third 'z' sound, immediately and completely release the abdominal wall so it relaxes over your waistband. This moment of relaxation, where the abdominal wall recoils, is an abdominal release.

An important fact that sometimes confuses untrained singers is this: the abdominal release *is* your in-breath. You don't need to breathe in once you have released; the breath has entered the body, filling your lungs with air. When you release the abdominal wall, the diaphragm flattens and moves downwards. At the same time the intercostal muscles move the ribcage upwards and outwards, increasing the size of the chest cavity. This lowers the internal air pressure in your lungs, causing air from outside the body (which is now of a higher density) to rush in to balance the pressure.

Sirening

Now you have an understanding of abdominal release, you are ready to programme your decisions about breathing into your muscle memory. A good way to do this is by 'sirening' the melody. Sirening – which takes its name from the sound of an ambulance or a fire engine – is a vocal exercise that involves gliding through pitch on an 'ng' sound. When you siren, the sides of your tongue should remain in contact with your upper molars and the soft palate should be lowered. The exercise is as follows:

1. Stand in front of a mirror. This will enable you to monitor the movements of your abdominals in your reflection. Ensure your feet are parallel and directly underneath your hips. Your knees should be soft and your neck long. Place your hand on your abdominal wall as in the previous awareness exercise.

2. Siren through the melody on an 'ng' sound. Use a piano, a backing track or a cast recording to ensure you remain in the right key. When you are sirening, ensure the sound is as quiet as possible. Keep the sides of your tongue against your molars as discussed.

3. Every time you reach one of the breath-points you have marked, release the abdominal wall, as you felt in the awareness exercise. Monitor the movements of the abdominal wall with your hand and in the mirror. When you are managing breath successfully you will feel the abdominal wall moving slowly inwards as you sing. The abdominals will then release forwards at the end of the phrase, to allow the breath to drop in. The longer the phrase, the more you will feel the navel travelling towards the spine. Importantly, you don't need to initiate this inward movement consciously – the body will do it for you. *You should never deliberately pull the abdominals in when you are singing.* Engaging in 'abdominal pumping' only serves to force the air out more quickly. Not only does this mean you run out of breath, it increases the pressure under your vocal folds, which can cause problems such as a constricted (raspy or gravelly) sound, cracking on top notes, and trauma to the vocal folds.

4. Complete the exercise for the entire song.

5. If you are struggling to access your abdominal release whilst standing up, you can try the exercise in alternative positions. You can sit on the edge of a chair with your legs wide apart, your feet planted firmly on the ground, and with a lengthened spine and neck. Working in this position can help you access your release more fully. You can also explore the exercise on all-fours – where the effect of gravity will assist your release – or by leaning your back against the wall with your feet about twenty centimetres away from the wall and your knees slightly bent.

6. Repeat the entire exercise several times until the release feels habitual.

Targeting Breaks in the Voice: the Thyroid Cartilage

Sirening the melody is an excellent initial exercise for working on a new song. Not only does it programme abdominal release into your muscle memory, it also has the same effect on the movements of your larynx (sometimes colloquially referred to as 'the voice box', the larynx is the organ in your neck which houses your vocal folds – the muscles which vibrate when you sing).

When you sing, your larynx changes position in two key ways as you progress through a song. Firstly, as the pitch rises and falls, your larynx moves up and down correspondingly. (If you gently hold your larynx with your fingers and siren on an 'ng' sound from the bottom of your range to the top and down again, you will notice how the larynx moves in relation to the pitch.) The second key laryngeal movement is that of the thyroid cartilage. To locate your thyroid cartilage run your index finger from the centre of your chin slowly down your neck. Stop at the first point of cartilage you encounter. This cartilage, in the centre of the larynx – which is sometimes called the 'Adam's apple' – is the thyroid cartilage. It usually sits in a horizontal position when you are speaking, but when you speak or sing in higher pitches it can tilt in a downward and forwards motion. When in a tilted position, the thyroid cartilage, as it is attached to the vocal folds, causes them to stretch and become thinner. This enables you to access higher pitches, makes your sound quieter and sweeter, and is a factor in helping you access vibrato. (If you hold the thyroid gently between your thumb and index finger and make a whimpering sound like a puppy, you will feel the thyroid tilt.) The movement of the thyroid cartilage from a horizontal to a tilted position is perhaps the most important in singing – and the previous exercise of sirening through the melody can help to make it smooth and controlled.

However, sometimes controlling your thyroid tilt can remain challenging. You may find at certain points of the song you flip from a horizontal to a tilted position – leading to a 'break' in your voice. This can often occur when you jump from a lower note to a higher note. At these moments you may experience a noticeable, and unwanted, shift in your vocal quality – like you are moving from a 'chest voice' to a 'head voice'. These terms are becoming outdated in modern singing training. A more accurate anatomical analysis is that, because of poor thyroid control, you are flipping from singing with thicker vocal folds to thinner vocal folds – or even that your vocal folds stop closing fully as you ascend in pitch and you end up singing in a Falsetto quality. To help finesse these transitions – and eradicate breaks in your voice – try the following exercise. As an example, I have described how you would practise the octave leap at the beginning of the chorus of 'Somewhere Over the Rainbow' from *The Wizard of Oz* – but the exercise would apply for any problematic interval between two notes.

1. Identify the correct pitches for the two notes you are targeting, either by using a piano or by listening to a recording. It is vital that you are practising in the right key.

2. Slide from the bottom note to the top note on a continuous 'ng' sound. (So in this example, you would slide from the note for the syllable 'some' to the note for 'where'.) Do this as quietly as possible, keeping the back of your neck long. Make sure you are not contracting the abdominal wall as you go up in pitch. Repeat this stage several times until you are able to control the slide and there are no sudden shifts in the sound quality.

3. Repeat the slide, but this time, instead of using the 'ng' sound, use the vowel of the bottom note. In this example, as the bottom note is the syllable 'some' you would there be sliding

on an 'uh' vowel. As you do so, keep the tip of the tongue behind your bottom front teeth. Repeat this stage until the slide is smooth and controlled.

4. Repeat stage 3, but now halfway through the slide move from the bottom vowel to the top vowel. In this example, you would therefore slide from an 'uh' vowel (for 'some') to an 'air' vowel (for 'where'), i.e. 'uh-air'. Try to keep the tongue as still as possible as you shift vowels.

5. Now sing the whole phrase with the actual words but still include the slide in the sound, i.e. 'Some-(*slide*)-where over the rainbow'. When you can do this without flipping, you will be successfully tilting your thyroid cartilage.

6. Finally, sing the phrase normally without sounding the slide – but still experience the same sensation you felt when the slide was included.

7. Repeat for all of the problematic intervals in the song.

Managing Breath

When working with new students who have had little prior training, I find that one of their most common concerns is about breath. They often fixate about not having enough breath to sing a long phrase or note. The warning words of their junior-school music teacher – *'Make sure you take a nice big breath'* – are lurking somewhere at the back of their minds. Lack of breath is actually rarely an issue in singing – contemporary research shows that vocal problems are more commonly caused when the singer uses *too much* breath.

The first principle of voice is contact – i.e. the vocal folds must meet for sound to be produced. Make the following sounds on a comfortable pitch and volume: 'oh oh' and 'eh eh'. If you focus on the muscular movements occurring inside of your larynx you will become aware of contact taking place as you make the sounds – this is the vocal folds joining. If you use too much breath pressure it can disrupt this efficient closure of the vocal folds, as the excess breath can blast the vocal folds apart. For example, when you try to sing a high note and you 'crack' – i.e. the sound momentarily cuts outs – this is because the subglottic pressure (the breath pressure created underneath your vocal folds when they close) became too great and the vocal folds were forced apart – so the sound stopped.

A major cause of too much subglottic pressure is what we previously described as 'abdominal pumping'. This is when you deliberately pull in the outer muscles of your abdominal wall. These outer muscles, which you can see if you have a 'six-pack', are called the external obliques.

Many singers erroneously believe that deliberately pulling in the obliques 'supports' their voice and is therefore to be encouraged, but in fact it causes problems. The science of the out-breath works on the premise of positive pressure, meaning that when you sing, the air comes out by itself because the air pressure in your lungs is greater than that in the room. As you sustain longer phrases you will indeed experience the abdominal wall contracting slowly – but this occurs *without you needing to try*. The contraction you feel is the underlying muscle – the transverse abdominis – not the obliques, and is automatic. This process occurs at the moment the balance of pressure changes, i.e. when the air pressure in your lungs becomes lower than the air pressure outside of your body.

Now that this premise is understood, you will find that one of the best ways you can improve the delivery of your song is to learn to avoid driving breath from the abdominal wall. Try and practise the following exercise on a daily basis to avoid overuse of the obliques whilst phonating (making voice):

1. Place your right hand on the abdominal wall and allow the muscles to relax. If you feel that the abdominals are tight then repeat the Accent Method breathing exercise outlined earlier to help you to find a true abdominal release. *Note:* In the Accent Method breathing you deliberately pull the abdominals inwards in order to feel a moment of abdominal release, but you should *not* pull the abdominals inwards at any other point during the rest of this exercise – you are trying to do the exact opposite and keep them relaxed.

2. Once the abdominal wall is released, make the following sounds as you did previously: 'oh oh' and 'eh eh'. Notice the contact in the vocal folds and monitor the abdominal wall, trying to ensure it remains relaxed and does not kick inwards

as you make the sounds. The effort should be in your vocal folds instead. Repeat this stage until you can produce the sounds without any abdominal contraction at all. *Note:* With the next four stages, which become progressively harder, you are aiming for the same physical sensation – the complete relaxation of the abdominal wall.

3. Now make a couple of short 'z' sounds ('zz zz') on a comfortable pitch. Again try to stay completely relaxed in the abdominal wall.

4. Next attempt a sustained 'z' sound of about ten seconds' duration. You will begin to feel the transverse abdominis contract underneath your hand towards the end of the sound, but ensure you don't engage the obliques.

5. Now start on a comfortable note in the lower half of your range and glide upwards and downwards for a few notes on a 'z' sound. Check you don't begin to activate the abdominals as the pitch rises.

6. Finally glide up and down through your full register on a 'z' sound. Go as high as you can whilst keeping the sound quiet and focused. Avoid any contraction in the obliques related to the ascending pitch.

This exercise is excellent for daily training as it helps to break the habit of driving breath when you begin to phonate or ascend in pitch. Personally, I found it had a hugely beneficial effect on my singing. When it was first taught to me, I was already a singer with significant experience, but even so it allowed me to extend my belt register several notes higher in just a few days. My progress had been held back because I was habitually pushing from the abdominals; this exercise helped free me from that poor musculature.

Raising the Soft Palate

As a singing teacher, one of the most common vocal problems I am called on to correct is nasality. A surprising number of singers suffer from a degree of nasality in their voice – even if they are not fully aware of it. This occurs when their vowel sounds are partially coming out through their nose, instead of their mouth, which can make your sound dull. To avoid this unwanted quality you must learn to gain control of the soft palate – a movable fold of muscular fibres and mucous membrane suspended from the back of the roof of the mouth.

As previously mentioned, the function of the soft palate in phonation is to direct sound either through the mouth, the nose, or both. The mouth and the nose are connected by a hole in the roof of the mouth called the 'nasal port'. When the soft palate is raised, it seals off the nasal port and subsequently all sound is directed through the mouth. This is the position you will want most of the time when singing. If you lower the soft palate it will make contact with the back of the tongue, sealing off the oral cavity, and all the sound will come out through the nose. This occurs when you produce what are known as the nasal consonants: 'm' 'n' and 'ng'. (If you hum on an 'm' sound and then hold your nose, the sound will stop – because the soft palate is directing all of the sound through the nose.) When the soft palate is in a mid-position, the sound comes out through both the mouth and the nose. It is when you sing in this set-up that your sound is heard as being nasal. To learn to raise the soft palate – and therefore avoid nasality – you must first become aware of its location and the sensations you feel when it moves. Try the following awareness exercise:

1. Make an 'ee' vowel on a comfortable pitch. Be aware that the tip of your tongue is behind your front teeth, and the sides of the tongue are in contact with your upper molars.

2. Keeping your tongue completely still, move back and forth between an 'ee' sound and an 'ng' sound, i.e. 'EE ng EE ng EE ng'. Every time you make the 'ng' sound you will feel something lowering in the roof of your mouth and making contact with the tongue. This is the soft palate.

Now that you can feel the movement of the soft palate you can begin to eradicate nasality from the song. Explore the following exercise:

1. The letter 'g' springs the soft palate up into a raised position. In a speaking position, practise moving from an extended 'n' sound (where the soft palate is down) to a vowel proceeded by the letter 'g'. For example: 'nnGee, nnGah, nnGoo'. You

should feel a sensation of lifting occur in the roof of the mouth – this is the soft palate. As you do this, rest a hand gently underneath the jaw to monitor that you are only raising the soft palate, rather than also lowering the jaw.

2. Sing through the song, placing the letter 'g' in front of all of the vowels. So for example, 'happy birthday to you' would become 'Gaa-Gee Geerr-Gay Goo Goo'. Again, practise with a hand underneath your chin.

3. Now try singing the song normally, a little slower than usual, focusing on the sensation of keeping the soft palate raised. You can check that you have achieved the correct position by pinching your nose occasionally as you sing. If there is no change in the sound when you pinch your nose then your soft palate is raised. (Avoid doing this on the letters 'm', 'n' and 'ng' as the soft palate will be down and the sound will stop.) If the sound quality changes on any of your vowels when you pinch your nose, then this means that your soft palate is in a mid-position for that word – and your sound is nasal.

4. Once you have worked through the entire song, go back and target any words that were nasal by placing a 'g' sound in front of the vowel you were struggling with. For example, if you identified the word 'walk' as being problematic, then your 'aw' vowel would be nasal. In a speech position practise repeatedly lifting the soft palate on this vowel, i.e. 'nnGaw, nnGaw, nnGaw'. This will help you build a new muscle memory for that particular word. Once you have repeated this stage for all problematic words/vowels, run the song again. With detailed practice the nasality should disappear.

Improving Articulation

In my experience of hosting audition workshops with casting directors, I have found that criticism of a singer's articulation is often a common piece of feedback. The reason for this is, if the panel are struggling to understand the lyric, it is hard for them to engage with the story being told.

Try the following exercise to work on your consonants. You may want to wash your hands before you begin.

1. Open your mouth slightly and rest the tip of your index finger gently between your front teeth. (You should twist your wrist so your fingernail is facing sideways towards the wall, rather than upwards towards the ceiling.)

2. During the exercise you want to avoid biting down on your finger – the aim is to keep the jaw relaxed. To test this, try biting very gently on your finger – then relax the jaw whilst maintaining the contact between your teeth and fingertip. As you relax you will find a feeling of ease and release in the muscles of the jaw; this is the sensation you should seek to sustain throughout the exercise. Once you can you access this lack of tension in the muscles controlling the jaw, move on to the next stage.

3. Keeping your finger between your teeth, slowly and clearly make the following consonant sounds: 'b', 'p', 'd', 't', 'r', 'j' 'ch', and 'k'. It is fine to move the lips but try to keep the jaw relaxed as you did previously.

4. Repeat Stage 3, but this time repeat each consonant in the sequence three times, i.e. 'b, b, b', 'p, p, p', etc. Make each consonant clearly without engaging the jaw.

5. You are now ready to work on the song. Maintaining your finger position, speak slowly through the lyric focusing on producing each consonant clearly.

6. Repeat the previous stage but now sing the song, rather than speak it.

7. Finally take your finger out and sing the song normally. Because your tongue had to work harder when your finger was in place, it will now be more agile when asked to work in its normal position – so you should notice an improvement in the clarity of your articulation.

Note: If you don't want to use your finger for these exercises, an alternative is to purchase a bone prop. These are available online from the vocal specialist Annie Morrison at www.themorrisonboneprop.com.

The following exercises are suitable for advanced vocalists.

Tongue Position

A feature of a well-trained musical-theatre voice is that the vowel sounds of the song are balanced, i.e. the resonance of those vowels is as equal as possible. When you produce different vowels, your tongue changes position. These modifications in position can unintentionally create big changes in the level of resonance – and make your vocal quality uneven. You therefore want to minimise these movements in order to make your sound more balanced. To achieve this, you should aim to keep the middle of the tongue as still as possible whilst singing. Not only will this help you to form vowel sounds with an equal resonance, it can also make your vocal production less effortful.

Try the following awareness exercise:

1. Sing an 'ee' vowel on a comfortable pitch and sustain the note for a few seconds. As you hold the note, become aware of the position of your tongue. You will notice that the tip of your tongue is in contact with your lower front teeth, and the sides of your tongue are touching your upper molars. This is an ideal tongue position for singing.

2. Now try speaking an 'ee' vowel followed by an 'ah'.

3. Repeat this several times. You will notice that the sides of your tongue drop downwards and lose contact with the molars each time you move into the 'ah' vowel.

As you can see from this exercise, habitually, the middle of your tongue can move significantly as you progress from one vowel to another. Aside from the change in resonance, this can be problematic when you try to sing high notes. As discussed previously, when you make higher pitches, your larynx needs to rise. Your tongue is attached to your larynx by a small bone called the hyoid bone. So if you allow the middle of the tongue to drop – as you just noticed when you made the 'ah' vowel – then the larynx will drop with it. This can make it hard to create and sustain higher pitches. Therefore it is doubly important to relearn how to produce your vowel sounds – by keeping the middle of the tongue as still as you can. Try this next exercise:

1. Make an 'ee' vowel on a comfortable pitch. Be aware of the tongue position described in the awareness exercise: the tip of the tongue behind the front teeth, the sides of the tongue in contact with the upper molars.

2. Speak through the following sequence of paired vowels: 'ee-ay', 'ee-ah', 'ee-aw', 'ee-oo'. With each pair, glide slowly from the first vowel to the second – keeping the sides of the tongue as still as possible. You are retraining your muscles to produce each vowel with a reduced movement of the tongue – by using the 'ee' sound as a basis for all of your vowels.

3. Repeat Stage 2, but this time sing, rather than speak, the paired vowels. Do this on a comfortable pitch. It is appropriate to breathe between each pair. Again try to minimise the movement of the tongue.

4. You are now ready to apply this technique to your song. Sing through the entire song on an 'ee' vowel, maintaining the prescribed tongue position. You will likely find the song easier to sing because of the efficient tongue position of the 'ee' vowel.

5. Now sing through the lyric on the vowel sounds, only with the consonants removed. Again focus on minimising the tongue movements.

6. Finally sing through the entire song with the consonants back in – but still keeping the tongue as still as possible. You should notice an improvement in the balance of your vowel sounds, and your voice may feel easier to produce.

Onset

Another great way to improve the delivery of your song is by enhancing your understanding and control of onset. The term 'onset' refers to what happens to your breath and your vocal folds when you begin to phonate. There are three different types of onset:

Aspirate – an aspirate onset occurs when the breath passes through the vocal folds before they begin to vibrate. Try holding your larynx gently with your fingers and make the following sounds: 'hhheee', 'fffaaahh', 'sshhaaww'. If you extend the first consonant you will notice the breath escaping before there is vibration. When singing you must use an aspirate onset every time a phrase starts with a word that begins with a devoiced consonant (i.e. 'f', 'k', 'p', 's', 't', 'ch', 'sh' and 'th' – as in the word 'thing'). Whilst it is therefore required when singing, unnecessary use of this particular onset, for example on a vowel sound, can lead to an undesired breathy tone.

Glottal – a glottal onset occurs when the breath is held momentarily behind the vocal folds, and then released in an explosive manner. Hold your larynx. Slowly make the sounds 'uh oh' – like a child realising they have done something wrong. You will be aware of a build-up of subglottic pressure before each sound. The explosive release, and the strong subsequent vocal-fold closure, is a glottal. Beginning with this onset in a song will help you access a Speech quality. However, if you use glottals too frequently it can be vocally tiring and make it harder to access thyroid tilt and higher pitches.

Simultaneous – a simultaneous onset occurs when the release of breath and the vocal-fold vibration occur at exactly the same time. Hold your larynx one more time and gently speak some extended vowels on a confortable pitch, i.e. 'eeee', 'aahh', 'oooo'. Glide into each sound, avoiding a glottal onset. You will feel under your fingers that the vibration in your larynx starts at the moment you begin to breath out. Simultaneous onsets are a key feature of nearly all singing – but particularly when using a legit or operatic style.

Any good singer uses each of the three onsets. All are important, safe, necessary and healthy, if used correctly. However, it is undoubtedly much easier to sing a majority of songs if you are able to access a simultaneous set-up consistently and avoid unintentional glottal and aspirate onsets. You can and should use the other two onsets at times for stylistic reasons – but if you use a simultaneous onset for the majority of the song your technical delivery will greatly improve.

The following exercise will help you improve your simultaneous onset:

1. Before you work on the onsets in your song, you first need to practise in a speaking position. First explore using an aspirate onset. Speak a series of vowels in a slow, elongated manner, placing an extended 'h' sound in front of each: i.e. 'hhaaahhh', 'hhhey', 'hhheee', 'hhhaw', 'hhhooo', 'hhhair', 'hhhigh'. Focus on making the transition from the 'h' sound into every vowel as smooth as possible. It can be beneficial to make a gliding gesture with your hands as you do this, as physicalising the work can help build greater awareness and control of what is occurring within the larynx.

2. Now try to apply the same feeling of a vocal glide to a simultaneous onset. Work through your vowels again. Start with an aspirate onset first, then repeat the vowel but removing the letter 'h' to give you a simultaneous onset. For example: 'hhaaahhh' then 'aahh', 'hhhey' then 'eeyy'. Try to achieve the same smooth beginning to the sound when the 'h' is removed. Be careful not to use a small glottal. You may again wish to use hand gestures to help build awareness of the internal sensations. Repeat this stage until you can affect a simultaneous onset on all vowels.

3. You are now ready to apply this work to your song. A good vowel for singing with a simultaneous onset is 'oo', so try singing through the entire song on that vowel, focusing on avoiding any glottal onsets. As with the sirening exercise, sing along to a backing track to ensure you are practising in the correct key. Repeat until you are able to deliver the entire song in a simultaneous onset.

4. Now sing through the song once more. This time use the vowels of the song, but with the consonants removed. So for example, 'happy birthday to you' would become 'aa-ee eerr-ey oo oo'. Work slowly through the lyric until you can achieve a simultaneous onset on all the vowels.

5. Finally sing through the song normally with the consonants back in. Use a simultaneous onset unless the word begins with a devoiced consonant, when an aspirate onset will be required. When that is the case, glide from the consonant

onto the vowel as you did in Stage 1 of the exercise. Avoid using glottals at any stage.

Torso Anchoring

As part of her research, Estill identified the importance of the use of the muscles in the back for the healthy production of the singing voice. Try the following awareness exercise:

1. Imagine you have an orange underneath each of your armpits. Squeeze gently downwards on these imaginary oranges. You will feel an engagement in the muscles in your back below your arm. (These muscles are commonly known as the 'lats'.)

2. Sustain an 'ah' vowel on a comfortable pitch. As you do so, play with engaging and releasing your lats as described above. You may notice the sound becoming clearer and stronger when your lats are engaged. Estill described this use of the lats as 'torso anchoring'.

Here is an exercise that will encourage an appropriate use of the back muscles when singing:

1. Stand in an upright position facing a wall. Your toes should be about fifteen centimetres from the wall, with your feet parallel and resting comfortably underneath your hips.

2. Rest your palms flat against wall, with your hands slightly wider than shoulder-width apart. As you do this, don't lean forwards into the wall; stand completely upright; the gentle pressure you are applying will engage your lats. Look directly in front of you so that your eyeline is horizontal and the back of the neck is long.

3. A key to the use of torso anchoring is isolation. As you engage your lats, you need to ensure your abdominals don't begin to work unnecessarily. To practise this, whilst maintaining your physical relationship to the wall, release your abdominals using the Accent Breathing method discussed previously (i.e. 'ZZ, zz, zz' – release).

4. Maintaining the same anchored posture, sing the first line of your song. At the end of the phrase release your abdominal

wall. Be sure that you have relaxed your obliques and allowed the breath to drop in, whilst maintaining the engagement in the back. Repeat if necessary.

5. Now sing through the entire song in this manner, releasing at the points where you had previously decided to breathe. You may notice that your vocal production feels more supported and stable.

6. Sing the song again, but this time replicate the marriage of release and anchoring without using the wall to help you. Stand upright in the space, keeping the same relationship with your feet and your neck alignment. To achieve the same degree of anchoring, you may want to return to the image of squeezing oranges underneath your armpits. This will engage your lats. Remember to release after each phrase.

Adding Twang/False-Fold Retraction

As noted previously, Twang is one of Estill's six voice qualities. In its purest form it can be perceived as strident and unpleasant. However, twang isn't only a voice quality, it is also an individual resonance that can be added to other vocal set-ups. For example, twang is an important component of Opera quality. It is one of the reasons you can hear an opera singer over a full orchestra.

The amount of twang in your voice is determined by how much you narrow and tighten your AES (see p. 32), the sphincter inside of your pharynx. Try the following awareness exercise:

1. Make the following sounds: cackle like a witch, taunt like a child in a playground ('na, na-na, na, na'), quack like a duck. When you make these noises you are tightening your AES and are therefore adding twang to the voice. It is a brash noise.

2. Repeat these three sounds and become aware of the sensations in your larynx. With each of them you should notice a feeling of narrowing in the vocal tract – this is the AES. If you experience any discomfort in the larynx making these sounds, or the sound is raspy/distorted, this may be because you are constricting. Constriction occurs when your false vocal folds, which sit above your true vocal folds, close over. To free

yourself of constriction, laugh silently for a moment. You will feel a sensation of width, or space, in the larynx. Here you have altered your musculature by widening your false vocal folds. This is called retraction. If you now repeat the twang sounds, maintaining the feeling of retraction – this should get rid of the distortion and allow you to produce a clear tone.

Now that you have a physical understanding of how twang is produced, you can learn to control the amount that is added to your sound – like pushing a fader on a mixing desk.

1. Make a 'NYeh' sound on a comfortable speaking pitch with a very tight, narrowed AES – adding a lot of twang.

2. Repeat, but now clench your right fist as you make the sound. You are using your fist to help you physicalise what is happening with your AES.

3. Now slowly make four 'NYeh' sounds. With each sound gradually relax and open your fist. As you do so, also gradually relax and widen your AES. You will progress from having lots of twang in the first sound to none by the fourth. The sensation you will feel during this exercise – moving from a narrowed to a widened position in the pharynx – helps to develop the muscle memory you need to add or remove twang on demand.

Having explored this element of vocal control, you can now choose to introduce twang into your song if that seems appropriate (most pop-based contemporary musical-theatre songs will benefit from the addition of some twang). Try using the exercise outlined below:

1. Siren the first phrase of the melody on an 'ng' sound. (Twang is made with thin vocal folds, so sirening helps you add the necessary thyroid tilt to create this position.)

2. Sing through the same phrase using a staccato 'ging' sound on each syllable. Use a very tight AES. This will produce nasal twang, as your soft palate will be in a mid-position (causing some of the sound to escape through your nose).

3. Now sing through the phrase once more, but this time use a 'NYee' sound for every syllable. Your AES should remain tight

as you do this. Sing the phrase legato, rather than staccato. (The soft palate will come down each time you make the 'n' consonant, but when you lift it to produce the 'ee' vowel the sound should come out entirely through your mouth and not be nasalised. If you do this successfully you will be producing oral twang. To check the sound is oral, rather than nasal, you can pinch your nose when making the vowel – there should be no change in the sound at all. Don't pinch on the 'n' consonant or the sound will cut out.)

4. Repeat Stage 3, but this time instead of using a 'NYee' sound, put the letters 'ny' in front of the vowels of the phrase. So 'happy birthday to you' would become 'NYaa-NYee NYeerr-NYay NYoo NYoo'.

5. Now sing the phrase normally. Think about still narrowing your AES to make the twang, whilst retaining the feeling of a silent laugh to retract the false vocal folds. You should notice a brighter resonance in your sound. If you wish to add more or less twang, tighten or widen your AES as you did in the previous exercise.

6. Repeat Stages 1 to 5 for every phrase in the song.

Practising Belt

Within many musical-theatre songs there are notes that should be delivered in a Belt quality. In well-written material, belting is used for moments of musical and dramatic climax. As such, it is rare for more than one or two notes in a song to be belted. In the self-rehearsal guides appropriate moments for the use of this voice quality are identified.

Belt in its pure form is very loud. As musical theatre is usually an amplified medium, it is therefore usually preferable to add some thyroid tilt to your belt set-up. This will quieten and sweeten the voice – and help you add some vibrato – making it a more appropriate sound for singing with a microphone. The described set-up is sometimes called a 'mixed belt'. When I am vocal coaching, this is the position I am most often asked to teach, as it is a highly desirable sound in commercial singing.

Below is a system for practising a mixed belt. Before you attempt the exercise, you should engage in a thorough vocal warm-up. (If you wish, you can use the previously outlined exercises to warm the voice.) You should also remind yourself of the sensations of thyroid tilt (p. 39), torso anchoring (p. 51), false-fold retraction (p. 52). Once you have done this preparation, you are ready to try the following:

1. Stand with your feet slightly wider than shoulder-width apart so you feel grounded and have a solid foundation. Ensure your knees are free and the abdominals are relaxed.

2. Make some glottal onsets on a comfortable pitch with the thyroid cartilage in a horizontal position (i.e. 'oh oh', 'ee ee', 'eh eh'). This will put you in a Speech quality.

3. Laugh silently to remind yourself of the posture of false-fold retraction – you will notice a sensation of width in the neck.

4. Repeat the glottal onsets whilst maintaining the silent laugh posture, but this time sustain the second sound, (i.e. 'oh ooohhh', 'ee eeeeee', 'eh eeehhh').

5. Now imagine you are holding the ends of a sixty-centimetre metal bar in front of your upper chest. Bend the ends of this imaginary bar downwards so your elbows finish by the sides of your body. In this position you will engage your lats and be provided with some torso anchoring, which is important when belting. Maintain this anchoring as you continue through the next stages.

6. Keeping the back of the neck long, lift your chin slightly so that you are 'looking up to the gods'. If you were in a theatre, you would be fixing your eyes on the back of the dress circle.

7. Maintaining this head/neck position, throw your voice across the room on a 'yeh' sound. This sound, like a happy yell or shout, requires you to maintain lots of retraction.

8. Still retaining the described physical posture, whimper on an 'ng' sound like a puppy. This is to remind yourself of the sensation of thyroid tilt (remember to focus on the cartilage tilting downwards and forwards).

9. Without changing your physicality throw your voice on a moaned 'yeh' sound. You are now adding thyroid tilt to the set-up and are very close to a mixed belt. (Done correctly, this sound can be quite amusing. In my studio I often describe it as 'how the Queen would belt'. It sounds like an empowered moaning.)

10. Now try Estill's famous belting phrase. In the same 'moaned' position, with an unchanged physical set-up, try exclaiming like an Italian market trader: 'Eh! Francesco!!!' (This sound should be as though you are exasperated, but not angry, with your beloved Francesco.)

11. Relax your body for a moment. Play an F♯4 on piano. Hold this pitch in your head. This is the pitch you will belt on in a moment. It is chosen because it sits in a comfortable part of the male belt register. (If you don't have access to a piano, you can find the same pitch using an online virtual piano.)

12. Repeat stages 1 to 10 whilst holding the pitch in your head. If each stage feels comfortable then try a belt on a moaned 'yeh' sound on the given male/female pitch. Remember to keep your chin lifted and back anchored. Maintain a feeling of retraction (silent laugh) in the false vocal folds. Hold the sound for as long as is comfortable. If the set-up is correct you will now be belting. It may surprise you how comfortable it feels and how easy it is to sustain the pitch for a long time. Repeat this stage a few times until it feels secure and that you are in full control.

13. If the last stage was successful, you are now ready to target the pitch that you will belt in your song. Repeat stages 1 to 12, but this time use the piano to ensure you are belting on the same pitch as the note in your song (this note will be identified in the self-rehearsal guide if you don't read music). If the belt in the song is currently too high for you, then gradually build up to this pitch in your practice, semitone by semitone. Remember: The higher you go the more thyroid tilt you will need to add (think of adding more 'moan' to the sound).

14. Once you are able to belt the requisite pitch on a 'yeh' sound, you can now target the vowel used in the song. Repeat stages

1 to 13, but this time instead of singing on a 'yeh' sound, belt on the vowel you will be singing in the song – but with the letter 'y' in front. So if you are trying to belt the word 'life' you would practise on a 'yi' sound. (If you struggle to access any particular vowel in belt, stop for a moment and try some spoken practice, moving from a moaned 'yeh' to the vowel under consideration, i.e. 'yeh, yi', 'yeh, yi', then try the singing again.)

15. Sing the phrase that contains the belt in its entirety, belting your desired note. Ensure that you add the required physicality (anchoring the torso, lifting the chin, retracting the false folds, tilting the thyroid) gradually *before* the belt – so you are already in position when the moment arrives. To achieve this, in some songs you may want to begin to alter your physicality during the preceding phrase.

16. Finally consider how you will deliver the belt in audition without 'showing' the panel your technique. Consider how you can use a gesture that is appropriate from an acting perspective to achieve the right degree of physical engagement – but so that the panel are not aware of the use of torso anchoring.

Note: When used correctly, belting is completely safe and healthy. It is also exhilarating to listen to. However, when executed poorly it can quickly tire the voice. If you feel any strain or 'scratching' of the vocal folds doing the above steps, then stop the exercise immediately and spend five minutes gently sirening on an 'ng' sound, using lots of false-fold retraction. Once you can siren through your full register, then you are usually safe to continue your practice. However, if you feel any signs of vocal fatigue, then once you have finished sirening, rest the voice and return to your belt practice another day. It is advisable to only practise belting in short sessions (no longer than twenty minutes), particularly if the set-up is new to you.

Despite this, I would encourage you not to be put off belting – even if you have not done it before. Whilst you should be careful and monitor your practice, don't be scared to experiment with your voice or to make a mistake. It is a rare student indeed who doesn't crack at times when they first learn to belt. As long as you don't practise incorrectly for long periods of time your work will be perfectly safe. However, belting can be one of the most difficult vocal set-ups – so if you find it difficult, tiring or intimidating then seek the advice of an experienced, qualified vocal coach to teach you the set-up rather than practise alone.

ACTING EXERCISES

It is a truism that a majority of candidates in a major singing audition will have good voices. Therefore if you want to excel, and stand out from the competition, you cannot simply sing well – you must also have great skills in acting through song. The following exercises will help you explore your song from an actor's perspective – and enable you to deliver the material successfully as a piece of dramatic text. All of the acting exercises are suitable for everyone.

Rehearsing as a Spoken Monologue: Images and Objectives

An excellent way to begin work on acting through song is to rehearse your performance as a spoken monologue. This temporarily frees you from the rhythmic structure of the music, allowing you the time needed in rehearsal to discover truthful impulses for the first time. However, as discussed earlier, in order to respond truthfully and spontaneously in an audition – where there are usually no other actors – you must see 'targets' in your imagination. Remember, these targets fall into four categories:

1. Something the character would see if they looked at their surroundings.

2. An image from the character's memory.

3. An image prompted by the character envisioning the future.

4. The physical behaviour of another person that your character is looking at.

Before you undertake this exercise, list on your working copy of the music the targets you'll need to see when acting the song. You may be surprised by how many there are. You will need to picture an image at all times — otherwise you will have nothing to respond to. The image will usually change every couple of lines, but in some songs may do so more frequently. The first image you see should occur before the opening line, so it engenders an impulse to start singing. For example, before the actress playing Maria can sing the first line of the title song from *The Sound of Music*, she needs to imagine a beautiful Austrian mountain range.

Once you have written down a list of images for the entire song, you are ready to undertake the exercise. You will need a friend or colleague to assist you.

1. Stand in the centre of the room. Give the working copy of your music to your partner. They should sit on the floor away from your eyeline.

2. Your partner should then read to you the first image you have written down, for example: 'an Austrian mountain range'. Picture that image in your mind, and describe out loud to your partner what you see. This should be done with your eyes open. Avoid giving intellectual answers where you are not really picturing anything. 'The large rocky mountains rise up into the summer sky' is problematic; whereas 'on the side of the nearest mountain there is a small dirt track that winds its way upwards, halfway up there is a single small tree with twisted branches and no leaves' is better.

3. To encourage you to imagine more clearly, your partner can ask you questions if they suspect that what you are describing is not truly imagined. It is helpful if they encourage you to focus on a detail, such as 'Describe the branches on the tree' or 'What do the clouds above the mountain look like?'

4. Once your partner is satisfied you have a clear mental picture of the first image on your list, they should then read out the next. Repeat Stage 3 for every image you have written down.

5. Having completed this work, act through your entire song as a spoken monologue. Allow the images you have just pictured to 'drop in' to your mind at the points you identified in the

lyric. Give yourself full permission to respond physically to those images. For example, if you had pictured someone crying, you might take a step towards them to offer comfort. If you had envisaged a clear blue sky, your impulse might be to look upwards at it and smile.

6. Rehearse your song as a monologue once more. This time, begin to play the objectives of the song, as well as seeing the images. (These objectives are outlined for you in the 'Textual Analysis' section of the self-rehearsal guides.) For example, in the opening line of 'The Sound of Music' the actress playing Maria might explore the following objective: to rejoice in the beauty of the natural world. As you rehearse, if your work is unclear, your partner should encourage you to go back and play an objective differently, or more strongly. Allow about two hours of rehearsal to explore each moment of the song till you can both play the objectives and respond impulsively to the images.

7. Finally, do a full run-through of the song, this time singing instead of speaking. See the images once more and trust yourself to respond to the impulses that are generated as a result of what you see. You shouldn't think about the objectives at this stage, instead clear your mind and trust that through rehearsal, and by seeing the images, the objectives will come to you in the moment of playing the song. Once you have finished, get your partner to feed back on what they observed.

Real Person/Imaginary Person

As mentioned in the previous exercise, if your song is directed towards another character in the musical, rather than being a soliloquy, then you will need to imagine that character's behaviour when acting it in audition. That can be difficult to sustain for the full duration of a song, but this next exercise will help you. The premise is that you work with another actor to discover what the other character's behaviour might be. You then repeat the work, but this time imagining the behaviour of the other character instead.

1. Before you start the exercise, you need to have worked on your objectives and memorised the lyrics so that you can look at the other actor.

2. Explain the given circumstances to your partner and agree an objective for them to play. It is helpful if their chosen objective works in opposition to your own, as this will create conflict in the scene and give you more to work off. For example, suppose the given circumstances are that the two characters are ex-partners and have recently broken up. If your objective is: to convince the other character to give the relationship another try, then a good choice for them to play would be: to try to avoid an intimate conversation.

3. Act through your song as a spoken scene between the two of you. Play your objectives. Your partner should also play their own objective fully and respond instinctively within the parameters of the given circumstances. So, for example, if the given circumstances were those outlined above, as you sing, your partner might choose to turn their back on you at certain points, or walk away. Pay careful attention to their behaviour and respond. At times you may feel that you are failing in your objective, which should provoke you to try something new. On other occasions you may notice that you are beginning to gain traction over your partner – which may prompt you to continue with your objective or encourage you to play a more conciliatory choice of action.

4. Now perform the song as a speech again, but this time without the other actor. Imagine the character's behaviour instead. This may include you remembering activities your partner just did, or might involve you making up something new in your head. (As you move towards a complete performance, beware of only replaying in your mind what the other actor did as this can limit your imaginative range.)

5. Finally, add the music and perform the full song, imagining the behaviour of the other character as you do so. You should find you have a much more detailed understanding of what your imaginary scene partner is doing, and will discover more impulses to respond as a result.

Incorporating Actions

As discussed earlier, playing an action (a transitive verb) on each line of your song can make your work more specific, credible and engaging. Whilst this is the strength of actioning as a system, its weakness is that it can lead to you 'getting stuck in your head'. You can end up thinking about the actions you have written down on your working copy, rather than acting spontaneously in the moment. The following exercise will help you avoid this pitfall and enable you to integrate your choices of action organically into your performance – helping you deliver a performance that is both specific and spontaneous.

Preparation

1. To undertake this exercise you are advised to purchase *Actions: The Actors' Thesaurus* by Marina Caldarone and Maggie Lloyd-Williams, available as both a book and an iOS app.

2. Firstly, you need to decide upon, and note down, your choice of actions on the working copy of your music. You will need to find a different choice for each sentence. Begin by acting out the first sentence of the lyric, whilst playing your objective. Speak the words, rather than sing them, then try and name the action you just played instinctively. For example, you may feel you were encouraging, mocking, undermining, soothing or seducing. (Remember, an action must fit into the format: 'I [action] you', or if the character is talking to themselves, 'I [action] myself'.)

3. Now look up the action you just identified in the book or the app, or using a thesaurus. This will provide you with a list of similar and related choices. For example, if you identified 'mock' as the choice you played, it would give further options such as: deride, patronise, ridicule, taunt, etc. Choose the word that you like the most from the list, the one you feel best suits your objective, and note it down clearly and legibly on your working copy. If none of them feel quite right, try another initial choice, and use the app/thesaurus again to provide further options.

4. Repeat this process, sentence by sentence, until you have noted down actions that you like for the entire song. Strive for

as much variety as possible, whilst still ensuring the actions you decide upon are logical for the character and situation. The self-rehearsal guides contain suggested actions that are appropriate for each song, but it will give you a greater sense of ownership of your performance if you are also able to identify your own choices.

Application

For this part of the work you will need the help of a colleague or friend.

1. Run your song as a spoken monologue, as you've done previously, ensuring you are still seeing images and are playing your objectives.

2. As you do this, your partner should stand about half a metre behind you with your working copy in their hand. A second or so before each sentence they should speak aloud your next action. They should do this in the form of a direct instruction. So if your action choice is 'I tempt you', and the character you are talking to is female, then you partner would simply say 'Tempt her'. If your action is 'I cross-examine myself' your partner would say 'Cross-examine yourself'. It is important that your partner says the actions loudly and clearly and doesn't worry about disturbing your work. The actions need to be delivered loud enough so that you can hear them whilst you are acting, and early enough so you have a second to process the word before it is time to play the choice. It is often necessary for your partner to say the next action whilst you are still acting the preceding sentence.

3. As your partner feeds you the actions, you shouldn't look at them – instead focus on the images you are seeing. Respond impulsively to what they say, like they are your inner thoughts.

4. Once you have completed the exercise, take a moment to clarify any hiccups. Identify any moments in which the action was incorrect, or in the wrong place. Ask if you needed a word to be spoken earlier. Change an action if you felt the chosen verb wasn't helping your performance.

5. Repeat Stages 2 and 3 again. It is usual for the first version to feel a little contrived, but by repeating the work, you will begin to take more ownership of the choices.

6. Once you have been through the process for the second time, immediately, and without discussion, act through the entire song as a monologue – this time without your partner feeding you the actions. Don't try to remember the actions you just heard, simply see your images and play your objectives. You will find that many of the actions 'stick', but you may also find you play different choices on some lines. Either eventuality is fine – don't feel obliged to stick to the actions from the exercise.

7. Finally – add the singing, ensuring you still continue to play actions now that you are no longer speaking. Get your partner to observe and feed back on what they saw. You should find your work is now much more specific.

Whispered Thoughts/Ownership of Words

This final exercise is to help you develop a deeper connection to the lyric, by allowing you to experience and find the full meaning of each individual word. You will require the assistance of two friends or colleagues.

1. Kneel on the floor with your eyes closed. Hold the working copy of your sheet music up in front of you.

2. Your two assistants should kneel either side of you, so they are in a position to whisper directly into one of your ears. One assistant should whisper into your right ear, the other into your left.

3. As you keep your eyes closed, your assistants should whisper alternative words in your ears by reading the lyrics off the sheet music. For example, if they were reading the first line of 'Happy Birthday', it would divide up as follows:

> Assistant 1: Happy
>
> Assistant 2: birthday
>
> Assistant 1: to
>
> Assistant 2: you

4. As your assistants whisper the words, they should do so with great intensity. They should aim to communicate the meaning of each individual word into your ear. Whilst they do this, you should try to clear your mind and receive the words as if you are hearing them for the first time. You may experience the exercise as though the words are your inner thoughts.

5. Once the task has been completed for the full lyric, stand up and act the full song as a monologue. You may find that you have made some new discoveries about the lyric and developed greater ownership of the words. Where previously you might have been neglecting particular words, receiving the lyric from your helpers in this way helps you to find new and fresh ways of delivering words that you might have been glossing over. Ask your assistants to feed back on this element of your performance.

The Audition

Delivering a song in an audition is different from acting on a stage. During an audition there are usually no other actors to work with; you sing to a panel rather than an audience, and you perform your song out of context. You must therefore modify the approach you would use in performance. This chapter will explore how you can do so.

When it comes to audition technique, I have often heard teachers and industry experts who claim to know the secret of how to audition successfully. However, in my role as course leader for several performing-arts programmes, I have been fortunate to lead masterclasses with many of the UK's leading casting directors. I have also sat on numerous audition panels for entry into leading drama schools. My overwhelming lesson from these experiences is this: when it comes to evaluating auditions, everyone has different preferences. It is subjective. Therefore this chapter is not simply a summary of my own opinions on auditions, rather it reflects a synthesis of the best advice I have heard from experts who regularly sit behind the audition table. So whilst I would, of course, recommend you consider these points carefully, I would encourage you to be discerning when receiving advice about auditions: it is only one person's opinion.

DO WHAT YOU DO

One of the best pieces of advice on auditioning I have heard comes from the actor Bryan Cranston, famous for the hit TV series *Breaking Bad*. You can find this short video yourself on YouTube. To summarise, Cranston's advice is: rather than going into an audition aiming to get a job (or a place at a drama school), you should simply 'present what you do'. He advocates that, rather than trying to always second-guess what the panel are after – which is completely out of your control – you should empower yourself to do what you do well, and then walk away. This is incredibly useful when preparing a song for audition. There can be a temptation to try to mould your performance into what you think the panel will want. Do they want me to sing to them, or over their heads? Would they prefer I was physically still, or used the space? Rather than hamstring yourself like this, I would suggest you follow Cranston's advice. Take ownership of the decisions you make; do what it is that you do well and make choices that you feel show you at your best. Remember: it is your audition.

PREPARATION

When I ask casting directors and performing-arts lecturers what they think is the most important factor in a good audition, they invariably give the same reply: preparation. Castings are usually friendly and supportive environments. The people behind the audition table need to cast their show, or find the right applicants for their course. *They want you to be good* – so they generally do all they can to put you at your ease so that you can demonstrate your talent and be the solution to their problem. However, though you will find that audition panels tend to be very considerate if you make a mistake through nerves – as this can happen to everyone – they can be less tolerant if you haven't prepared properly. But what should your preparation involve? Here is a checklist:

1. Ensure you know the song(s) you have prepared inside out – both musically and lyrically. When you are nervous in audition it can affect your ability to perform and you can make silly mistakes. Allied to this, your songs may be redirected in the room – which can also throw you a little. To avoid making unnecessary errors, you therefore need to know the material especially well.

2. Find out about the people on the panel. A simple internet search will allow you to research the background of a casting director you are auditioning for, find out about a

director's previous shows and achievements, or read up on the career of the course leader of the drama school you want to attend. If possible, go and watch the work of the people on the panel, or a graduation performance of the course you want to take. This kind of research will give you an insight into the type of actors, material and performance styles the panel might favour. It also gives you the opportunity to strike up a conversation about something that interested you or that you admired. This helps suggest that you take the audition seriously and have a genuine interest in the panel members and their work. If you are auditioning for a musical at school, or with your local amateur group, if possible, take the opportunity to speak to the person leading the auditions in advance to get an idea what they may be looking for.

3. Go through your song in advance with a pianist. Many auditionees fail to do this, and it really affects their performance in the room. Working with a piano in advance will allow you to be completely certain about key musical issues, such as how you pitch your first note, when you come in during the introduction, and how the vocal line fits with the accompaniment.

4. Prepare what is asked. If you are auditioning for a performing-arts course, you will often be given a clear brief about the type and length of audition song to bring with you. For professional auditions, the casting director will usually provide a breakdown (through your agent) about the style of song that is required. Presenting the right type of material gives you the best chance of showing the panel what they need to see. It can be hard to cast an actor in *Hamilton* if they audition with a song by Rodgers and Hammerstein.

5. Memorise key information about the show your audition song is from and the character you are playing. This will help you address any questions that the panel may have. They might ask about the given circumstances, or the overall context of the piece. Sometimes they may enquire

about the vocal range of the song, particularly what the top note is. Most of this information is contained within these pages, but there is further research you can do. If the show is currently running, go and see it. If that is not possible, you can watch footage of previous productions online. If you are auditioning for a full-length production, you may have been sent a script; if so, always read it in its entirety. In early-round auditions for musicals, you will normally sing material of your own choosing, rather than songs from the show you are up for. But whether you are auditioning for a professional show or for the faculty of a drama school, it is likely that the panel will know the canon very well. So if you are aware of the key information, it gives you an opportunity to demonstrate that you have done your research, are well prepared – and are therefore someone they may want to work with.

6. Dress appropriately for the audition. Deciding what to wear for a professional audition is relatively simple. A good benchmark is 'smart-casual'. You shouldn't overdress, as you need to feel comfortable to physically inhabit your song, but on the other hand, you don't want it to appear that you have made no effort. I sometimes say to my students: 'If you are not comfortable walking down the street in your audition outfit then you have probably got it wrong.' When you are auditioning for a drama school you are often asked on your invitation letter to wear loose, comfortable clothing, or dance attire, as there will usually be a movement component to the audition. However, it can be advisable to bring a change of clothing (similar to that suggested for a professional audition – i.e. smart-casual) for the singing component of a drama-school audition. In my experience, if you enter the singing audition with your hair still done for the ballet class, or wearing jogging bottoms, then it can make you appear and feel like a dancer. This can make it harder for the panel to take you seriously as an actor-singer.

THE PROCESS

When you first start auditioning, if you are not sure what to expect, then the structure of the process can be quite unsettling. There are lots of small things that can throw you on the day, which can mean that when you get to the most important part – the singing – you are not as focused as you might be. In truth, every casting is different – so some of the best advice you can have is to expect the unexpected. However, there are certain things that are fairly typical in most singing auditions, and if you enter those situations with a good understanding of the way they are likely to be structured, you give yourself the best opportunity to do well. The following sequence describes what you might expect in an early round of auditions for a big commercial musical, and how that might differ if you are taking part in a singing audition in a drama school.

1. In a professional scenario, you are brought into the room by the casting director – who introduces you to the team. In a drama-school audition this task may be done by a tutor, or by a student who is already on the course. (Alternatively you may already be in the room with a group of fellow applicants, as the whole group sing in front of each other.)

2. There is a short greeting. In a drama-school audition someone may ask your name. The panel – who could range anywhere from two to twenty people (in auditions for big-budget musicals) – will normally remain behind the table.

3. Someone, perhaps the musical director (or a tutor in a drama-school audition), will ask you what you want to sing. A choice is agreed between you and them.

4. You go over to the pianist and discuss how you would like your music played.

5. You come into the centre of the room and sing the song.

6. The panel may, or may not, ask you to sing something else, they might redirect the song, or hear you do some vocal exercises.

7. They then thank you for your time and you leave, often without any feedback.

8. The whole process normally lasts between five and ten minutes.

As you can see, this is a fairly brief opportunity for you to showcase your abilities. It is therefore important to make the most of every moment in the room. Let's consider how you should approach each stage of the process.

ENTERING THE ROOM

When I've sat on audition panels for shows, I've found that the actors that often seemed to get cast were those that came across as open, positive and professional – someone that the panel felt they wanted to work with. Although tutors at drama schools may put less emphasis on this and look more for raw potential (at this stage of their careers, few applicants are great at auditioning), the impression you make as an individual is still highly important.

As previously mentioned, in a musical-theatre audition you get very little time to put across a positive impression. It is unlike a casting for a play, where your audition slot is usually longer and you get the opportunity to talk with the director and strike up a rapport. The panel have very little time to form opinions about you, so what you do when you enter the room is crucial.

Here are a few things to try:

1. Enter with purpose. Make eye contact from the moment you come through the door and walk energetically to the centre of the room. Take control of the space. You want to appear upbeat and pleased to be there.

2. Sometimes the panel may still be talking amongst themselves about the last audition when you're coming in. If so, hold your ground in the centre of the space, breathe, and wait for them to look up. Don't wander aimlessly over

to the pianist until you have had the chance to greet them and agree your song choice.

3. Unless instigated by the panel, don't shake their hands. This process can become tiresome for them if they have to repeat it all day, so it is often not welcomed. They will offer their hand if they want to greet you in that manner.

4. Don't convey anything negative. You get to say very little in a musical-theatre audition, so opinions can be shaped by the smallest ill-thought-out comments. No one wants to hear about your sore throat or that you've had a terrible journey.

5. You will frequently be asked to prepare two songs for an audition. But when you are asked what you are going to sing, don't offer the panel a choice. Tell them which song you intend to sing. This approach is wise for two reasons. Firstly, most panels are happy for you to make this decision, as it saves time and stops them having to make the choice. Secondly, and more importantly, you will usually get to sing the song that showcases you best. (Don't worry, the panel will tell you if they want to hear an alternative!)

THE PIANIST

Once you have agreed your song choice you should make your way straight to the piano. Again, take control of this moment. Don't wait to be told. There is nearly always a time pressure in singing auditions, and your efficiency will be appreciated. As you head towards the piano it is worth reminding yourself that the performance you are about to give will rely a great deal on how well the pianist plays for you. So take a moment to greet them and ask them how they are. Be polite and professional. Taking a second to say hello costs you nothing and can help get the pianist on your side. It is important to understand that the panel may also be taking an interest in these interactions at the piano. When I am behind the table I often listen to how the singer interacts with the pianist. It gives me a sense of whether they will be somebody who I want to be in the room with.

After you have greeted the pianist, you should then explain how you would like your song to be played. If you are not very experienced at auditioning, or are not a musician yourself, it can be intimidating giving musical instructions to a professional pianist. Don't worry though – a pianist is looking for and expecting instructions about the tempo, etc. Take the time you need and don't feel rushed. Of course, the more clearly and efficiently you can communicate your requirements to the pianist, the better. To help you with this it is hugely beneficial to have laid out and marked up your music correctly in advance. As someone who has spent a lot of time sight-reading, as both a musical director and a vocal coach, I can't tell you how much easier it is when the actor has prepared their music properly and can explain clearly what they want.

Before the audition you should have done the following:

1. Marked up your sheet music. Use your clean copy to do this, rather than your working/rehearsal copy. Start by ensuring any cuts are crossed out. To mark these clearly, draw brackets around where a cut begins and where it ends. Score out the cut section with several lines unmistakably in pen. When whole pages are cut out they should be taken out entirely. If you are cutting an entire verse, and the lyrics for one verse are printed on top of the other, rule out any unsung lyrics with a ruler and pen.

2. Once you have marked the cuts, highlight any repeat marks, codas, or important dynamics with a highlighter pen. Do this in a single colour. Colour-coding is not necessary – the pianist knows what the musical instructions mean. You are simply highlighting these to draw their attention to them. If you are not sure what to highlight, seek the advice of a singing coach or music teacher, or a friend who is a musician. They can help you to mark up the music appropriately.

3. Put the marked and highlighted sheet music into a display file (a folder with in-built plastic pockets) as this makes it easy for the pianist to turn the pages. Avoid using a ring-binder, as these are very hard for quick page-turns. An alternative to using a display file is to tape the music together. If you do this, ensure you tape down the full length of the page on both sides (if you only tape one side the music can stick together), then fold the pages so the music concertinas into a book.

4. Ensure there isn't any old music lurking at the back of your display file. It is not uncommon for one of the panellists to flick through your portfolio if they didn't fancy hearing your original song choice. If there are other songs in your folder you may find they ask you to sing them instead – even if you haven't performed them for years and have forgotten half of the words!

Knowing that your music is well prepared will help you be assured in your dealings with the pianist. Here is how you should use your time at the piano:

1. Once you have greeted the pianist, put your music on the piano stand. A good trick is to enter the room with a finger tucked inside your folder at the first page of your song. This will help you find it immediately.

2. Begin by pointing out any repeats in the music. These will be easy to find as you will have highlighted them. If there are no repeats, tell the pianist: 'It goes straight through.'

3. You should then indicate your desired tempo. The best way to do this is to sing a section at the speed you require, tapping a clear pulse on your leg as you do so. It is advisable to ask the pianist to play the first note of the section before you demonstrate. This will help ensure you are singing in the correct key when you set the tempo.

4. If the sections are marked '*colla voce*', '*rubato*' or '*freely*' then the pianist will follow you at these points and it is unnecessary to provide them with a tempo. Instead give the speed for the moment when the music drops into a steady

pulse. If there is more than one tempo in your song, you should go through each one, as indicated in Step 5.

5. Once you have finished going through the music and thanked the pianist, ask them if they wouldn't mind waiting until you indicate that you are ready to sing. This will allow you a moment once you get to the centre of the room to focus your thoughts before they begin to play, and allow you to act from the first note of the introduction.

MAKING CHOICES

Once you leave the pianist you have a couple of key decisions to make. Firstly: where will you start in the space? This will often be your first time in this particular audition room, so you need to make a quick assessment of your options. A majority of auditionees will begin their song standing roughly in the centre of room, facing the panel about two to five metres from the table – depending on the size of the space. This is a standard convention, and if you make this choice it will certainly do you no harm. However, in my experience facilitating workshops with leading industry professionals, they have often revealed to my students how performers at the top of their profession make much bolder use of the space. I have witnessed casting director Neil Rutherford, who has vast experience of auditions at the highest levels from both sides of the table, encourage my students to start their performance from a corner of the audition room. On many occasions I have observed award-winning actress Rosalie Craig begin a song in an audition masterclass leaning casually against the wall or lying on the floor. Such choices give the impression that the actor is comfortable in the space. It also allows the panel to get a sense of how you might use your physicality on stage. So don't be afraid to start kneeling, or to make use of a chair; just ensure that your decisions make sense in the context of song. For example, if you are singing 'Bring Him Home' from *Les Misérables*, the character Valjean is praying. So it would be a sensible choice to start kneeling on the floor, perhaps at a slight angle to the table, looking up towards an imaginary heaven. If you are singing 'Heaven on the Minds' from *Jesus Christ Superstar*, Judas is brooding on his darkening relationship with Jesus. This might make leaning against the wall, or sat hugging your knees in the corner, an appropriate starting point.

The second important decision you need to make is whether to sing directly to the panel, or not. This is a choice you should have made – and practised – in advance of your audition. Your options are:

1. To sing to the panel, making direct eye contact with them.

2. To sing to a fixed point above their heads.

3. To direct your focus to a variety of circles of attentions.

It is worth noting that leading casting professionals have different preferences when it comes to this issue. Some feel involved when they are engaged with eye contact; others prefer for you to look above them so they can sit back and assess your work without feeling they need to be directly involved in your performance. As opinions differ, the best advice is for you to make an informed choice about which style works best for your song and for you as an actor. In audition workshops with Olivier Award-winning director Timothy Sheader, I have often heard him remonstrate with students about the need for them to make clear and definite choices about where they place their focus. But what factors should determine your decision?

Singing to the Panel

This manner of presentation works particularly well if you are performing a comedy number, or a narrative song. It can also suit songs that are written as conversations with a group of other characters, or with the audience. You may discover this style suits you if you are an actor that usually thrives on interaction with other performers. Singing to the panel often has the benefit of making them feel included and engaged.

However, there are certain styles of song that don't suit this mode of presentation. Pieces in which the content is aggressive or confrontational can be awkward, as they can make the panel feel as though they are the ones under attack. Similarly, songs that are flirtatious or seductive can be a little uncomfortable to watch. It is also worth understanding that the panel might be making notes or whispering to each other during your performance (they are not being rude – they are doing their job). If you think this might throw you, then you may want to consider one of the other styles of song presentation. Below are a few tips for singing directly to the panel:

1. Don't sing for too long at one individual person, as it can become uncomfortable for them, particularly if they want to make a note, or discuss you with their colleague. If you make eye contact with a panel member and they look away, or seem uneasy – shift your focus to another person. It is important to share your performance with the entire panel in any case.

2. Avoid getting too close to the table, as again this can be a little disconcerting for the audition panel.

3. Don't neglect thoughts that are found in your imagination, e.g. mental pictures that are located in the first or third circles of attention (see pp. 28–29). In life we rarely deliver an entire conversation directly into someone's eyes.

Singing to a Fixed Point

This style of presentation is perhaps the most commonly used by musical-theatre professionals. It is a method of acting through song where you sing to a single focal point over the heads of the panel. For songs that are addressed to one character, it can work particularly well, as you can put all your focus on seeing that imaginary person. It also means you are less likely to feel self-conscious because you are not making eye contact with those assessing you. It also allows them to discuss you, and write notes about you. On a different point, some actors struggle to know what physical choices to make when they are singing in audition – they worry about using too many gestures. Although I would encourage you to trust your impulses – and always move if it feels correct – this style of auditioning can help, as it lends itself to a stiller form of presentation. It also allows the panel to concentrate on your voice, which is normally the crucial component being assessed in early-round musical-theatre auditions. Below is some advice about singing to a fixed point:

1. As discussed in the previous chapter, you must see mental pictures in your imagination at all times. So if you are singing to another character, for example, you must visualise the behaviour of the person to whom you are singing. Imagine them walking into a room, winking at you, shrugging their shoulders, etc., as this will give you something to respond to.

2. Ensure your imaginary person is positioned behind the table so you are not singing on too much of an angle; otherwise the people who need to be able to see you end up looking at the side of your head.

3. When you are singing to an imaginary person, don't have them sat down, or stood on top of something. As the casting team are not privy to what you are picturing, it can appear as if you are talking to a dwarf or a giant! This can look very odd.

4. In this mode it is easy to feel physically inhibited. Always give yourself permission to move and follow your impulses.

Varied Circles of Attention

This approach is useful for songs where the character is singing in soliloquy, i.e. when they are alone. When delivering soliloquies in audition, try mixing the focus of your delivery so that you find some thoughts in the first and third circles of attention – and address the panel in other moments. This approach has the benefit of allowing you to display an element of stagecraft in your song presentation, and to demonstrate physical choices that bear a similarity to those you might do on stage. However, you need to be physically articulate to pull off this approach so that your choices make logical sense to those watching – otherwise your performance can easily be criticised as lacking in focus.

Here are some tips for this style of presentation to make your focal points specific:

1. Try putting your focus in the first or third circles when the character is remembering something, or envisaging a future event. See an image each time you do this. For example, in 'Empty Chairs and Empty Tables' from *Les Misérables* – which is a soliloquy – if you were playing Marius, you would see images such as the memory of your dead friends at the barricade.

2. The best thoughts to address directly to the panel are lyrics in which the character asks themselves a question, confesses a secret, or has a moment of self-discovery. In these instances, use the panel as though they are your inner-consciousness – try to seek their advice as though you are searching your own soul.

THE MOMENT OF ORIENTATION

Whichever method of delivery you decide upon, perhaps the most difficult moment of your audition is the transition between the conversational element of the meeting and the start of your performance. It is a challenge to shift quickly and successfully from talking to the pianist, to getting yourself in the necessary frame of mind to begin the song. A majority of young actors don't handle this as well as they might, and consequently the first thirty seconds of their audition song can often be acted poorly – until they get into their stride. By that point the panel may already have made an unfavourable decision.

Outlined below is a process to help you act successfully from the moment the music begins. We will use another song from *Les Misérables*, 'Bring Him Home', as an example.

1. As you walk away from your conversation with the pianist, take a brief second to remind yourself of the immediate previous circumstances, i.e. what has happened just prior to the song. You want to focus on elements of the story that will engage you imaginatively, change your inner tempo and get you thinking as the character. In *Les Misérables*, Valjean is at the barricade, having chosen to stand alongside the student revolutionaries. If you were performing this song you might reflect on the recent onslaught by the French army, and the danger this caused to the life of Marius, the future husband of your adoptive daughter Cosette.

2. Once you feel your imagination is activated, bring the first objective of your song to the forefront of your mind. Pretend that you desperately want that objective. So, with Valjean, you would focus on how much you want God to hear your prayer for Marius.

3. See your first image in your head. This should be the image that you respond to at the beginning of the song. This might be the behaviour of the imaginary person your character is talking to, a memory, an imagined possible future event, or an aspect of the character's surroundings. With Valjean he might be looking at the night sky, as he searches it for the presence of God.

Once you have these three key points clear in your mind, you can indicate to the pianist you are ready. This entire process should take no more than a few seconds in total, as it can be awkward for the panel if your preparation takes too long. By readying yourself in this manner, and beginning the song in the correct mind-set, you will find it easier to act well and avoid feeling self-conscious about being watched by the panel.

ACTING THE INTRODUCTION

Once the music starts, you have your next big opportunity to make a favourable impression: by making the best use of the musical introduction. It is standard practice in audition to cut down an introduction to about two bars – and this is something you should do whenever possible. Yet even with such a short opening instrumental, it is important to recognise that the starting note of the music is the beginning of your performance and therefore the first chance the panel have to assess your acting. You should use this opportunity to stimulate the panel's interest. A good way to do this is through an imaginative use of the space. For example, in the song 'Anthem' from *Chess*, The Russian is addressing a group of journalists and news reporters. So you might choose to start the song a few metres off the centre of the room, then walk into the middle of the space during the introduction, as if entering the press conference. Making such a choice can get the panel sitting forward in their seats ready for the first lyric.

THE OPENING LINES

What you do next – in the first few lines – is crucial. You should make clear decisions in advance about what your first two actions (see pp. 27–28) will be. Although this approach is necessarily premeditated, knowing what you will play on the first line, and how the action changes on the second thought, can help set you running from the start of the song – which can be very hard to do in an audition when you are nervous. You may find that using a structured beginning can actually make you more spontaneous as the song progresses. Because you have started changing action on each new thought from the very start of your performance, you will find it easier to achieve the ideal use of actions with a different choice on every line.

FOLLOWING YOUR IMPULSES

Once you are into the flow of your song – if you have done the required preparation and rehearsal – then your job is actually uncomplicated: you merely need to see something, allow an impulse to develop inside you, and then trust your instincts enough to respond to it. Acting, though difficult to do well, is actually very simple. If instead of blocking yourself – by self-editing your choices through fear of failure – you give yourself permission to do whatever feels right in the moment, then you allow yourself a greater opportunity to be successful.

When you are acting in audition you should aim to follow this cyclical process:

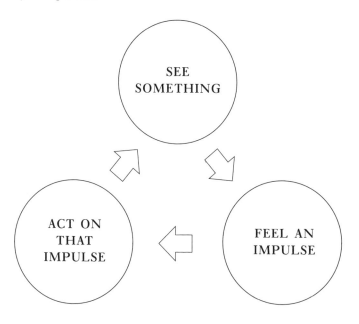

In an audition context, the instruction to 'see something' most usually refers to the mental images you will have practised, e.g. the character's memories, their visions of the future, their surroundings, or the imagined behaviour of the person to whom they are singing. When working in direct address, it refers to something you observe in the behaviour of the panel. For example, if you are working on 'Anthem' from *Chess*, you could imagine that the panel are the news reporters. So if one of the panellists smiles at you whilst you are singing, you could pretend they were a reporter who was smirking at you. This might give you an impulse to challenge them.

When you act on an impulse this can take several forms. It may cause you to move in the space, to use a gesture, or to a play an internal action – such as to comfort, to amuse, or to antagonise. A genuine impulse is a precious gift, and when one comes along you only have a split-second to take advantage of it. To do so you must act before you think. Because when you are in the moment, if you stop to analyse a choice, instead of just doing it, then spontaneity dies. Remember: *your impulse is always right*. When you are in that audition room you need to trust yourself, avoid second-guessing your choices, and give yourself total permission to follow your instincts in the moment.

EVENTS

In her fine book, *The Director's Craft: A Handbook for the Theatre*, Katie Mitchell talks about the idea of 'events'. An event is a fundamental shift. It is the instant the character makes an important discovery, takes a great decision, or has a moment of emotional catharsis. For instance, in 'Soliloquy' from *Carousel*, there are two events. Firstly, when Billy realises that his future child may be a girl, rather than a boy, and secondly when he decides that he will provide for that child no matter what, even if that means stealing or dying. Where there is an event in a song, this is identified in the self-rehearsal guides. As they are the most important moments in the story, they should be highlighted as the crucial moments of the narrative. You can emphasise an event successfully in the following ways:

1. Through a moment of stillness. This works particularly well when the character has a sudden realisation, or makes a fundamental internal decision.

2. By playing the strongest action of the entire song. This can highlight instances when the character finally communicates something they strongly feel – which has been suppressed for a long time.

3. By finding a genuine emotional connection at that point. This can be appropriate for moments of catharsis for the character.

CONCLUDING THE SONG

A simple way to refine and improve your audition technique is to take particular care of the moment at the end of the song, when you break out of the imaginary world of the character. You achieve this by staying in the thought-process of the song for a second or two after the music concludes, before clearly breaking character and bringing your focus back into the real world of the audition room. By marking this transition, it draws a clear delineation between yourself and the role. When you are on a panel and you see this transformation occur, it is very exciting to watch; you feel you have witnessed the end of a clear and defined piece of storytelling.

REDIRECTION

After you have performed your song you might be asked to sing it again following a piece of redirection from the panel. This might be a vocal instruction – you could be asked to belt a high note, rather than sing it in a Twang quality, for example – but more usually it will be related to acting.

When a director asks you to act your song differently, this isn't necessarily because they didn't like your original choices – it is usually an indication that they are interested in you and want to know more. A good piece of redirection will be an invitation for you to demonstrate a quality that wasn't present in your initial performance. The director, or drama-school tutor, might want you to play a different choice of action, so they may encourage you to charm, to cross-examine, to amuse, or to belittle. They might ask you to work for more stillness, or to make greater use of the space. On other occasions they may ask you to alter the given circumstances. For example: play the song as if you have just learned that your lover has abandoned you, or sing it as if you have just returned home after a romantic first date.

The redirection you are offered can sometimes be radically different from the given circumstances in the musical. This may be because the director is unfamiliar with your song, or more usually because they want to see if you can change your performance and be responsive to feedback. So even if the instructions seem strange or nonsensical, *don't ever be resistant to what is asked.* The first rule of being redirected is to respond positively to what is suggested. It is valid to engage with this redirection – to ask the panel to clarify or go further with their note – but this should always be done in a constructive and non-confrontational manner. You want to convey that you are someone who understands notes and will be good to work with.

When you act your song for the second time, you should be bold in your choices and fully engage with the redirection. However, playing a note successfully doesn't simply mean delivering only what was asked of you in a narrow, confined manner. See the note as a springboard to a wide range of new choices. This might mean starting in a different part of the room, being freer physically, and even allowing your vocal performance to alter radically. It is important to remember a basic fact: the panel witnessed your first version! They will have noted the original choices you made. So when you are redirected you should try to show something new on every line.

EXERCISES

As well as redirecting you, the panel may also ask you to sing some vocal exercises as a way of learning more about your voice. When you are auditioning for a production, this is usually because your song choice didn't demonstrate the vocal range required for the role you are being considered for. In drama-school auditions, you are often asked to sing exercises so the tutors can get a better picture of your full vocal potential. Exercises typically might include scales, arpeggios, or sirening on octave slides. The given exercise will usually be repeated, ascending a semitone at a time. When you deliver the requested exercise, give yourself the best opportunity to sing well by standing with good alignment of the head, neck and spine, with your feet directly below your hips and your weight evenly distributed. Release your abdominal wall between each repetition, as there can be a tendency for your breath to become tight as the exercise gets progressively higher. It is useful to understand that you will most usually be asked to continue progressing upwards in pitch *until your voice cracks*. Whilst this can be disconcerting, try not to let it worry you – it is just a method a panel uses to ascertain the top note of your range. You may well have sung the note the panel needed to hear several semitones before.

FEEDBACK

One of the hardest aspects of auditioning is that you rarely receive any detailed or meaningful feedback. Despite the recent #YesOrNo Twitter campaign, which has seen many leading theatres commit to informing all actors about the outcome of their audition, when trying out for many professional productions you still may not even be informed that you didn't get the job – only learning you have not got a part through the gradual passage of time. Undergoing a nerve-racking audition, and then not being told why you've been unsuccessful, can be wearing and demoralising. You can spend the weeks that follow an audition reliving it, second-guessing yourself and wondering whether you could have done something differently. Although to some extent this is unavoidable, it is also counterproductive and can make it hard to sustain yourself emotionally – whether through a season of drama-school auditions, or over a long career as a working actor.

A sensible way to manage this is to allow yourself a brief period of reflection – perhaps on your journey home from the audition – where you make a few notes on how you could improve next time around. You should then encourage yourself to forget about the audition – accept that the odds are that you will have been unsuccessful, that there is nothing you can do to change the outcome – and then ready yourself for the next opportunity. Responding in this manner can be an effective self-protection strategy that enables you to better cope with periods of uncertainty and rejection. In between auditions, if you are able to clear your mind and focus on the future, then on the occasions when the phone does ring, the positive outcomes are wonderful and uplifting surprises.

For further exercises and advice to aid you in the preparation and performance of your songs, you might look at the following books:

Acting Through Song: Techniques and Exercises for Musical-Theatre Actors by Paul Harvard

Successful Singing Auditions by Gillyanne Kayes

The Actor and the Target by Declan Donnellan

Finally, may I wish you the all very best for your audition, whatever it may be for. Remember that ultimately it is *your* audition. The exercises outlined in this book, followed carefully, will help you to prepare in the best possible way – but on the day the most important thing is to trust your own instincts and express yourself. Good luck!

PART TWO:
THE SONGS

Tenor/High Baritone

'Almost Like Being in Love' from *Brigadoon*

Music by Frederick Loewe, lyrics by Alan Jay Lerner

Choose this song if: you enjoy playing the love-struck, romantic lead, and have a warm, high-baritone voice that suits songs written in a legit style.

Given Circumstances

WHO ARE YOU: Tommy Albright, a successful, attractive young city professional in your early twenties from New York.

WHERE ARE YOU: Outside the house of Andrew MacLaren in the magical village of Brigadoon in the Scottish Highlands.

WHEN IS IT: Early evening, a summer's night, 1947.

WHAT HAS HAPPENED BEFORE: You have been dissatisfied with your life recently, and felt that something was lacking – particularly in regards to your relationship with your fiancée, Jane. You have begun to lose faith in love. Three days ago you left New York with your friend Jeff Douglas for a game-hunting vacation in Scotland. Before leaving your home city, you had postponed your marriage to Jane.

On the first morning after arriving in Scotland, you and Jeff got lost walking in the hills. Whilst trying to figure out where you were, you realised that you had stumbled upon a village. This was a great surprise to you, as there was no reference to it on the map. (You learn later from the village's schoolteacher, Mr Lundie, that the village, Brigadoon, only appears for one day every hundred years. This magical circumstance has come about because, two hundred years ago, the local minister asked God if life in village might remain the same for ever and his prayer was granted.)

When you first entered the village a fair was taking place. There you met one of the villagers, Andrew MacLaren, and his two daughters, Fiona and Jean – who were buying supplies for Jean's imminent wedding. As you were feeling hungry, you accepted the invitation of the eldest daughter, Fiona, to go back to their family home for a meal.

That afternoon you accompanied Fiona on a trip to gather heather for her sister's forthcoming nuptials. Whilst on the hillside you revealed to her that you were not happy in your own engagement. She in turn confessed that she thought she was falling for you. The afternoon was very exciting for you both, as you felt such a strong connection to each other. Having just returned to the village you decided to seek out Jeff to tell him how happy you were feeling.

WHO ELSE IS THERE: You are alone with Jeff.

WHO SHOULD YOU SING TO: You should sing to Jeff. In the stage version, during the middle section of the song you sing to Fiona – as though in a memory – but this dramatic conceit is hard to make clear in an audition. Instead, sing the entire song to your friend, as Gene Kelly does in the film version.

CLASSICAL

Textual Analysis

At the beginning of the song you are excited and energised, as you have just returned from your romantic afternoon with Fiona. This should express itself in positive, uplifting actions and a playful and expressive physicality. This is reflected in the fact that you say that you could swim Loch Lomond in half an hour. Your objective in this opening verse is: to work out why you feel so fantastic. At this point you are talking to yourself as much as you are to Jeff.

When the main melody starts a new unit begins and your objective changes. You now want: to get Jeff to appreciate your amazing day – and the new feelings it has ignited in you. In this section, your physical energy becomes calmer, your conversation more intimate and focused. There should be greater desire for advice and validation from your friend. You want Jeff to validate that the new feelings you have are love.

In the second chorus, when you recall your walk with Fiona, you are reacting to the memories of the afternoon. See these images in the third circle of attention, let them warm and delight you. You objective in this section is: to indulge in the memory of your afternoon with Fiona.

After the key change there is a feeling of joyous celebration in the music. This reflects your belief that you are now in love. Your objective here is: to celebrate the dramatic change in your fortunes. You are transformed, and are no longer a pessimist, but a romantic. This represents a huge conversion for you as you were depressed and cynical when you left New York. The end of the song is thus an emotional catharsis, a joyous emotional release, and is the event of the song.

KEY MOMENTS/TOP TIPS

1. Tommy is feeling entirely free of self-consciousness during this song, as he is ecstatic. Give yourself permission to be physically bold and expressive.

2. When delivering this song in an audition room, you can either talk to an imaginary Jeff, located behind the table, or use direct address and sing to the entire panel as though they are all your best friends.

3. During the opening section in particular you have a renewed connection to the natural world that surrounds you – to the sun, the fresh air and the beautiful countryside. Let the beauty of these images inspire you.

4. As you approach the key change, and say for the second time that you think that the bells are ringing for you, you should say a metaphorical 'yes' to that statement. You feel that finally love has come your way. This moment of celebration should fuel that joyous musical modulation.

5. Loewe cleverly puts a crotchet rest before the title lyric on several occasions during the first verse. Make sense of these momentary pauses – they are there to demonstrate

Tommy is still trying to weigh up at that point whether it is really love that he is feeling.

6. You repeat the title of the song several times, so try a range of different actions to ensure it doesn't become repetitive. When you are talking to Jeff you can try playing actions such as: to excite, to mesmerise, to charm. When you are speaking to yourself you can explore choices like: to warm, to uplift, to amuse and to thrill.

Vocal and Musical Analysis

WHO TO LISTEN TO: Gene Kelly in the 1954 film. This will give you the correct style, but has long dance breaks. For a version that marries with the sheet music listen to Jack Cassidy on the 1957 studio cast recording.

VOCAL RANGE: C3 to F♯4 (optional ending to A4).

ORIGINAL KEY: B♭ major.

ACCENT: New York.

STYLE OF MUSICAL: Book musical.

CLASSICAL

VOCAL SET-UP/MUSICAL TIPS

1. This version of the sheet music is a duet for Tommy and Fiona. You should sing all of the lyrics, including those assigned to Fiona. This requires a couple of minor changes. In the middle section, after you have just spoken about walking up the brae, change the word 'we' to 'she' and the word 'your' to 'her', as Kelly does in the film. You should also sing the melody at all times, as per the suggested recording. This therefore means singing the top line of the music at the key change leading into p. 100 of the sheet music, and the bottom line for the last four bars.

2. The song was originally written to be sung with a crooner's style, which you can very much hear in the film version recommended above. To achieve this style you can make a

liberal use of pitch-glides (where you slide from one note to another). You can hear Kelly do this on the words 'day' and 'smile'. You can also add tiny grace notes, which Kelly demonstrates on the word 'be' and also on the final note.

3. The song starts in a Speech quality, but should still feel fluid and romantic rather than conversational, so try to use a simultaneous onset wherever possible.

4. The line about feeling aglow and alive is the most important in the opening section and should be highlighted. Try lifting the larynx at this point, tilting the thyroid cartilage and delivering it in a Cry quality.

5. In the first chorus return to a Speech quality, as you did at the beginning.

6. In the second chorus, which is more reflective, try returning to a Cry position – but play with a strong use of consonants and some aspirate onsets. This will help convey a sense of thoughtfulness. To move out of this set-up, you should crescendo on the line before the key change when you talk about the ringing of bells. Effect this crescendo by removing your thyroid tilt and adding torso anchoring to allow you to deliver the key change in a loud, rich anchored Speech quality.

7. The last line is delivered in an Advanced-Speech quality rather than Belt. To achieve this add anchoring in your torso and don't lift the chin. As an alternative finish you could sing the line written for Fiona which ends on a high A. If you choose this option you should belt the final note.

Sheet Music

The correct sheet music for this song is available at www.scribd.com.

'It Ain't Necessarily So'
from *Porgy and Bess*

*Music by George Gershwin, lyrics by DuBose Heyward and
Ira Gershwin*

Choose this song if: you are a tenor who enjoys singing music
influenced by jazz and are good at playing the charming,
manipulative villain. The role was originally written for an
African-American actor.

Given Circumstances

WHO ARE YOU: Sporting Life, a small-time, but elegant and
persuasive, drug-dealer in his mid-twenties.

WHERE ARE YOU: At the church picnic on Kittiwah Island, near
Charleston, South Carolina, USA.

WHEN IS IT: 3.00 p.m., a hot summer's afternoon, 1930.

WHAT HAS HAPPENED BEFORE: A month ago you were involved
in a crap game with the male residents of Catfish Row, a run-
down tenement on the waterfront of Charleston. Whilst you
were in the midst of the game, Crown, a physically
intimidating dockworker, arrived with his lover Bess. She was
received coolly by the women of Catfish Row as a woman of
disrepute, but you managed to sell Crown some cheap
whiskey and 'happy dust' (cocaine). During the game the
players withdrew one by one, until eventually only the now
drunken Crown and a player called Robbins remained. When
Robbins won the game and tried to take his winnings Crown
reacted angrily and murdered him with a cotton hook. Crown
chose to flee, telling Bess that she should fend for herself until
he could return. Seeing a chance to seize the woman you
desired, you gave Bess some 'happy dust' and asked her to
come to New York with you. Bess, who is an addict, was
tempted but eventually refused. With nowhere to stay, Bess

98

was refused shelter by all of the local residents – except the cripple Porgy who let her live with him. Rejecting her life with Crown, Bess gradually came to be accepted by the community and her affection for Porgy grew.

This morning you turned up at Catfish Row and once more tried to tempt Bess with cocaine and the offer to take her to New York – where you intend to turn her to prostitution. She refused and told you she had given up taking drugs. You taunted her that no addict ever gave up cocaine (which turns out to be true, as at the end of musical Bess does give in to her addiction and accompanies you to New York, destroying her chance of happiness). When Porgy caught you trying to pressurise Bess, he chased you off. The residents of Catfish Row then boarded the boat to Kittiwah Island where the church picnic was taking place that evening. Bess was encouraged to attend by the virtuous Maria, even though she was reluctant, as Porgy was unable to make the crossing due to his disability.

This evening, with all of the churchgoers enjoying the picnic, you arrived at the island. You have just decided to take this opportunity to offer them your ironic opinions on some of the stories of the Bible.

WHO ELSE IS THERE: The crowd of churchgoers. Bess is not present.

WHO SHOULD YOU SING TO: The churchgoers.

Textual Analysis

During the song you try to convince the churchgoing picnickers that the stories of the Bible are ridiculous. You hold up some of the most fantastical stories – that a small man such as David managed to slay the giant Goliath, that Jonah lived inside a whale, and that King Methuselah lived to be nine hundred years old – to ridicule. Your objective in the first verse is: to undermine the Christian beliefs of the congregation. You try to achieve this objective in the most charming and seductive manner. For each of the three verses this objective remains the same, so if the song is to be engaging, you must use a wide range of appealing actions to lure the picnickers into believing your heresy. Actions you might play in the verses might include: I amuse, titillate, enthrall, beguile, tempt, delight and entertain you.

As the lyrics of the two choruses contain no proper words at all, the objective in these sections could be many things. Try playing the following on the scat lyrics in the first chorus: to dismiss the Bible stories as ridiculous. In the second chorus, for the sake of variety you may want to alter this objective. You could play: to celebrate and glorify your rebellious behaviour. Alternatively you could try: to mock the picnickers for their blind obedience to the church.

During the short bridge section, you reveal your true self to the churchgoers. You confess that you twist the rules of the Bible to your own ends. But that is an unusual confession in that you are almost bragging about you sinful nature. Your objective here is: to antagonise the Christians with your attitude towards sin.

In the last two lines you have a final objective: to explain your reasoning for this unconventional sermon. Your rationale being that you genuinely believe the stories of the Bible to be false.

KEY MOMENTS/TOP TIPS

1. As the song makes constant reference to the Bible, you may want to research the following Biblical stories if they are unfamiliar to you: David and Goliath, Jonah and the whale, Moses being found as a baby in the bulrushes, and Methuselah. By knowing the stories well, as Sporting Life does, you will be able to sing about them with more authority.

2. This song works particularly well if sung directly to the panel, as if they are the parishioners.

3. Sporting Life is sexually charismatic. Your performance should reflect a person who is very much confident in his physicality.

Vocal and Musical Analysis

WHO TO LISTEN TO: Cedric Neal in the 2014 Regent's Park Open Air Theatre production. This version is a great example of the required style, but it is full of improvisation and deviates wildly from the score. Listen to Damon Evans on the 1993 television recording to hear a version that more closely follows the original music.

VOCAL RANGE: D3 to G♭4 (with the possibility to riff to higher pitches).

ORIGINAL KEY: G minor.

ACCENT: New York.

STYLE OF MUSICAL: Book musical.

VOCAL SET-UP/MUSICAL TIPS

1. Some lyrics are assigned to members of the ensemble in this version of the score – you should sing all of these, including the call-and-answer sections in the choruses.

2. The predominant vocal set-up is typical of many jazz and blues singers. The sound should contain twang, but with the larynx lowered to remove any sense of harshness, giving the voice a mellow quality. Neal ably demonstrates this on the suggested recording.

3. In the chorus, which is sung as a jazz scat, you should use an Advanced-Speech quality – add some torso anchoring tilt and thyroid to allow you to access the higher pitches.

4. Liberal use of pitch-glides and 'bending' the pitch of a note is stylistically appropriate. You can hear numerous examples of this in Neal's performance.

5. As a jazz song this piece can include a degree of vocal improvisation. If you feel confident to do this it is usually best to create your own musical version, rather than copying another artist's riffs. If this is something you find difficult, you may wish to work on this in conjunction with a singing teacher.

6. The word 'yeah' at the end of each chorus is notated to be spoken – but is a good example of an instant where you could add a vocal riff.

Sheet Music

The correct sheet music for this song is available at www.scribd.com.

CLASSICAL

'Soliloquy'
from *Carousel*

Music by Richard Rodgers, lyrics by Oscar Hammerstein II

Choose this song if: you have rich baritone legit voice, and have the gravitas to play a charming, ultra-masculine and flawed leading man who has the capacity to be a rogue at times, and can make poor, impulsive decisions.

Given Circumstances

WHO ARE YOU: Billy Bigelow, a very attractive, strong, working-class young American who, at the beginning of the musical, is working as a fairground barker on a carousel. You are a troubled man who, despite a desire to do the right thing, often lets temper and pride get the better of you. Your arrogance and flirtatiousness hide a deep-rooted lack of self-worth.

WHERE ARE YOU: Outside of Nettie Fowler's Spa on the oceanfront in Maine, New England, USA (unlike the film version which takes place on a rocky beach).

WHEN IS IT: 11.00 a.m., a bright June morning, 1873.

WHAT HAS HAPPENED BEFORE: You had previously been working on the carousel for a middle-aged widow named Mrs Mullin. She is in love with you, though her feelings are not reciprocated. Over a month ago an attractive young millworker named Julie Jordan came to the fairground. Julie allowed you to put your arm around her whilst riding the carousel (something that was viewed as scandalous for a single woman at this time). Witnessing this, and incensed with jealousy, Mrs Mullin confronted Julie and told her to never return to the carousel. Annoyed by Mrs Mullin's possessiveness, you didn't attempt to stop her when she threatened to fire you – which she eventually did. Despite being out of a job, or perhaps because of that fact, you asked Julie to have a drink with you that evening. Julie agreed, even though it meant she would lose her own job at the millhouse – because she would be returning home late to the mill boarding house. During a night spent talking under the stars you both tried hard to conceal the growing attraction you felt towards the other.

In the month since that first meeting you and Julie have had a hasty marriage. However, because you have no other skills, you had been unable to find a new job. With both of you unemployed you were forced to move in with Julie's cousin, Nettie. This situation created a lot of tension between yourself and Julie, and recently you hit her. You felt ashamed – but conversely those feelings only served to make you increasingly angry towards, and dismissive of, Julie.

In the past few weeks you have struck up a friendship with a man called Jigger, who is a whaler by profession, but who is also a small-time criminal. A few minutes ago he tried to convince you to become involved in an armed robbery of the house of the rich mill-owner, Mr Bascombe. You refused, as the plan might potentially involve murder. After Jigger left, Mrs Mullin, who had heard that you had beaten Julie and was concerned about your friendship with Jigger, tried to convince you to leave your wife and return to work at the carousel and be with her. Julie interrupted you and so Mrs Mullin left, but not before she had asked you to think through her proposition. The reason Julie interrupted was to tell you that she was pregnant, after which she went back in the Spa. A moment ago Mrs Mullin returned, expecting you to agree to her offer, but you told her that you were going to be a father and therefore would be staying with Julie. With this news she has just departed for good.

WHO ELSE IS THERE: You are alone.

WHO SHOULD YOU SING TO: Yourself, though in an audition you can share many of your thoughts with the panel as though they are your inner-consciousness.

Textual Analysis

Note: The song is far too long for most auditions, but can be easily cut down and still make sense dramatically. The following cuts are therefore suggested.

Start at the beginning. Sing until you almost reach the end of the first chorus – including the first syllable of the word 'around'. Then make a large cut so you complete the word with the second syllable four pages later when the word 'around' is repeated. (This will mean you cut from the beginning of bar 73 to the end of bar 146.) Then continue onwards until you reach the important discovery on the word 'girl' (at bar 185). At this point make a second cut, starting at the end of bar 184 and coming back in at bar 228 with the four bars of the descending bassline that lead into the final section. Mark on the music that you will speak the word 'girl' instead of the word 'me' on the first beat of bar 228. From there you should continue till the end of the song. The textual analysis that follows assumes those two cuts have been made.

At the start of the song you are very introspective. In the preceding scene, your instinctive response to the news that you are to become a father was exhilaration, but having been left alone, this feeling has turned to worry and reflection. Your objective in the opening lyric is: to imagine what your son will make of you as a father. In the second half of the first verse you then try to imagine what kind of person your son will be. Your imagination quickly begins to run wild with this subject and you are pleased with what you envisage: you reckon that your son will just be like you – but with more common sense.

In the section marked '*più mosso*' your objective becomes: to imagine the fun you will have with your child. You take great delight in thinking about teaching him to wrestle and swim. As you move into the chorus, and decide that you will name your son after yourself, your objective is: to celebrate how strong Bill will grow up to be. You believe he will never be bullied by his boss, as you were by Mrs Mullin.

After the first cut section your thoughts return very much to the argument you have just had with your former employer. This makes you vow that Bill will never marry anyone he doesn't want to.

Of all the daydreams you have, perhaps the thought that gives you most pleasure is imagining when Bill is seventeen and old enough to date women. You delight in thinking about how you will be able to advise and guide him. Your objective in this section is: to indulge your belief that you are wise about women. At the end of that unit the first event of the song occurs: when you realise that you future child might not be a boy at all, but a girl. This thought fills you with a sense of dread and responsibility, for you acknowledge that you must find a way to provide for and protect a daughter. Thinking of having a little girl warms and softens you and the thought that she will come home to you every night needing food, shelter and protection leads you to arrive at a massive decision. Your objective then becomes: to spur yourself into action. You decide that you will get the money you need to provide for your daughter, even if it means stealing, or dying. This is the second and final event of the song.

KEY MOMENTS/TOP TIPS

1. I once heard this song described by the Olivier Award-winning director Timothy Sheader as 'the "To be or not to be" of classical American musical theatre'. This weight of expectation can mean many people are afraid to choose it as an audition piece. It is a famous song because it is exceptionally well-written, and therefore great to act, so if the material suits you then you shouldn't be put off using it.

2. The song requires a great deal of charm and swagger. Find enjoyment when indulging in Billy's self-important fantasies, as this will help the panel warm to you. When talking to the panel, play: to amuse, exhilarate, impress, delight and tickle them.

3. Another event occurs when Billy lands on the idea that he would name his son after himself. This idea fires him up with feelings of fatherly pride.

4. Try playing around with physical stillness on the vital discovery that the child may, in fact, be a girl. This will help highlight this crucial moment in the song.

5. Remember that underneath Billy's brash, hard confidence lies a man who is filled with a lack of self-esteem. Explore the idea that he is fiercely driven by a desire for his daughter to have everything she needs, so that she can lead a better life than he ever had.

Vocal and Musical Analysis

WHO TO LISTEN TO: Hugh Jackman singing live in concert at the Carnegie Hall in 2002.

VOCAL RANGE: B2 to G4.

ORIGINAL KEY: B minor.

ACCENT: General American.

STYLE OF MUSICAL: Book musical.

VOCAL SET-UP/MUSICAL TIPS

1. The main voice quality used in the song is Speech – though try modifying this set-up to include a lowered laryngeal position to achieve a classical musical-theatre sound. This is clearly demonstrated by Jackman on the suggested recording.

2. Sing the long phrases found throughout the song with a legato line wherever possible.

3. The chorus about your son Bill should sound strong and athletic. Use a modified Speech quality at this point, by adding some torso anchoring to make the sound strong and full.

4. The more reflective sections, such as the opening, and later on when you imagine Bill being seventeen, should be delivered in a Cry quality, as this helps demonstrate Billy's sensitivity in these moments.

5. Listen to a recording of the accompaniment. In such a well-written piece of dramatic music, the constant changes of tempo and accompaniment reveal how Rodgers has written the subtext for you in the score – providing many clues about the changes in Billy's emotional state.

6. The last note should be belted to give the song a thrilling vocal conclusion.

Sheet Music

The correct sheet music for this song is available at www.musicnotes.com.

CLASSICAL

'Something's Coming'
from *West Side Story*

Music by Leonard Bernstein, lyrics by Stephen Sondheim

Choose this song if: you suit playing the young, romantic lead
and have a tenor voice that sits stylistically somewhere between
a contemporary and a legit sound. You need to be accomplished
at singing with dynamic control and a legato line.

Given Circumstances

WHO ARE YOU: Tony Wyzek, a young, working-class man in his
late teens, who was formerly the leader of a street gang called
the Jets.

WHERE ARE YOU: In the backyard of Doc's Drugstore in the
Upper West Side of New York, USA.

WHEN IS IT: 4.30 p.m., late afternoon in the hot summer of
1957, towards the end of your shift at work.

WHAT HAS HAPPENED BEFORE: In the last six months or so, your
local neighbourhood has been terrorised by violence between
two gangs of teenagers: the Jets (which is comprised of white,
second- and third-generation immigrants) and the Sharks
(whose members are first-generation Puerto Rican
immigrants). Tired of the violence, and wanting to make a
better life for yourself, you quit the Jets a few months ago and
took a regular job working for Doc, the owner of the
drugstore who is something of a father figure to the Jets. Your
best friend Riff, whom you have known for over four years
and who lives with you and your family, became the leader of
the Jets. Many of the other members of the gang feel that you
betrayed them by leaving the gang, though Riff has been
trying to protect your reputation.

Recently the violence between the two gangs has escalated.
About ten minutes ago Riff came to visit you at the drugstore.

He described the latest tensions with the Sharks and implored you to come to the dance at the gym tonight at 10.00 p.m. – which both gangs would be attending. You were reluctant. During the conversation you confided to Riff that for the last month you have been having a nightly dream in which you are expecting something amazing to happen, an undefined event that you are constantly reaching for, yet are unable to identify. After opening up to Riff you reluctantly agreed to attend the dance when he told you that he had already promised the other Jets you would be coming. A few seconds ago, as he walked off, Riff suggested – somewhat in jest – that the something you have been twitching for might be at the dance tonight. (Of course, this turns out to be true, as tonight you will meet and fall instantly in love with Maria, a Puerto Rican girl who is the younger sister of Bernado – the leader of the Sharks.)

WHO ELSE IS THERE: You are alone. Riff has exited just before you sing.

WHO SHOULD YOU SING TO: You are mainly talking to yourself, but on occasion you address the 'unknown something' you are searching for. It is useful in these moments to behave as though you are talking to Fate.

CLASSICAL

Textual Analysis

When the introduction begins you are considering whether Riff could be right, that you might indeed discover what you are searching for at the dance tonight. In the first two verses your objective is: to work out what this life-changing event might be. Try playing actions such as: to analyse, cross-examine, investigate, scrutinise and dissect yourself.

Although you remain unable to identify what it might be, in the middle section, when the time signature changes into 2/4, your objective becomes: to excite yourself about the prospect of this imminent event. Possible actions at this point might include: to uplift, exhilarate, thrill, rouse, stimulate, accelerate, encourage and electrify yourself.

During the next verse you begin to directly address this 'unknown something'. Twice in this section you sing the lyric 'come on'. In these moments your objective is: to urge this life-changing event to arrive. (Briefly you are personifying it.) By the final verse your objective becomes: to revel in your sense of expectancy. You truly feel that your life is on the cusp of changing forever.

KEY MOMENTS/TOP TIPS

1. In some productions of this show Tony is presented as an overly romantic, saccharine figure – which doesn't reflect his tough social background. He is ultimately a character who demonstrates the ability to commit murder, so it is important your characterisation is credible as a former leader of a street gang. Although Tony is working hard to avoid his violent past, playing characteristics such as masculine, driven, ambitious and passionate will help deliver a performance that is believable.

2. Tony is alone in a space he is familiar with: his workplace. He therefore is without self-consciousness. Give yourself permission to be physically free and playful when that feels appropriate.

3. Unusually for a lyric by Sondheim, there is not a clearly defined journey in the text. At both the beginning and the end of the song Tony is essentially expressing the same idea: that it's possible that the great event he has been expecting may happen tonight. If you are not careful this can lead to the dramaturgy feeling a little stagnant. To help make your audition dynamic, try to find the following arc to the storytelling: at the beginning of the song Tony is hopeful, but uncertain as to whether the dance will provide the answer to his expectations, but by the end he genuinely anticipates it will. At the conclusion of the song he looks forward to attending the dance at the gym with excitement and expectancy.

Vocal and Musical Analysis

WHO TO LISTEN TO: Richard Beymer on the film soundtrack (1961).

VOCAL RANGE: E2 to G4.

ORIGINAL KEY: C major.

ACCENT: New York. If this is an accent you find difficult, then General American will also work.

STYLE OF MUSICAL: Book musical.

VOCAL SET-UP/MUSICAL TIPS

1. *West Side Story* is a score that has sometimes been sung in an operatic style. This is due in large part to the complexities of Bernstein's score – which requires much of the vocal finesse of an opera singer – and that the composer himself wrote for both the theatre and the concert hall. However, this can lead to vocal performances that lack credibility. For example, the 1985 recording that Bernstein himself conducted features a performance by José Carreras which is simply impossible to believe as a New York teenager from the streets of the Upper West Side. As an alternative, try to work for a sound that is more youthful and rooted in a contemporary musical-theatre style.

2. The starting point for a modern delivery of this song must be to ensure the sound is based in Tony's speaking voice, so a strong use of the colloquial dialect is helpful. The verses of the song are conversational and staccato, so the use of Speech quality is suggested at these points; but bear in mind that the back of the tongue should be higher than usual in this quality due to the New York accent.

3. Make use of all three onsets, particularly an aspirate onset, to create an excited breathy sound. In these verses pay particular emphasis to the end consonants, as Sondheim has provided a lyric with lots of vocal bite.

4. In the more lyrical sections – such as the bridge – work for long, sustained phrases. To achieve this, use simultaneous onsets and keep the tongue high near the upper molars. Avoid lowering the larynx too much, as this will begin to make the sound too operatic.

5. Bernstein's music typically contains a great deal of dynamic contrast, and 'Something's Coming' is no exception. Study the score for where crescendos and decrescendos are marked. Where you need to crescendo, gradually take some of the thyroid tilt out and then add torso anchoring. This will cause you to get louder. Reverse this process when you wish to decrescendo.

6. Try delivering both the first and last sections in a Cry quality, as this gives them a reflective quality that is appropriate for the lyric.

7. You should sing the extended ending, which is used on the recording suggested above. Some versions of the score do not contain this conclusion. If your music does not, then tell the audition pianist that you will be singing the extended ending and they should be able to do this for you, as it is very well known. It is appropriate to deliver the last note in a Falsetto quality.

Sheet Music

The correct sheet music for this song is available at www.musicnotes.com.

'Younger Than Springtime'
from *South Pacific*

Music by Richard Rodgers, lyrics by Oscar Hammerstein II

Choose this song if: you can play the masculine, heroic,
romantic lead, are good at singing in a legit style, and like to
sing high and quietly.

Given Circumstances

WHO ARE YOU: Joseph Cable, a handsome, no-nonsense young
lieutenant in the United States Marine Corps.

WHERE ARE YOU: Inside a simple, but beautiful hut on the
island of Bali Ha'i in the South Pacific.

WHEN IS IT: 7.00 p.m., a summer's night, 1942.

WHAT HAS HAPPENED BEFORE: It is the middle of the Second
World War. Recently you were posted to an undisclosed island
in the South Pacific – having previously been on active service
on the island of Guadalcanal. You were assigned to this new
location as you are due to undertake a dangerous and
important spying mission against Japan, who are currently in
the ascendancy in the war against the United States.

Not long after your arrival, a Tonkinese woman, a native of the
island nicknamed 'Bloody Mary', tried to tempt you to visit the
nearby volcanic island of Bali Ha'i. Overhearing her invitation,
Seabee Luther Billis (a sailor of junior rank) tried to persuade
you to accept her offer – and to take him with you. Billis
wanted to meet some of the French girls who live on Bali Ha'i
as the only other women on this island – the nurses stationed
there – were off-limits to sailors of his rank, and as an officer
you are allowed to sail to Bali Ha'i. You refused his request.

The spying mission for which you have been posted requires a
guide, and your commanding officer, Commander William

Harbison, recently asked Emile de Becque, a local French plantation owner, to fulfil this task. When he refused, Harbison ordered you to take a few days leave of absence until the mission could take place. Meanwhile, Billis had managed to commandeer a boat. After your commander's order, you decided to accept to accept his offer to take you to Bali Ha'i.

Tonight when you arrived on the volcanic island you were greeted by Bloody Mary, who led you straight to an empty native hut. She left you alone for a few minutes, but when she returned she brought along her beautiful Tonkinese daughter, Liat, whom you were meeting for the first time. There was a strong initial attraction between you both, but as Liat only spoke French your conversation was stilted and you wondered if she was afraid of you. Moments ago, when she heard the ship's bell indicate it was time for you to leave, she threw herself on you and kissed you, as she didn't want you to go.

WHO ELSE IS THERE: You are alone with Liat.

WHO SHOULD YOU SING TO: Liat.

Textual Analysis

At the beginning of the song you are trying to make sense of your feelings towards Liat, as you have never had this strong, initial connection with a woman before. Your objective in this opening section is: to make Liat understand the effect she has had on you. You want her to understand that holding her in your arms makes you feel vital and masculine. This behaviour, so soon after meeting her, may seem superficial and reflect outdated and even inappropriate attitudes towards women in a modern context. But it is worth remembering the context in which this encounter is taking place. As a member of the armed forces you are in the middle of the most terrible war the world has known. The tenderness and intimacy you are experiencing is a complete contrast to the world outside, which perhaps serves to heighten how strange and wonderful these new feelings are to you.

When the first chorus begins your objective changes: you now want Liat to understand how innocent and beautiful she is. For you this is inextricably linked to her youthfulness. A key line here is when you discuss her lips: one of the reasons you are feeling so love-struck is because it is a hangover from the wonderful surprise of Liat suddenly kissing you.

During the bridge and into the second chorus your focus returns to the mesmerising effect Liat has had on you. Your objective in this section is: to get Liat to understand that she makes you feel as youthful as her. You want Liat to comprehend how meeting her has affected and changed you; it has lifted the cares of war from your shoulders and made you feel like a young man again.

KEY MOMENTS/TOP TIPS

1. Over sixty years after it was written, the sentiments and lyric of this song can now seem a little saccharine. It can seem implausible that Cable has such strong feelings having met Liat only moments before. To make the lyric seem credible, try to make your acting choices as simple and honest as possible – so that the lyrics seem motivated by a youthful innocence, rather than a forced romanticism.

2. One of the key facts of the scene is that, as they speak different languages, Liat does not fully understand Cable. He therefore has to communicate with her using more than just language. It is the only through the combination of his simple words, emotional honesty and strength of feeling that he can get Liat to understand him.

3. The title of the song is a key to Cable's thoughts. It is Liat's youth and purity that he is obsessed by, that he finds infectious. This suggests that, perhaps due to the effects of the war, Cable has been feeling world-weary and older than his years.

4. It is worth considering how Liat would be feeling: nervous, shy and vulnerable. This means Cable would have to work

CLASSICAL

hard to convince her that he is sincere. Try actions such as: to soothe, content, captivate, charm, compliment, uplift and amuse her.

5. The song has an instrumental break, after which the bridge and final chorus are repeated. This repetition is unnecessary in audition, so finish the song after you say the words 'am I with you' for the first time.

Vocal and Musical Analysis

WHO TO LISTEN TO: Mandy Patinkin on the 1986 studio recording.

VOCAL RANGE: E3 to G4.

ORIGINAL KEY: F major.

ACCENT: General American.

STYLE OF MUSICAL: Book musical.

VOCAL SET-UP/MUSICAL TIPS

1. The song is unusual in that it is best delivered almost entirely in one voice quality: Cry. Maintaining this lifted larynx position helps give the song the required simplicity and innocence.

2. To add variety and interest to the set-up, use aspirate onsets to put emphasis on particular words, as Patinkin does so successfully on the suggested recording.

3. As with much of Rodgers and Hammerstein's work, try to sing long legato phrases wherever the music demands it – for example in the bridge.

4. The bridge is the one place where you could perhaps lower the larynx to get a richer tone and find some variety from the Cry position.

5. The last line can either be delivered in Cry, or in a Falsetto position if you find that easier and are able to blend easily between those two qualities.

Sheet Music

The correct sheet music for this song is available at www.scribd.com.

'A World Without You'
from *Children of Eden*

Music and lyrics by Stephen Schwartz

Choose this song if: you have a contemporary pop voice and can belt to a top A♭. This role suits actors who can portray naivety, innocence and vulnerability.

Given Circumstances

WHO ARE YOU: Adam, based on the biblical figure of the same name – husband of Eve. You are an innocent, as you have never experienced pain, suffering, want or neglect. Although the passage of time is not clearly indicated in the script, it is useful to suppose at this point you are about seventeen years old, as you are on the verge of becoming a man.

WHERE ARE YOU: In an unspecified location in the Garden of Eden. The exact surroundings are for you to imagine, but undoubtedly this is a place of astonishing beauty.

WHEN IS IT: Late afternoon, an hour or so before dark, in the time of the Book of Genesis, seventeen years after the Creation.

WHAT HAS HAPPENED BEFORE: At the dawn of time, God (called Father in the musical) created the universe. In six days and six nights he made the Heavens and the Earth – populating it with all living creatures. On the seventh day he made you – the first man – in his own image, and he created Eve to be your wife. Father loved you both greatly as his children, and you wanted for nothing in the perfect paradise that he had made for you.

You were very content with your life in the Garden, and in particular took great pleasure in naming and listing all of the animals of Creation. At first Eve was also content, but as she grew older she began to become bored with the repetitive nature of her life.

One day Eve questioned Father about a strange, glistening tree that grew on a hilltop beyond a distant waterfall. When Father became defensive at Eve's persistent questioning you warned her to stop, but still she continued asking. Eventually Father revealed that the tree was called the Tree of Knowledge, but warned you both that you were forbidden from eating the fruit that grew in its branches. He made you promise that you would never do so. You immediately agreed, but Eve remained curious and wanted to know why she could not eat the forbidden fruit. Father did not answer her questions, instead telling her to trust that what he was doing was in their best interest. Reluctantly she also promised not to eat the fruit, or even go near it.

This morning Eve led you to the tree. She had made an amazing discovery that she wanted to show you. Whenever you stepped near the tree the daylight temporarily disappeared – turning the day into night – and the fruit glowed with an eerie light. Not wanting to displease Father by being near the forbidden tree, you left to continue listing the animals.

Whilst you were gone, the Devil – taking the form of a serpent – tempted Eve to eat from the Tree of Knowledge. The strange fruit gave Eve the newfound ability to see all of the possibilities of the world: how she could invent tools, travel the Earth and bear children. She was a child herself no longer. Excited by her new knowledge, and comforted by her belief that Father's warnings had proved unfounded, Eve tricked you into drinking cider made from the forbidden fruit when she returned home.

Discovering that he had been disobeyed, Father was furious and a few minutes ago he sought you both out. You tried to hide, but he discovered you concealed amongst the trees. Eve tried to explain to Father that the fruit had simply given her knowledge, and told you that she had learned you could have children together, but Father was not interested in hearing her excited protestations. Blaming Eve for tricking you, he has just ordered her to leave the Garden. He then told you that he would make you a new wife to replace her. When you replied that you only wanted Eve, Father retorted that either you must choose to stay with him – and never see Eve again – or leave the Garden with her and never return.

WHO ELSE IS THERE: Father and Eve.

WHO SHOULD YOU SING TO: For the majority of the song you move between talking to Father and to Eve. However, there are two crucial moments in the text: where you address the Garden, and where you speak to yourself.

Textual Analysis

At the beginning of the song you face a terrible decision and are in a state of disbelief. Father has always loved you and protected you and, having lived your life as a loved and protective child, you have never known suffering. Now you are being forced to make a painful choice between the two people you love. In the first verse your objective is: to stop Father from making you choose. You do this in a very respectful manner. You say how much you love and honour him; you try to make him understand how devastated you would be if you had to choose between him and Eve. In this section, explore actions such as: I credit, elevate and beseech you.

In the second verse all of your attention turns to Eve. Your objective here is: to get her to understand you would be heartbroken if you never saw her again. Looking at your wife at this point should melt you; all the love you feel for her should come flooding to the surface.

In the bridge you once more address Father. Your objective is similar to the first verse; you are imploring Father not to make you choose. The fractured rhythms and shifting time signature here indicate that you should make more urgent choices, as if you are feeling emotional distress. At this point try playing actions such as: I beg, beseech, urge and rattle you.

When you address the Garden at the beginning of the third verse your objective is: to mourn the loss of your home. After a few lines your thought process then takes an unexpected course. You turn to Father and tell him that you want to stay. But you are now in a state of utter turmoil. After one final appeal to Eve for advice, and realising Father will not change his mind, you accept you must make a choice. So in the last few lines you finally play your most important objective: to decide whether to leave the Garden. The event of the song occurs when you choose to leave with Eve on the final word of the lyric.

KEY MOMENTS/TOP TIPS

1. As this song is addressed to two other characters, to make this clear, try locating Father just to the left of the audition table, and Eve just to the right of it. Address those points each time you are speaking to the relevant character – imagining their behaviour as you look in their direction.

2. At the end of each verse you ask a question that contains the title of the song – first to Father, and then to Eve. Ask these questions ferociously as though they might reply to you. Adam is doing all he can to seek advice and avoid making the decision himself.

3. It is significant that the first time you belt you are addressing the Garden, rather than Father or Eve. As the Garden is Adam's home this moment of great emotional distress occurs because he realises he will never see it again, and the happy times that were shared in that place – as a united family – can never be repeated.

4. As the story of Adam and Eve is so famous, those watching your performance will already know the decision that Adam makes. *But you mustn't show this in the performance.*

You must live through his dilemma, and behave as if he is grappling with this decision in the moment. A good way to sustain the drama to the last moment is to sing the last line towards Father (as if you are going to choose to stay with him), before shifting your focus to Eve during the musical pause that precedes the very last word.

Vocal and Musical Analysis

WHO TO LISTEN TO: Adrian Zmed on the American premiere recording (1998).

VOCAL RANGE: D3 to A♭4.

ORIGINAL KEY: A♭ major.

ACCENT: The song is written to be sung in General American, and it is undoubtedly easier to deliver in that accent due to the higher tongue position prevalent in that dialect. However, if you are performing the song in a UK audition, there is a strong argument for delivering it in Standard English, which will sound more neutral to British ears. This can be a good choice as the location of the Garden of Eden is so nebulous.

STYLE OF MUSICAL: Contemporary musical (pop-based).

VOCAL SET-UP/MUSICAL TIPS

1. On the recording there is a section in the middle of the song sung by Father and Eve. This should not be delivered in audition, and is already cut on the version of the music listed below.

2. To reflect Adam's innocence and vulnerability, the opening verse should be delivered as purely as possible. Lift your larynx to a raised position, tilt your thyroid cartilage and use simultaneous onsets to make your sound very smooth and sweet, and allow you to access a Cry quality.

3. In the final line of the first verse, crescendo by gradually releasing your thyroid from a tilted to a horizontal position

so that you can sing the second verse in a louder Speech quality.

4. In the bridge, where the time signature moves between 5/4 and 6/4, trying pushing the tempo forward a little, as this helps convey Adam's desperation at this stage.

5. When you sing the word 'oh' on the high A♭ you should access a Belt quality. Use the same set-up when you sing the next A♭ on the word 'I'.

6. After the first belt, the next section of the song should be delivered in a Speech quality, but with some torso anchoring added to provide extra resonance and presence to the sound.

7. Try delivering the last few words in a sweet, intimate Cry quality.

Sheet Music

The correct sheet music for this song is available at www.musicnotes.com.

'And the Rain Keeps Falling Down' from *Elegies for Angels, Punks and Raging Queens*

Music by Janet Hood, lyrics by Bill Russell

Choose this song if: you have a contemporary pop voice and enjoy songs that require a strong emotional connection. The song enables you to showcase a variety of voice qualities, including Falsetto.

Given Circumstances

Note: This show has usually been staged in a very simple fashion as a charity gala. As the context of the song is only provided by the one short poem that precedes it, the given circumstances are, to a large degree, open to interpretation. Therefore those outlined below, though firmly rooted in the limited information provided by the script, are in large part invented. You may therefore wish to alter them to suit your own needs.

WHO ARE YOU: Brian, a handsome, sporty and athletic heterosexual man of thirty-five.

WHERE ARE YOU: Central Park, New York City, USA.

WHEN IS IT: 2.05 p.m., a rainy Thursday, February, 1989.

WHAT HAS HAPPENED BEFORE: Six years ago you married a girl named Charlotte. During your marriage you became good friends with her gay older brother, Ray. You first got to know him when you visited him in Miami where they were both from. You stayed for a glorious, sunny month in the height of summer, 1985. Before meeting Ray you had not had any homosexual friends, and you wrongly imagined that you would have little in common. In fact, you quickly discovered he shared your love of baseball, rock music and, most particularly, the beach. A year later Ray moved back to New York to be closer to his sister, as he'd been through a period of feeling very unwell.

Early in 1987 you divorced amicably from Charlotte, as you had been arguing frequently and you both felt you would be happier apart. Despite the separation, your friendship with Ray endured the divorce, and you grew even closer when Charlotte moved back to Miami. You became virtually inseparable and did everything together – whether that be watching the Mets play baseball, or partying all night in the nightclubs of Manhattan.

A year ago Ray started to become unwell again. At first he thought he had a heavy bout of flu, but after a series of different illnesses during the next few months you encouraged him to have an HIV test. The test came back positive. By the end of the year his health had declined significantly and he was given an AIDS diagnosis.

With Ray perhaps having only months to live, you suggested that he return to Miami as you thought that he should be with his family. Although he sometimes complained how much he missed the hot weather, he didn't want his parents to see how ill he was.

Shortly after New Year, Ray's mood became very dark. To try and cheer him up you booked a holiday for you both in Jamaica. It would prove to be a marvellous week. As the trip approached Ray had a period of respite from feeling unwell, the holiday was blessed by unremitting sunshine. The whole week was full of laughter; it was like having the old Ray back.

However, just a few weeks after you returned to New York, Ray's health began to worsen once more and he was diagnosed with pneumonia. He was hospitalised as the full effects of late-stage HIV began to take hold. He died a week ago.

Ray stated in his will that that he wanted to be buried in New York. You attended the funeral this morning. Despite the strong feelings of friendship you felt towards him, and the sight of his family uncontrollable with grief, you found that you were unable to cry. This troubled, confused and angered you. Straight after the funeral you offered your condolences to his parents and to Charlotte – and then made your way to Central Park so you could have some time alone. You arrived about ten minutes ago and it has just begun to rain.

WHO ELSE IS THERE: You are alone.

WHO SHOULD YOU SING TO: Ray, your dead friend.

Textual Analysis

As the musical introduction begins you should take in the rain clouds. At this point you find the bad weather ironic. Ray comes into your mind, and you begin to address him. In the first line your objective is: to amuse him with the irony of the rain. But from the second line onwards this objective quickly shifts. You now want Ray to explain his decision to stay in a cold and rainy New York, rather than go home to Miami. This is something you found hard to understand, as you know how much he loved the sun.

During the first chorus you begin to protest about the bad weather. But you are not really complaining about the rain, but what it means as a metaphor. You are really bemoaning the entire epidemic, as you view the rain as a terrible analogy for all of the tears that have been shed for the victims of the AIDS crisis. In this moment you not only want the rain to stop, you are pleading for the whole epidemic – and the suffering it causes – to cease as well.

During the second verse you become more introspective. Your objective at this point is existential: to examine the value and purpose of your life. This is prompted by feelings of guilt related to Ray's death. You worry that you have wasted your adulthood partying, and despise yourself for not having developed the emotional maturity to cry over the death of your best friend. You rebuke yourself for this inability to shed a single tear when the heavens themselves are pouring forth countless tears of rain.

Having reached a point of self-loathing, in the bridge your objective becomes simply: to cry. You want the tears to flow as you hope that might be a release valve for the pain you are feeling. During the second chorus your objective is the same as in the first – to protest about the unfairness of the weather and the epidemic – though you may find some different moments by altering who you are singing to (see point 3 below).

KEY MOMENTS/TOP TIPS

1. During the song you frequently address you dead friend Ray. To make this clear for the panel you should make use of the third circle of attention. As you will also use this circle when looking at the rainy sky, decide on one clear place – perhaps over the heads of the panel – to look at, each time you talk to Ray.

2. When you talk to yourself in the second verse, you can make this clear by finding more thoughts in the first circle of attention. The actions you could play at this point might include: I cross-examine, mock, berate and castigate myself.

3. The song poses a challenge for you as an actor, in that both choruses have exactly the same lyric. In order to find variety, try singing the first chorus to yourself, and the second to Ray. This will alter the physical choices and actions you use.

4. Before you say 'one more tear' for the second and final time, there is a pause in the music. This is the event of the song. It is the point in which Brian finally connects emotionally to the death of Ray. If you are able to access tears, this might be the moment when you begin to cry.

5. The song ends with the title lyric, which you have already sung several times. However, the high falsetto note at this point suggests something different is occurring from earlier in the song. Previously when you said these words

on this lyric you had been protesting about the never-ending rain, and the relentless flow of tears that this represented. When you sing the title lyric for the final time explore the idea that, rather than this being a protest, this is a moment of acceptance: that you realise that you are powerless to stop the flood of the sorrow caused by the epidemic. This last line then becomes a moment of catharsis: it is the first stage of you beginning to come to terms with the terrible death of your friend.

Vocal and Musical Analysis

WHO TO LISTEN TO: Simon Green on the original London cast recording (1993).

VOCAL RANGE: C3 to G4.

ORIGINAL KEY: E♭ major.

ACCENT: General American.

STYLE OF MUSICAL: Contemporary musical (pop-based).

VOCAL SET–UP/MUSICAL TIPS

1. The beginning of the song should be very gentle and reflective. As such, it is appropriate to deliver the first verse in a Cry quality. The word 'loved' on the high G♭ can be difficult in this quality. If you find it easier, and can blend the vocal transition successfully, you may want to flip into a Falsetto quality for this single note.

2. As you sing the title lyric for the first time, crescendo gradually by taking the position of your thyroid cartilage from tilted to horizontal. This will allow you to access a Speech quality by the beginning of the first chorus.

3. Having sung the chorus in Speech, the second verse should once more be in a Cry quality, but explore using some aspirate onsets to give this section the thoughtful, introspective quality that the lyric demands. At the end of

the verse make a similar transition into Speech quality as you did at the end of the first verse.

4. When you sing about wishing to let go in the bridge, your voice should be full and rich. Use a Speech quality for this section with some torso anchoring on the higher notes to give added resonance and power.

5. As indicated by the music, it is very evocative to make your voice suddenly very quiet and vulnerable on the word 'heaven'. Add as much thyroid tilt as possible and lift your larynx just before you sing this word.

6. You then need to create a very sudden and dramatic crescendo in the next phrase. Start by removing thyroid tilt when you reach the word 'reason' and add torso anchoring on the word 'I' – to achieve an anchored Speech set-up. Continue using this vocal quality in the second chorus.

7. You want to repeat the same dynamics and vocal set-ups you used in point 5 at the end of the second chorus. Become suddenly quiet when you sing the words 'one more tear', begin to remove the thyroid tilt and crescendo on the word 'town' and add lots of torso anchoring on the word 'down', as this should be the strongest note of the whole song.

8. The last time you sing the word 'rain', flip into a very pure Falsetto quality. Use lots of false-fold retraction at this point. This vocal shift is particularly effective if the two preceding words remain in an anchored Speech quality, and therefore the vocal shift is swift and dynamic.

Sheet Music

The correct sheet music for this song is available at www.scribd.com.

'Endless Night'
from *The Lion King*

Music by Lebo M., Hans Zimmer and Jay Rifkin, lyrics by Julie Taymor

Choose this song if: you have a tenor pop voice and are able to riff and belt up to a top A. The show is set in Africa, so is particularly appropriate for black actors. You may suit this role if you enjoy playing characters that mix heroism with moments of self-doubt.

Given Circumstances

WHO ARE YOU: Simba, a lion. You are a young prince, the son of your late father, King Mufasa, and rightful heir to the kingdom of Pride Rock. Although you have the potential to be a brave and heroic leader, you battle with uncertainties and insecurities, and worry that you are not able to be a great king like your father.

WHERE ARE YOU: In a forest in the Serengeti, Northern Tanzania, Africa.

WHEN IS IT: Shortly before sunrise, the early hours of the morning, after a summer's night, in an unspecified time before Africa was touched by colonialism.

WHAT HAS HAPPENED BEFORE: When you were born it was a momentous and joyful day for your father, as you were his first and only son. He loved you greatly, but this feeling was not reciprocated by your uncle, Scar, who coveted the throne for himself and who was now no longer next in line. Scar began to plot to have you killed.

As soon as you were old enough, your father began to teach you about the world. He taught you to respect the natural order of the world – the circle of life – and told you that when you became king it would be your duty to respect all of the creatures in the kingdom. He also warned you that you must never cross the northern border of the Pride Lands – to a dangerous and shadowy place called the Elephants' Graveyard.

As a young prince, though, you were adventurous, naive, vain and easily manipulated. These were characteristics Scar decided to use to his advantage. Playing on your egotistical nature, he taunted you by saying that only the bravest lions dared go to the Elephants' Graveyard. To prove your courage, you decided to visit this forbidden place, taking young Nala with you – a lioness that you are expected to marry when you are both old enough.

By leaving the Pride Lands, you were walking into a trap Scar had laid for you. In the Elephants' Graveyard you were cornered by three hyenas who tried to kill and eat you. Facing certain death, you were saved at the last moment by Mufasa, who fought off the hyenas, rescuing yourself and Nala.

Back at Pride Rock Mufasa told you that he was disappointed with you for disobeying him. You explained that you had only done so because you wanted to prove that you could be brave, just like him. He replied by teaching you that kings should only be brave when they needed to be, and that today he had been afraid of losing you. This helped you understand that even kings experience fear. Feeling great love for your father in that moment, you asked him if he would always be there for you. In response Mufasa pointed in the direction of the night sky. He told you a story that his father told him: that the great kings of the past look down at you from the stars, as he will one day when he is gone. He said that if you ever felt alone in the future you should look to the stars and remember that he would be there to guide you.

In the meantime, Scar formed an alliance with the hyenas to help destroy Mufasa and take the throne for himself. A few days later he led you down into a rocky gorge, told you to stay there and to await a surprise for you and your father. The hyenas then provoked a herd of wildebeest into stampeding the gorge. Afraid of being crushed to death, you ran for your life. With you trapped, Scar went and told Mufasa that you were in danger in the ravine. Your father set out to rescue you. Once he'd arrived he managed to haul you to safety, but he was badly hurt when the herd trampled him. After he struggled to climb the walls of the gorge, he found Scar waiting for him at the top. Mufasa pleaded for Scar to help him climb out, but instead his brother sank his claws into the king, before throwing him to the bottom of the gulley and to his death. When you rounded the corner and discovered your father's dead body you were distraught. Scar told you that you were to blame. As you ran off, broken-hearted, he ordered the hyenas to chase and kill you – but they allowed you to escape into the desert and to exile.

Whilst you were out in the wilderness you became friends with a meerkat, Timon, and a warthog, Pumbaa, who were outcasts like yourself. You began to grow into adulthood, safe in your friendship with them, but racked by a niggling doubt that you were not all that you should be – that you should be king.

In the Pride Lands, Scar, having taken the throne for himself, was slowly destroying the kingdom. He had allowed the hyenas into Pride Rock – where they were killing off all of the other beasts, leaving the lions dying of starvation. The now fully grown Nala knew the situation had become intolerable and set out to find you.

Tonight Pumbaa and Timon were discussing why the stars were in the sky. You recounted the story your father had told you. Thinking this was ridiculous, they have just laughed at you and left, leaving you feeling alone and upset.

WHO ELSE IS THERE: You are alone.

WHO SHOULD YOU SING TO: You shift between talking to yourself and to your dead father.

Textual Analysis

At the beginning of the song you are searching the night sky. Your objective is: to find a star (which you believe would be a signal that you father is looking down on you). The sky remains resolutely black. You assume this to be a fatalistic sign and resolve yourself to the fact that you will never be able to return home. In the chorus you suddenly begin to talk directly to your absent father, which is prompted by the emergence of the stars (see point 1). In the first half of the chorus your objective is: to get Mufasa to take responsibility for abandoning you. In the second half that objective develops, and you now want: Mufasa to send you a sign so that you know he can hear you.

In the second verse you continue to address your father. Your objective here is: to get Mufasa to tell you when you will have a change of fortune. During the second chorus, as the lyric is identical, your objectives are the same as in the first. To ensure this section remains engaging, try using different actions (see point 3).

When the musical accompaniment changes at the end of the second chorus, the event of the song occurs: the sun begins to rise. At this moment, for the first time, you begin to imagine a hopeful future. Your objective here is: to convince yourself that life will get better. To achieve this objective, try playing actions such as: I galvanise, uplift, regenerate, hearten, and bolster myself.

KEY MOMENTS/TOP TIPS

1. A key to acting this song well is to be clear what you imagine when Simba is looking at the sky. In the Broadway/West End production the solo is staged before a stunning backdrop of stars throughout. Although this is visually spectacular, it does not reflect what Simba would actually see. At the beginning of the song, he clearly can't see the stars – evidenced by the first lyric. So in the opening stanza you should imagine that the sky is

completely black, perhaps because clouds have rolled across. The moment that the starlight re-emerges then becomes very significant as Simba believes the presence of the stars means his father is now looking down on him. I would suggest you see the stars emerge on the last line of the first verse when you tell your father you feel alone. When the music changes at the end of the second chorus you then need to imagine the rising sun – which, as described above, is the event of the song.

2. The accompaniment provides a clue on how to approach acting the two verses. The piano is very still and sustained in the first verse, but has more rhythmic movement in the second. Try to mirror this by using more dynamic actions second time around. So, during the first, try actions like: I question, cross-examine, quiz and investigate myself. In the second explore options, such as: I interrogate, confront, pressure and implore Musafa.

3. The repetition of the same lyric in both choruses needs to be handled with some thought so that your performance doesn't become repetitive. In one chorus try playing direct choices to pressurise Mufasa such as: I grill, challenge and contradict you. In the other you might try more positive choices such as: I awaken, rouse and vitalise him.

4. This song is a turning point in Simba's story. It is the moment at which he first envisages that his story may end positively, and grows from a boy into a man. To successfully inhabit this transition, try to shape your performance so that at the end of the second chorus Simba is at his lowest ebb, as this will make the change more pronounced when the event of the sun arising occurs.

Vocal and Musical Analysis

WHO TO LISTEN TO: Jason Raize on the original Broadway cast recording (1997).

VOCAL RANGE: E3 to A4.

ORIGINAL KEY: D major.

ACCENT: On the original Broadway cast recording and in the West End production, the song is performed in a General American accent, so that would be a suitable choice. However, if you are from an African country then it would appropriate to use your own accent.

STYLE OF MUSICAL: Contemporary musical (pop-based).

VOCAL SET-UP/MUSICAL TIPS

1. This piece has the harmonic structure of a pop song and should be sung as such. To help achieve a pop style it is advisable to add some twang to your fundamental sound. The rhythms in this style of music can also be afforded some freedom for interpretation, and it is appropriate to make occasional use of pitch-slides.

2. In the first verse raise the larynx and try to make the sound as pure and as possible. Minimise the use of vibrato and keep the tongue still as you move vowel position. This should produce a very uncluttered vocal delivery – giving your performance an innocent, vulnerable quality.

3. The last section requires you to riff. If this is something you find difficult, you can copy the riffs on the suggested recording or work with a singing teacher to devise something that works for you. It is not advisable to improvise riffs in the audition.

4. The last note on the word 'rise' should sung be in a Belt quality.

Sheet Music

The correct sheet music for this song is available at www.musicnotes.com.

'Finishing the Hat'
from *Sunday in the Park with George*

Music and lyrics by Stephen Sondheim

Choose this song if: you excel at acting very complex lyrics.
The song requires a great deal of acting skill, allied with a
developed ability to sing high baritone in a legit position. It is
a suitable choice for the advanced performer.

Given Circumstances

WHO ARE YOU: George Seurat, a brilliant, innovative twenty-
six-year-old painter. Despite being a genius who
revolutionised painting (George was real person), at this point
of your career you are struggling for recognition. You can be
intense, obsessive and self-absorbed.

WHERE ARE YOU: In the popular park on the island of La
Grande Jatte, on the River Seine, Paris, France. (In the
musical, the action takes place in an abstract setting, where
the park itself appears as pieces of two-dimensional set that
resemble Seurat's famous painting *A Sunday Afternoon on the
Island of La Grande Jatte* – where the persona of the painting
are played by actors. In this abstract world, George retains an
element of control over the *mise-en-scène*. For example, he can
make a tree disappear from the park by rubbing it out on his
sketchbook. However, for the purposes of audition you should
simply behave as if you are in a park.)

WHEN IS IT: 10.30 a.m., a Sunday, summer, 1884.

WHAT HAS HAPPENED BEFORE: You have been sketching studies
for your second major work, *A Sunday Afternoon on the Island
of La Grande Jatte*, for many months now. Your previous
large-scale work, *Une baignade à Asnières*, was heavily
criticised, which has made you defensive and eager for your
next work to be recognised as a success.

Dot, your mistress, has been modelling for your new painting. Over a month ago, after a long day of sketching her, you promised to take her to see a performance of her much-loved Follies. Back at your studio, Dot was getting ready whilst you were painting up the day's sketch of a hat. When it became time to leave, you told her that you couldn't go, as you needed to finish the painting instead. She left alone, very upset.

This was a turning point in your relationship, and Dot began to see someone new: a baker called Louis. You met him for the first time a few weeks ago in the park where he was accompanying Dot. The conversation between yourself and her was awkward and frosty.

Today you have had a difficult day. Jules, a friend and another artist, criticised you. He complained that your behaviour was isolating you from those who care about you, and that the new style of painting you've created, pointillism (where the image is formed by small, distinct dots of colour), is alienating collectors. He also told you that he thought you should be painting people in high society, rather than working-class park-dwellers. You then had another uncomfortable meeting with Dot and Louis. Dot was looking for you, but you ran away before she could speak to you (by this point Dot is actually pregnant with your child). Dot then decided that, although she loves you, Louis takes care of her needs in a way that you are not capable of – so she will make a life with him. Shortly after she had left, you returned to the park and began to reflect on which is more important to you: your love for Dot or art.

WHO ELSE IS THERE: You are alone. (In the production, you deliver some of the song to a dog called Fifi, but this is not useful or necessary in audition.)

WHO SHOULD YOU SING TO: Yourself, though in this situation you can share many of your thoughts with the panel as though they are your inner-consciousness.

Textual Analysis

Note: The full song begins with a few fractured phrases that George sings as he flicks through his sketchbook. It is hard to make sense of these out of context, so in audition it is advisable to cut them and begin from the word 'yes' when you acknowledge that Dot is looking for you. The sheet music suggested below contains this cut.

Before you start to sing you need to imagine Dot in the distance. This image will provide the impulse you need to play your first objective, which is: to ignore Dot and let her suffer. Although this objective might seem cruel, you have been very hurt by her leaving you for Louis. So although you can see she is desperately searching for you – to tell you she is pregnant – you don't call out to her. A new unit begins on the third line that starts with the words 'I had thought'. Your objective here is: to convince yourself that any relationship with a woman is doomed to fail. This again is a very negative choice to play, but it is a means of self-preservation. You feel you must protect yourself from being hurt again. The internal struggle this causes manifests itself when you wonder 'if anybody could' love you. At that moment you feel that if anyone might be your soulmate, it would be Dot. Explore at this moment an impulse to run after her – an impulse that you don't follow.

The music then changes, when the main piano figure is introduced to accompany the first verse. This musical development signifies an important change in your thought processes. In both verses – which contain this repetitive, hypnotic accompaniment – rather than longing for Dot, your objective becomes: to articulate your compulsive, obsessive need to finish a work of art. In articulating your love for the process of painting, you are trying to convince yourself that, by choosing your work over Dot, you are making the correct decision.

In contrast to the flowing verses, the two choruses are musical and emotional outbursts. At these moments, despite trying to focus on your art, the pain of losing Dot suddenly rushes back to you. In the first chorus your objective is: to punish yourself for not giving Dot the attention she deserved. You are angry that you were too consumed in what you were painting – whether that be the grass, a stick or a dog – to cherish your relationship. Try delivering the second chorus towards the absent Dot. Get her to understand that you could never have given her what she needed, that there would have always been a part of you – the artist – that would have been consumed by painting the sky, rather giving your full attention to her.

At first, you may find to difficult to empathise with why George sacrificed his relationship for his art. In the last two lines he makes his reason clear. He believes that he has not just painted a hat, he has painted a hat *that did not previously exist*. If you have ever written a poem, a song or a play, you may relate to this unparalleled sense of achievement that comes from bringing a new piece of art into the world.

KEY MOMENTS/TOP TIPS

1. The song is a soliloquy and in performance you would share some of George's inner thoughts with the audience. In audition it works well to share lines directly with the panel. For example, when George is trying to convince himself of the importance of finishing a piece of art, you can play that objective on the panel, as if they are a part of your soul.

2. The crux of the song is George's internal struggle with what is most important to him: his art, or his love for Dot. In the end George chooses his art. This is clarified immediately prior to the second chorus, when he states that the act of painting is the only way to see. At this moment, which is the event of the song, you should articulate something deeply felt by George: that he can only make sense of life through the act of making art.

3. The song contains several references to 'windows'. One of the themes Sondheim is exploring in *Sunday in the Park with George* is the loneliness of the creative artist. At times during the song the window becomes a metaphor for a

CONTEMPORARY BALLADS

barrier that can exist between the busy artist and the real world when he is consumed in his work. Yet a window is also something through which you can see. When George talks about reaching through the window, he says that by really studying the subject of a painting – a hat, the light, or Dot – he can learn to see the world as it really is. Just like looking through a window. The window therefore represents George's relationship to his work. Sometimes it is the barrier between him and Dot, at other times it is his means of seeing the world.

4. In the song George sings about the night. For George the night represents an escape from the all-consuming busyness of his mind when he is working (which he describes as a 'dizzying height'). He feels that only Dot can turn off the tiring genius of his creativity – and allow him to find peace in the night-time.

5. This song is arguably Sondheim's most autobiographical. As a man who found love late in life, he perhaps could closely relate to Seurat as man whose obsessive work ethic at times interfered with his romantic life. Whilst you may not be a painter, you might be able to relate, as Sondheim surely did when he wrote the material, to a time when you have been totally immersed in your art (when you were rehearsing a show, for example) – and this had a negative effect on your personal relationships.

6. The last line is very telling. George articulates that the act of creativity – of having painted something that didn't previously exist – is ultimately what defines his existence, rather than love.

Vocal and Musical Analysis

WHO TO LISTEN TO: Mandy Patinkin on the original Broadway cast recording (1984).

VOCAL RANGE: B♭2 to A♭4.

ORIGINAL KEY: G♭ major.

ACCENT: Received Pronunciation. Although Seurat is French, when this show is performed in the UK this role is normally sung in RP to reflect that Seurat is from the upper echelons of society. If you are French, of course, you should use your own accent.

STYLE OF MUSICAL: Concept musical.

VOCAL SET-UP/MUSICAL TIPS

1. As with much Sondheim material, the fundamental set-up for this song is Speech. It is the best voice quality to help you communicate such complex lyrics. To land in Speech from the beginning of the song, use some glottal onsets in the opening phrase to help you access thick vocal folds.

2. Several times in the song George longs to escape from his work, either to return to Dot or to just be a full participant in the world outside of his studio. Try using Cry quality to highlight these moments of longing. For example, on the line 'but if anybody could', and the first time you say the word 'window'.

3. In the verses, take particular notice of the note-lengths at the ends of phrases. Most are short, leaving rests between each lyric. This clipped musical phrasing helps portray George as meticulous and obsessive. When a note is then finally sustained – such as on the word 'sky' – it lets the audience into something new about George: his sense of wonder when taking in the beauty of the world.

4. In the first verse, on the words 'window go', Sondheim provides the singer with an unusually detailed level of musical instruction – he gives each of the three syllables of those two words an individual dynamic marking. Each syllable gets successively quieter, they are marked: '*mf*' (medium loud), '*mp*' (medium soft), '*p*' (soft). These dynamics come in a phrase where you sing about the sound of voices passing the studio window whilst you paint. By

achieving this decrescendo you embody for the listener the idea of voices gradually disappearing into the distance. To realise this technically, sing the first syllable in an anchored Speech quality, remove the torso anchoring for the second, and then tilt the thyroid for the third to finish in a Cry quality.

5. The choruses are challenging to deliver, as the phrases are set to consistently high pitches. In order to sing this well, lower your larynx slightly (like in a Sob quality), tilt your thyroid cartilage and anchor your torso. Then focus on keeping the sides of your tongue as close to your upper molars as possible. Done correctly, this set-up should make the chorus achievable.

Sheet Music

The correct sheet music for this song is available at www.musicnotes.com.

'The Journey Home'
from *Bombay Dreams*

Music by A.R. Rahman, lyrics by Don Black

Choose this song if: you enjoy playing the idealistic young hero. This role was originally written for an actor of Indian descent – and there are two short sections of riffs written in the character's native tongue. However, if you don't feel comfortable doing these, then those sections can be cut.

Given Circumstances

WHO ARE YOU: Akaash, a handsome young man in your early twenties known as 'an untouchable' – someone from the lowest level of India's caste system. You are optimistic and aspirational but also have the capacity to be easily led.

WHERE ARE YOU: A street in an uptown area of Bombay (now Mumbai), outside of a Bollywood party.

WHEN IS IT: 11.30 p.m., summer, 1995.

WHAT HAS HAPPENED BEFORE: Several months ago you were living in the slums of Bombay, as you had done since you were a child. As an idealist you had always dreamt of escaping your impoverished existence and becoming a Bollywood star – which, perhaps unsurprisingly, always seemed fantastical to your mother, Shanti. Whilst she often reprimanded you for your daydreams, your friend Sweetie, a eunuch, saw something special in you and believed that realising your aspirations was one day a possibility.

Around this time your life suddenly took an unexpected turn for the worse when some property developers named Money Singh and Honey Singh arrived. They announced that everyone who lived in the neighbourhood had thirty days to leave as the slums were to be torn down in order to make way for a new development. In the aftermath of this terrible news, salvation seemed to quickly appear in the shape of a wealthy couple, a lawyer named Vikram and his girlfriend, a young documentary film director called Priya – who also happened to be the daughter of a famous Bollywood producer. Upon hearing of the plight of you and your friends, Vikram promised to save all of your homes through a legal battle. When he also pledged to waive his usual fees he was cast as a hero by the local community. (In fact, the truth was that Vikram – unbeknownst to Priya – was secretly plotting to tear down the slums and make himself a fortune through property development, as she discovers later in the story.)

After Vikram's announcement you got talking to the pair, and Priya revealed her film background to you. Excited that this might be your opportunity to break into Bollywood, with the help of Sweetie, you pleaded with her to introduce you to her father. She agreed to get you an audition for his next film – *The Diamond in the Rough* – and told you to come to the film studio the next morning. Upon meeting her father, Madan, you delivered an impressive audition and he decided to give you the lead part.

On the first day of filming you met your co-star Rani, a beautiful, famous and demanding Bollywood actress. She was immediately attracted to you, but your interest lay in the unavailable Priya – who was being kind and generous to you as you tried to accustom yourself to your new job. In particular she helped by rehearsing the romantic scenes of the film with you – which only made you fall for her more. When Rani saw this occurring she grew jealous and tried to seduce you. You eventually succumbed to her advances and made the mistake of going back to her hotel with her.

When the film opened a few weeks ago your performance was received as a critical and popular success. However, at the opening-night party, in the midst of the celebrations, tragedy occurred when Madan was shot dead by an unknown assassin (who was secretly working for Vikram). To avoid being implicated, Vikram blamed the incident on you – saying that

Madan had made himself lots of enemies by casting you in the film. A few days later, when Sweetie walked in on Vikram plotting with Honey Singh and Money Singh, Vikram shot him too in order to keep his secrets hidden.

Tonight you have been at a Bollywood party attended by Vikram and Priya. A few minutes ago Vikram had a jealous argument with Priya on the street outside, as at the party you both had been constantly looking at each other across the room. He then stormed off, leaving Priya alone. Shortly afterwards you came out to join her. You had not talked to her for some time, as she had been keeping her own company since her father's death. Taking the chance to open up, you confessed to Priya that you were worried that she blamed you for her father's death. She reassured you that this was not the case and told you that she was about to direct her first movie. A few moments ago Vikram came outside once more – and caught you both embracing. He warned you to stay away from his girlfriend. Priya, still oblivious to the truth that Vikram was responsible for her father's murder, and thinking him to be a hero, began to think with her head, rather than her heart. She responded by telling you that she loved Vikram, and that she wanted to say goodbye to you forever. Priya and Vikram have just returned to the party together, leaving you heartbroken on the street.

WHO ELSE IS THERE: You are alone.

WHO SHOULD YOU SING TO: Yourself.

Textual Analysis

As the introduction plays, you find yourself in the midst of a moment of great decision and inner conflict. Having always longed to be a successful Bollywood star, the thought of turning your back on that new life – and of leaving Priya behind – is exceptionally difficult. Yet making it in Bollywood has not turned out the way you intended, and with your dreams of a life with Priya apparently shattered, you now must decide whether you would be better off returning home.

With your heart leading you towards returning to your old life, your objective in the first verse thus becomes: to remind yourself of how good it would feel to return home.

During the second verse you begin to imagine the reception that would await you back in the slums. Your objective at this point is: to indulge the prospect of a happy return. This starts to give you great comfort. In the bridge that follows, the event of the song occurs. At this point you make a fundamental discovery – when you realise that you made the wrong decision to search for the fame and riches of Bollywood. Your objective in this section is: to convince yourself that home is where your heart is.

Having embraced this truth about yourself, a great moment of emotional catharsis then occurs when you sing in your native language: you have finally realised what your home, your friends and family really mean to you. In the final verse your objective then becomes: to take comfort in your decision to return home. At this moment you feel relieved of all of your troubles and manage to achieve a sense of contentment and inner peace.

KEY MOMENTS/TOP TIPS

1. This song is the key point in the entirety of Akaash's story. It is where he finally realises that the pursuit of fame and riches is a poor substitute for his friends, his family, his roots. The number should therefore be a moment of self-awakening.

2. As discussed, the bridge is the crucial moment of self-discovery for Akaash. In order to inhabit this struggle to understand his true nature, try playing actions such as: I cross-examine, scrutinise and challenge myself at this point.

3. It is worth considering the immense fame of a Bollywood star, and how the pressures of such a life would affect a young man such as Akaash, who rises very quickly from a

humble background. He was totally unprepared for his new lifestyle – which reveals itself in the behaviour of someone who is struggling to cope.

Vocal and Musical Analysis

WHO TO LISTEN TO: Raza Jaffrey on the original London cast recording (2002).

VOCAL RANGE: F♯3 to G4.

ORIGINAL KEY: D major.

ACCENT: In the original London production this song was performed in Standard English – and therefore would be an acceptable choice in audition. However, there is no logical reason for this. If you are of Indian descent, and can deliver a Mumbai accent, then that would be a good choice for you to make.

STYLE OF MUSICAL: Contemporary musical (pop-based).

VOCAL SET-UP/MUSICAL TIPS

1. The piano accompaniment on the published sheet music does not have the same rhythmic drive that you will hear on the suggested recording. To counteract this, ensure that you remain on the front foot in your vocal delivery, and don't allow the tempo to sag.

2. The majority of this song is delivered in a single vocal set-up: Twang quality. To achieve this, remember to keep your larynx high, your soft palate lifted and your AES narrowed.

3. The song contains lots of long legato phrases. To achieve this successfully, use simultaneous onsets wherever possible and minimise the movements of the back of the tongue. Try to form all your vowels with a tongue position as similar to the 'ee' vowel as possible.

148

4. Try starting the bridge very quietly in a Cry position. This helps to reflect that this is a moment of great contemplation. You can help portray a sense of soul-searching through the use of aspirate onsets, which makes your sound thoughtful and introspective, as Jaffrey demonstrates on the suggested recording. In the final line of the section, when you talk about standing still, switch to a simultaneous onset, begin to release your thyroid tilt and add torso anchoring to affect a massive crescendo.

5. If you wish to sing the riffs, be aware that they are not notated on the sheet music. Simply ask the pianist to play the full piece of music, and deliver the riffs as they occur on the suggested recording. If you wish to remove the riffs, you should place a cut in the instrumental section. Keep the first seven bars of the fifth page of the sheet music (where you are sustaining a long note on the word 'make'), then cut the rest of the page and the first bar of the sixth page. On the final page you should also cut all of the last nine bars, except the very final one. This will shorten the play-out if you are not doing the riffs that occur at the end.

Sheet Music

The correct sheet music for this song is available at www.musicnotes.com.

'Stranger in this World' from *Taboo*

Music by John Themis and Boy George, lyrics by Boy George

Choose this song if: you have contemporary pop voice and suit sensitive, flamboyant and androgynous roles. The song has a belt to a top G.

Given Circumstances

WHO ARE YOU: George O'Dowd, better known as Boy George – the real-life gay pop superstar of the 1980s. You are currently twenty-one years old and have yet too achieve your world-wide success and fame. You are a follower of the New Romantic movement, a pop-culture phenomenon prevalent during this period that was notable for eccentric and ostentatious fashion. It centred around the Blitz nightclub in London, which you regularly attend, along with other well-known personalities from that period, such as Steve Strange, Marilyn, Philip Sallon, the artist Leigh Bowery and the group Spandau Ballet.

WHERE ARE YOU: Outside a telephone box near Warren Street in Central London.

WHEN IS IT: 11.30 a.m., summer, 1981.

WHAT HAS HAPPENED BEFORE: This song occurs in your first scene of the musical. Today you were kicked out of your shared flat for the bizarre crime of stealing a headdress. In need of financial help, you have just telephoned your Irish working-class parents, Dinah and Gerry O'Dowd, who live in suburban Eltham in South London. You wanted to talk to your mother, but she would not come to the phone. Your father, who you have a difficult relationship with due to your sexuality and outlandish behaviour, answered instead. When he heard your voice he immediately hung up the phone. He had long found it difficult to accept the provocative and androgynous way you dressed. Growing up with four brothers, you felt very uncomfortable in this male-dominated household, and you described yourself as the 'pink sheep' of the family. This phone call brought these feelings into focus for you. Alone on the street, you began to reflect on your lonely adolescence growing up in the O'Dowd household, and to resolve to turn your back on that past.

WHO ELSE IS THERE: You are alone.

WHO SHOULD YOU SING TO: At some points you sing to yourself, at other times to your mother – who is not present.

Textual Analysis

During the introduction you are reflecting on the fact that your father has just hung up the telephone. Try to connect to feelings of rejection, as this will help lead you into your first objective, which is: to turn your back on your family. This objective is for the opening line only. The second thought – when you ask to be a star – is directed towards a higher power: Fate. Your objective in this moment is: to implore Fate to make you successful and famous. For the remainder of the verse your objective is: to convince yourself that you are making the right decision by moving on from your current life.

You then experience a moment of epiphany. In the first chorus of the song you discover and articulate, perhaps for the very first time, that your mother knew that you never fitted in as a child. You realise that she always understood that you have felt isolated and ostracised. In this chorus, as that idea becomes clear to you, you should play actions such as: I question, query, investigate, quiz, search and inspect myself.

Your attitude towards your mother hardens in the second verse, as you've now realised that, even though she knew you were sensitive and vulnerable, she never did anything to intervene or help. So you begin to attack her. Your objective in this section is: to criticise your mother. You want to prove to her that you can survive on your own. Explore actions such as: to ridicule, antagonise, provoke and harass her. This confrontational attitude continues in the second chorus. Your objective in this section is: to get your mother to confess. You want her to admit that she didn't stand up for you.

In the final section there is a sudden and significant shift. When you talk about how you feel on a clear day, the event of the song occurs. At this moment you try to convince your mother that, despite your difficult past, you can envisage a bright future for yourself. For an instant you see the superstar that you will eventually become.

KEY MOMENTS/TOP TIPS

1. It is not advisable to perform the song in an audition scenario as if you are in a telephone box. Instead, simply act as if you are alone.

2. A weakness of the song as a piece of dramatic text is that both choruses have identical lyrics. This issue can be successfully resolved by talking to yourself in the first chorus, and to your absent mother in the second. This gives both sections a very different dramatic thrust and imbues the structure of the song with a sense of progression.

3. Because the song shifts between George talking to himself, and talking to his absent mother, you need to be clear in your use of circles of attention. When talking to your mother, try addressing a clear spot behind the panel in the third circle of attention.

4. George describes himself as 'fragile and clever'. This lyric can be open to many interpretations – but an interesting way to play this moment is that George is proud of his sensitivity, that he feels that it makes him in some way superior.

5. There is a section in the song for the character Josie. For audition purposes this should be cut, so you should jump

straight from the second chorus into the final section, in which George talks about how he feels on a clear day.

6. It is interesting to consider that, for a period in the mid-1980s, Boy George was one of the most famous people in the world. This helps you to gauge his level of drive and determination, which must have been extraordinary. This should influence your performance of this song, as this moment – where he decides to leave his previous life behind, and look to the future – must be highly significant.

Vocal and Musical Analysis

WHO TO LISTEN TO: Euan Morton on the original London cast recording (2002).

VOCAL RANGE: C3 to G4.

ORIGINAL KEY: C minor.

ACCENT: General London.

STYLE OF MUSICAL: Contemporary musical (pop-based).

VOCAL SET-UP/MUSICAL TIPS

1. The harmonic structure of this song is that of a pop song, and should be delivered as such. To achieve an appropriate vocal style it is advisable to add some twang to your fundamental sound. The rhythms that are notated in the score can also be afforded some freedom of interpretation. Don't make them too precise; you can alter note-lengths to make the song feel conversational. It is also appropriate to make occasional use of pitch-slides.

2. The first verse and chorus should be very quiet and reflective, so try delivering them in a Cry quality. During the first chorus pay particular attention to the use of simultaneous onsets and a tilted thyroid cartilage to achieve a sweet, legato sound.

3. The second verse and chorus need to be louder and stronger in comparison, so should be delivered with thick vocal folds in a Speech quality. To transition into this set-up smoothly, crescendo at the very end of the first chorus (on the word 'world') by gradually removing your thyroid tilt as you sing this word.

4. After the second chorus, as you move into the final section, the song jumps higher and you need to shift into an Advanced-Speech quality. To achieve this, add some torso anchoring to your normal Speech set-up, lift the chin slightly and add a little thyroid tilt.

5. The penultimate time you sing the word 'mother' should be in a Belt quality. This doesn't want to be too overpowering so add some thyroid tilt in the sound to achieve a mixed belt.

Sheet Music

The correct sheet music for this song is available at www.scribd.com.

''Til I Hear You Sing'
from *Love Never Dies*

Music by Andrew Lloyd Webber, lyrics by Glenn Slater

Choose this song if: you have an outstanding tenor legit voice and enjoy singing huge, romantic ballads. This song is rightly recognised in the industry as being vocally demanding, so if you can sing it well it offers an opportunity to impress a panel with your vocal ability.

Given Circumstances

Note: *Love Never Dies* is the sequel to *The Phantom of the Opera* and features many of the major characters from that show. The details below provide a plot summary of the first piece, and the key information from the reworked 2012 version of *Love Never Dies*.

WHO ARE YOU: The Phantom, a reclusive, romantic, yet deranged composer. Born with a severely deformed face, you spent most of your life living alone in the catacombs beneath the Paris Opera House. The rejection, revulsion and isolation you endured for many years left you mentally unstable. (In *The Phantom of the Opera* you murdered several people.)

WHERE ARE YOU: Coney Island, New York, USA.

WHEN IS IT: Dawn, summer, 1907.

WHAT HAS HAPPENED BEFORE: Ten years ago, you left the Paris Opera House after a series of dramatic and tragic events. Haven fallen in love with Christine Daaé, a beautiful young ballet dancer and soprano, you became enraged when she began a romantic relationship with her childhood sweetheart Raoul, the Vicomte de Chagny. After the pair became engaged, you held the entire Opera House to ransom through murder, threats and intimidation – forcing them to mount your twisted opera *Don Juan* with Christine as the female leading role. During the performance you kidnapped Christine (for a second time), taking her to your secret lair in the bowels of the Opera House. When Raoul came to try and rescue Christine, you captured and threatened to kill him, unless Christine agreed to spend the rest of her life with you. Despite this ultimatum, you relented. And when Christine showed you pity and compassion – and kissed you – you let them both go. With the authorities apparently about to capture you, you disappeared without trace.

That night you were secretly smuggled from the Opera House by Madame Giry, the ballet mistress, and her daughter Meg. A decade on, you have now settled on Coney Island, where you have become the impresario of a new fairground attraction known as Phantasma. Tortured by the absence of Christine, you feel that your life has little meaning and you long to see her again… and to hear her sing.

WHO ELSE IS THERE: You are alone.

WHO SHOULD YOU SING TO: Yourself and the absent Christine.

Textual Analysis

The dramatic arc of this lyric is relatively simple, so the delivery of this song should, to an unusually large degree, be informed by the music, rather than the text (see point 1 below). However, there are some important changes of objective to be noted.

The song begins at the start of yet another day of solitude for the Phantom. In the first two verses your objective is: to reconcile yourself to the slow passing of time. You are trying to do so because your days are incredibly lonely and your feelings of isolation are seemingly without end. At the first bridge your intention changes when you suddenly remember dreams you have had about Christine. Your objective at this point becomes: to come to terms with your dreams. Memories of her have been plaguing your sleep, so you try to soothe yourself in order keep a hold on to your sanity.

Your focus in the third verse is on the long years you have been without Christine. At this moment your objective is: to protest the cruelty of time. During the second bridge you are then unexpectedly haunted by a daydream of Christine's voice. Your objective at this point, which reveals you are of troubled mind, is: to stop hearing Christine's singing in your ears.

In the fourth verse your mental state begins to deteriorate still further. You feel that you can never be at peace until Christine is back with you and you can hear her sing. Your objective here is a negative one: to force yourself to accept the hopelessness of the situation. This seems a strange objective to play, but you feel at this point that if you can abandon all hope of seeing Christine, then you might protect yourself from the pain of wanting her.

The event of the song occurs in the last three lines, when you resolve that you cannot be complete without Christine – so you will do all you can to see her again.

KEY MOMENTS/TOP TIPS

1. As suggested above, the drama of this song is largely dictated by the composer rather than the lyricist, so allow Lloyd Webber's dynamics and your own musicality to shape your performance – rather than simply rely upon a textual analysis of the lyric. This song requires you to trust your instincts as a musician and follow the sweeping crescendos and decrescendos of the score.

2. There are two musical high points in the piece: on the lyrics 'you're not here' and the final ''til I hear you sing'. These musical peaks must be justified by strong acting choices if the audience is to understand why the character is expressing themselves through an extended part of the voice. Try exploring the following choices to make these moments work. In the first, the Phantom is releasing, perhaps for the first time, the full strength of his feelings about Christine's absence, so try playing this musical release as a moment of protest, an emotional outburst. In the second, he is making a decision: he concludes he must get Christine to come to Coney Island. Try exploring this as a moment of great resolve, when he finally decides to seek out

Christine. Only by fully realising these moments as an actor will the musical scoring make sense dramatically.

3. Lloyd Webber's music, particularly in his ballads, often benefits from a degree of rhythmic interpretation of the melodic line. Therefore don't stick too rigidly to the note lengths as they are written; allow natural speech rhythms to influence the delivery.

4. The emotional highs and lows of this song are very extreme. At some points the Phantom is almost catatonic with melancholy, at others he is restless with a sense of suffocating panic, or a desperate urge for action. Explore how these extremes might be realised physically. At times you could use extended moments of stillness, at others you might move dynamically in the space.

5. This song provides the narrative lift-off for the entire show: it is from this moment onwards that the Phantom decides he will find Christine again. By the end of the song we should therefore feel that he has moved past his melancholy and that he is now ready to take action.

Vocal and Musical Analysis

WHO TO LISTEN TO: Ramin Karimloo on the original London cast recording (2010).

VOCAL RANGE: C3 to B♭4.

ORIGINAL KEY: F major.

ACCENT: Received Pronunciation. (In reality the Phantom would be French, but the role has always been delivered in RP when performed in English.)

STYLE OF MUSICAL: Contemporary musical (legit-based).

VOCAL SET-UP/MUSICAL TIPS

1. The correct vocal set-up for this style of musical theatre is sometimes unkindly called 'poperetta' – and is a mix

between a pop sound and operatic set-up. (Many singers have used a similar vocal style in productions of *Les Misérables* and *The Phantom of the Opera*.) The fundamental colour of the sound is achieved through a lowered laryngeal position. The set-up also contains thyroid tilt, some twang and an anchored torso. You should use simultaneous onsets wherever possible.

2. The opening of the song should be very quiet and intense. Try singing this in a Cry quality with thin vocal folds and also explore the use of aspirate onsets, as some breathiness can help portray a tortured sensibility. You can hear Karimloo demonstrate this on the suggested recording.

3. From the second verse onwards, when you talk about weeks passing, your sound should become louder. Thicken the vocal-fold mass and lower the larynx slightly to achieve this in a stylistically appropriate manner.

4. From the third verse, which begins with 'and years come' through to the big musical peak on 'you're not here' the volume of sound needs to increase again. Gradually thicken the vocal-fold mass further and add torso anchoring to achieve this.

5. In the two bridge sections, try moving the tempo forward to give the song a feeling of momentum. This helps portray the Phantom's desperation and fractured state of mind at these points.

6. The top notes of the song should not be belted. Instead maintain a legit sound. To realise this, instead of lifting the chin and tilting the cricoid (as you would do in Belt quality), add more torso anchoring, a little twang and some thyroid tilt as you ascend in pitch.

Sheet Music

The correct sheet music for this song is available at www.musicnotes.com.

'What Is It About Her?'
from *The Wild Party*

Music and lyrics by Andrew Lippa

Choose this song if: you belt to an A♭, have a good control of vocal dynamics, and like to play intense, brooding and vicious characters.

Given Circumstances

WHO ARE YOU: Burrs, a violent, sexually possessive vaudeville comedian with a huge appetite for women.

WHERE ARE YOU: The bedroom of your apartment, Hollywood, Los Angeles, USA.

WHEN IS IT: The early hours of the morning after a Saturday night, late summer in 1928, during the period of Prohibition in the USA (when alcohol was banned).

WHAT HAS HAPPENED BEFORE: Several months ago you met a stunningly good-looking, but emotionally fragile, vaudeville dancer by the name of Queenie. From your first meeting there was a strong, animalistic sexual attraction between you both, and you quickly fell into a passionate, intense love affair. Shortly afterwards she moved into your apartment.

Despite its exciting beginning, over the past months the relationship has begun to sour. Queenie felt increasingly trapped by your possessive nature and you became violent towards her. A few days ago, Queenie suggested that you have a party. You readily agreed and you both decided to invite some hell-raising guests, in particular some who were new to your circle. What you didn't know at the time was that Queenie was intent on taking a form of revenge.

Several hours ago the guests began to arrive. As the title of the musical suggests, the party was an outrageous one. Illegal

alcohol and drugs flowed freely. In the highly sexualised
atmosphere you made a move on Nadine, a guest who was
under the age of consent. Shortly after the party began,
Queenie – who had been changing in the other room – made
her entrance. She looked even more stunning than usual. You
publicly complimented her on her appearance, but she used
this as an opportunity to slight and ignore you.

Shortly afterwards an emotionally damaged, alcoholic party-
girl named Kate arrived with her mysterious new friend and
lover, Mr Black. You knew Kate previously, having slept with
her before you met Queenie. You'd dismissed her at the time
as you saw her as promiscuous, so had treated her with little
respect.

As soon as they saw one other, Queenie and Black felt an
instant mutual attraction. Kate spotted this and decided to
flirt with you in order to get back at Black. The music for a
dance number called 'The Juggernaut' began to play and
Queenie invited Black to the dance floor. They danced
together very provocatively. This display was nothing short of
a public humiliation for you and made you feel incredibly
angry. Sensing your growing rage, and worried what you
might do out of temper, Kate tried to distract you. But once
you got the opportunity, you interrupted Queenie and Black
and led her away. You warned her to stay away from Black,
but she laughed at you, declaring she could do whatever she
wanted. In response you became violent, twisting her arm.

The party galloped on towards its restless climax, and as a
result an hour ago it was interrupted by an angry neighbour
who came round to complain about the noise. This unwanted
visitor was chased off by insults from some of the guests.

A few minutes ago Queenie and Black disappeared to have a
private conversation. You went into the bedroom and were
followed by Kate. She tried to make a move on you but you
rejected her advances. With no one else to talk to, you decided
to confide in Kate about your darkening feelings towards
Queenie.

WHO ELSE IS THERE: Kate.

WHO SHOULD YOU SING TO: Kate, though in many ways you are talking to yourself (see point 1). In audition, as this is a song of confession, you can address some thoughts to the panel as though they are all your confidants.

Textual Analysis

The lyric is notable because it is full of questions. You are searching for fundamental answers about why your relationship is breaking down and the reasons for your violent behaviour. In the first verse your objective is: to understand why you desire Queenie. You have a similar aim during the second verse, although at this point you are asking specifically why you find Queenie arousing. (The images about parting the waters and hoisting the sail are sexual metaphors.)

The first chorus, which begins when you say that Queenie makes you cry, is a sudden emotional outburst. During it you want Kate to understand the damage and pain that Queenie causes you. But once more you are really talking to yourself. Your objective in this section is: to understand why you choose to remain in a destructive relationship.

In the third verse your emotions become calmer for a time, and you begin to once more ask questions of both Kate and yourself. Your objective here is: to discover what it is about Queenie that is pushing you over the edge. You want to comprehend what is fuelling your obsessive behaviour. At the end of this verse you resolve to keep Queenie forever. This leads to another huge emotional outburst in the second chorus. Your objective in this moment is: to lay down a challenge to Mr Black. You want him to understand the pain that you have been through with Queenie – and why you will not give her up.

You can argue that in the final verse we clearly see that you are mentally ill, and that this relationship is destroying you. In this final section, in which you are desperately trying to

CONTEMPORARY BALLADS

162

understand why you love Queenie, your objective is: to get
someone – anyone – to help you with the inner turmoil you
are grappling with. During the final two lines you play an
ultimate objective: to decide whether you can let Queenie go.
The answer to this final and fatal question is: no.

KEY MOMENTS/TOP TIPS

1. Because the song is full of questions, it suggests Burrs has
   a burning need to understand his relationship with
   Queenie. That relationship is often destructive and violent,
   so he is grappling with himself during the song: he wants
   to know why he is attracted to someone who causes him
   such pain. In order to portray this deep-rooted need for an
   answer, you must employ a variety of strong actions. Try
   playing choices such as: I interrogate, cross-examine,
   challenge, dissect, analyse, scrutinise, shake and grill
   myself.

2. At the end of the third verse, when you resolve that
   Queenie will be forever yours, an important decision is
   made. This is the event of the song. At this point you
   resolve that you will hold on to this relationship, no matter
   what the cost.

3. An interesting detail is the moment at which you comment
   on the way Queenie catches the light. This reflects how
   Burrs observes Queenie obsessively. Try making this
   moment very still, and become fascinated by the image of
   Queenie that you have in your memory. Exaggerating the
   rapid change in dynamic at this moment from loud to quiet
   can help portray the fact that Burrs's feelings towards her
   are now in the realms of the fanatical.

4. It is important to understand that at the end of the musical
   Burrs tries to shoot Queenie and Black (though he fails in
   this attempt and it results in his own death). He therefore
   has an ominous capacity for violence. That internal furnace
   should be always burning during this song.

Vocal and Musical Analysis

WHO TO LISTEN TO: Brian d'Arcy James on the original Off-Broadway cast recording (1999).

VOCAL RANGE: F minor.

ORIGINAL KEY: C3 to A♭4.

ACCENT: General American.

STYLE OF MUSICAL: Concept musical.

VOCAL SET-UP/MUSICAL TIPS

1. The tense, repetitive, staccato bassline in the verses reflects Burrs's inner tempo: he is brooding and ready to explode. When the music is suddenly much louder in the choruses it is because these moments are outbursts of anger and frustration.

2. Try delivering the verses in a sweet Cry quality. This helps portray the deep level of thoughtfulness and soul-searching that is occurring. By also making use of aspirate onsets, you can convey that Burrs is grappling with the questions.

3. The choruses should be very full and strong. To achieve this sound, try using an Advanced-Speech quality, by keeping the vocal folds thick whilst high in the range. In order to achieve this safely, you should add some torso anchoring and a tiny amount of thyroid tilt on the top notes.

4. The last word 'no' should be belted.

Sheet Music

The correct sheet music for this song is available at www.musicnotes.com.

CONTEMPORARY BALLADS

'Corner of the Sky'
from *Pippin*

Music and lyrics by Stephen Schwartz

Choose this song if: you can play a handsome, optimistic, yet
self-absorbed leading man. The song demands a beautiful,
contemporary musical-theatre sound and an excellent falsetto.

Given Circumstances

WHO ARE YOU: Pippin, son of Charlemagne the Great – who
united much of Europe through his conquests in the early
Middle Ages, before going on to become the Emperor of the
Holy Roman Empire: the first to hold that title since the fall
of the Western Roman Empire three hundred years earlier.
Charlemagne is famously a real person, and the character of
Pippin is very loosely based on his real-life eldest son, Pepin
the Hunchback – though Pippin does not share the physical
deformity of the real man on whom is based.

WHERE ARE YOU: The University of Padua, in what is now
Veneto, a province in Northern Italy.

WHEN IS IT: About 11.30 a.m., a spring morning, 780AD – in
the time preceding the formation of the Holy Roman Empire
(though the world of the play bears little resemblance to this
historical period, which instead takes on much of its
atmosphere from the 1970s, when the piece was written).

WHAT HAS HAPPENED BEFORE: The story of *Pippin* began when
the audience were welcomed to a performance by a group of
theatrical players, most notably the Leading Player. They
announced that this evening they would be telling the story of
Pippin, son of Charlemagne – which they proceeded to do in
the most theatrical manner. Having briefly described your
early years, in which you proved to be a child with a
tremendous thirst for knowledge, they then moved the

narrative forward to the moment of your graduation from university. With you having just completed your graduation ceremony, your tutors then invited you to remain at the university and accept the honorary title of 'scholar of the house'. In response, you politely declined, saying that, although you were extremely grateful for the knowledge they had given you, you were searching for something that could not be found in books. You then made a pledge to not waste your life in what you considered to be commonplace ordinary pursuits – and to instead search for a purpose to your life that would be completely fulfilling. (During the course of the story you will try to find the meaning of your existence through many pursuits, including: going to war, in love and sex, through religion, in writing poetry and by going into politics. Ultimately, having found none of these fulfilling, you will eventually find contentment by building a simple family life with a woman named Catherine and her son Theo. Of course, you know nothing of this right now, as you are just about to begin your quest.)

WHO ELSE IS THERE: The scholars of the university.

WHO SHOULD YOU SING TO: Although the scholars are present, for audition purposes you should behave as if you are alone. At points you sing to yourself, at others to the universe.

Textual Analysis

At the start of the song you are feeling lost and directionless. You do not know what to do now you have finished university. So in the first verse your objective is: to understand why your life seems to have no meaning. Looking around, it perplexes you that everything else in the universe seems to have a purpose, even cats and children. This realisation engenders feelings of frustration in you that nonetheless imbue you with a sense of mission. Your objective for the first chorus thus becomes: to inspire yourself to find something fulfilling and purposeful to do with your life. This objective is repeated in all subsequent choruses.

During the first verse you were baffled and irritated by your observations of the world. You felt isolated. However, during the second verse this changes. You become inspired that everything else in the world appears to have a purpose, as you figure that surely this must also apply to you. Your objective in this section is therefore: to convince yourself that every entity has a calling, including yourself. This positive discovery means that when you get to the second chorus your actions should be more overtly upbeat than they were previously. Try actions such as: I convince, motivate, assure and bolster myself during the first chorus, and choices such as: I excite, galvanise, awaken and spark myself during the second.

In the third verse, with your self-confidence now growing, you broaden your outlook and start to address the entire universe. Your objective in this section is: to swear to the universe that you will be successful in your quest. By the end of the song you have thus laid down a clear marker to the world: you are going to seek out your destiny, no matter how long it takes or what obstacles you may encounter.

KEY MOMENTS/TOP TIPS

1. A difficulty in performing this song successfully is that there are three choruses with an identical lyric, which can lead to your performance seeming repetitive. To avoid this, try approaching each chorus in a different manner. In the first chorus you should *discover* your need to seek out the purpose of life, as if you are articulating it for the first time. During the second, you should *resolve* to take action on those feelings. In the third you should *promise* yourself and the universe that you will complete this quest.

2. The first verse involves a great deal of soul-searching. To answer your inner questions, explore using actions such as: I analyse, question, evaluate, investigate and scrutinise. You may direct some of these thoughts to the panel, as though they might be able to help you answer them.

3. Stephen Schwartz wrote *Pippin* in his early twenties, and his youthfulness is reflected in the writing. A key to this song is therefore the character's optimism about the future, and his sense of drive and purpose. To portray this from the third verse onwards, try using actions such as: I uplift, inspire, motivate, invigorate, thrill, electrify and fire myself.

4. To acknowledge the title of the song, try directing the title lyric towards a corner of the audition room, as though the goal you are striving for is currently far away and out of reach.

5. This song is the engine for the entire show. It is the moment that Pippin resolves to begin his quest. By the last note of the music we should therefore feel that he has thrown off any self-doubt, and is now ready to set off on his journey to find fulfilment. This is therefore the event of the song.

Vocal and Musical Analysis

WHO TO LISTEN TO: Matthew James Thomas on the Broadway revival cast recording (2013).

VOCAL RANGE: C3 to C5.

ORIGINAL KEY: C major.

ACCENT: General American.

STYLE OF MUSICAL: Contemporary musical (pop-based).

VOCAL SET-UP/MUSICAL TIPS

1. The introduction of the song is too long for an audition. You should cut the first five bars to leave a two-bar introduction.

2. The majority of the song should be delivered in an oral Twang quality. In this quality remember to keep the

thyroid tilted, the larynx high and the soft palate high. Thomas expertly demonstrates this sound in the suggested recording. You can also afford to mix your onsets – using glottals at times – to give the song a conversational feeling. Use this vocal set-up for the first three verses and two choruses.

3. During the third verse it is usual to improvise the vocal line and move away from the melody that is notated. If you find this difficult, it is advisable to base what you do on Thomas's performance on the suggested recording. Alternatively you can repeat the same melody as in the previous verses, which is notated on the sheet music.

4. The first two lines of the third chorus should be sung in a quiet Cry quality. To achieve this, thin your vocal folds as much as possible, lift your larynx and relax your AES to remove any twang from your voice. On the word 'fly', slowly remove your thyroid tilt to affect a crescendo and arrive in a Speech quality. The word 'corner' in the third chorus should then be belted – all of which Thomas demonstrates.

5. The final note on the word 'sky' should be sung in a Falsetto quality.

Sheet Music

The correct sheet music for this song is available at www.musicnotes.com.

'I'll Be There'
from *The Pirate Queen*

Music by Claude-Michel Schönberg, lyrics by Alain Boublil and John Dempsey

Choose this song if: you have strong tenor voice and your voice sits within that stylistic crossover between a pop and operatic quality (i.e. a sound suitable for *Les Misérables*). This song suits actors who might usually play the romantic lead.

Given Circumstances

Note: *The Pirate Queen* references some real-life historical figures and events, but for narrative purposes liberties were taken with the timeline of events. The facts that appear below work within the context of the show, but are not always historically accurate.

WHO ARE YOU: Tiernan, an Irish sailor in his early thirties, and member of the O'Malley Clan.

WHERE ARE YOU: Clew Bay, County Mayo, Ireland.

WHEN IS IT: 4.00 p.m., late autumn, 1558.

WHAT HAS HAPPENED BEFORE: A few years previously, King Henry VIII of England had decided to conquer Ireland. His aggressive action prompted the various feuding clans of Ireland to take arms against him. As part of this action the O'Malley Clan of seafarers and pirates, of whom you were a member, decided to plunder English treasure ships returning from India, China and the Caribbean. At this time, Dubhdara, the chieftain of the O'Malley Clan, had just christened a new ship: *The Pirate Queen*. Dubhdara was about to set sail when his daughter Grace – your childhood sweetheart – implored him to let her join the expedition. He refused. Grace remonstrated with you about her father's decision, arguing that she was as capable a sailor as you, and that the only reason she was not allowed to sail was because she was a woman. Following this heated discussion, you boarded the ship and told her to remain behind. Not to be deterred, Grace disguised herself as a cabin boy and boarded in secret.

On the voyage Grace proved her heroism by climbing the mast to pull down the mainsail in the midst of a vicious storm. Dubhdara, discovering that the heroic 'cabin boy' who had saved the ship was, in fact, his daughter, was at first angry that he has been disobeyed. In his rage he threatened to throw Grace overboard, but his pride in, and love for, her caused him to quickly relent, and he allowed her to join the crew. You were both overjoyed. That night you and Grace made love and swore yourself to each other.

The next day, in the midst of a thick fog, *The Pirate Queen* was attacked by a much larger English warship. In the mêlée Dubhdara was injured and Grace took command of the ship – leading the crew to a famous victory over the English. Witnessing this remarkable feat, Dubhdara decided to break with tradition and train his daughter as a sea captain.

Several years passed, and Elizabeth I ascended to the throne of England. Her commander in Ireland, Sir Richard Bingham, then came to court to inform her that there was a rebellion in Ireland and that many of her ships were being sunk by a group of pirates led by Grace O'Malley – who was by now renowned as a fearsome sea captain. Elizabeth ordered Bingham to crush the rebellion and have Grace killed.

Back in Ireland, you and Grace had grown ever closer and everyone expected you soon to marry. But with the renewed ferocity of the English attacks there was pressure for the O'Malleys to set aside their differences with their ancient rivals the O'Flahertys and form an alliance against Queen Elizabeth's army. Under pressure from the chieftain of the O'Flahertys, Grace agreed to marry his son Donal, as this would be the only way to unite the clans against the English.

Today you watched Grace and Donal marry, knowing that she still loves you and has married for duty's sake. Moments ago the wedding party departed, to take Grace from Clew Bay to Rockfleet – the home of the O'Flahertys – leaving you alone.

WHO ELSE IS THERE: You are alone.

WHO SHOULD YOU SING TO: During the song you alternate between singing to yourself and to the absent Grace.

Textual Analysis

The song starts with an opening phrase containing three questions. Your objective with these questions is: to try and understand how you will cope with the loss of Grace. Try playing a different action on each one, such as: to search, interrogate and cross-examine yourself. These quick to rapid changes of action will help portray your desperation in this moment. In the second phrase, instead of talking to yourself, you now address the absent Grace. Your objective at this point is: to ask her how she can expect your loyalty when she has married another man (though Grace has placed no such obligation on you).

Halfway through the first verse your anger and disappointment momentarily get the better of you. You feel that you want to get away from Clew Bay and forget about Grace forever. But that feeling is transient. In the final lines of the verse you realise that one day Grace will need you, and you resolve to be around for her when that time comes.

In the first chorus you heroically promise Grace that you will always be there for her, no matter what the circumstances, or the suffering you might endure. Your objective at this point is: to convince Grace that you will never abandon her.

Your thoughts then turn towards Donal at the beginning of the second verse. Your objective here is: to get the absent Grace to accept that Donal doesn't really love her. You want her to understand that, despite the lavish wedding and the gifts that Donal might bestow on her, his offerings mean nothing compared to the love you feel towards her.

During the second chorus you play the same objective as in the first, and once more promise Grace that you will not abandon her. On this occasion you particularly want her to understand how much that sacrifice will hurt you. Despite your good intentions, a great bitterness and resentment arises in the bridge. You seek to antagonise Grace in this section, pressing her to go and throw her life away on a marriage that is based on expedience, not on love. This objective is, in fact, counterproductive, as you are acting spitefully and out of jealousy.

After this outburst you gain control of your temper once more, and in the final chorus you promise for one last time to never abandon Grace. The difference on this occasion is that this vow is not accompanied by any negative comments – your love for her is now unconditional. This thus makes the final repetition of the title lyric the event of the song.

KEY MOMENTS/TOP TIPS

1. The urgent piano accompaniment of the verses reflects Tiernan's state of mind: he is agitated and thinking quickly. Try to reflect this by working with a quick inner tempo, like your heart is racing.

2. When you talk to the absent Grace, explore directing your thoughts towards the spot from which she has just exited. For the purposes of the audition, try locating this point at an angle somewhere behind the panel so they can clearly see your face.

3. A challenge when singing this song is the repetition of the title lyric. In order to keep the panel engaged, try to play a different action each time you repeat the lyric. Suitable choices might be: I assure, comfort, uplift, hearten, strengthen and sustain you.

4. Immediately after the bridge, there is a single bar of instrumental music. This momentary break from singing is important, as it allows you the space to discover the

question contained in the next thought. For the first time you wonder if you are, in fact, deceiving yourself.

Vocal and Musical Analysis

WHO TO LISTEN TO: Hadley Fraser on the original Broadway cast recording (2007).

VOCAL RANGE: C3 to A4.

ORIGINAL KEY: E♭ major.

ACCENT: An Irish accent would be appropriate for this song, but many of the Broadway cast chose to sing in Received Pronunciation – so if you struggle with Irish accents that is an alternative option.

STYLE OF MUSICAL: Contemporary musical (legit-based).

VOCAL SET-UP/MUSICAL TIPS

1. The correct vocal set-up for this style of musical theatre is sometimes unkindly called 'poperetta' – and is a mix between a pop sound and operatic set-up. (Many singers have used a similar vocal style in productions of *Les Misérables* and *The Phantom of the Opera*.) The fundamental colour of the sound – which is used in the choruses of this song – is achieved through a lowered laryngeal position. The set-up also contains thyroid tilt, some twang and an anchored torso. Use a simultaneous onset wherever possible.

2. Sing the verses in a Speech quality, but with a slightly lowered larynx. This helps give those sections a similar vocal style to the choruses.

3. The repeated high notes on the word 'I'll' should be loud and full, but are not belted. (The vocal set-up is that described in point 1.) Usually when you sing higher the larynx raises, but in this style you want to maintain a degree of laryngeal lowering to achieve a rich, deep vocal

colour. On these high notes, instead of raising the larynx, add more thyroid tilt and anchor your torso. This will give the sound a moaned/poppy quality. A good example of this position on the suggested recording is when Fraser sings the words 'sorrow' and 'morrow'.

4. The bridge requires a great deal of vocal attack. Explore using hard glottal onsets and speaking some words to achieve this, as Fraser admirably demonstrates.

5. The final note should be belted. Belting on an 'oo' vowel is challenging. Alongside the usual requirements for a belt set-up, you must therefore pay particular attention to the position of your tongue (the sides of the tongue must be as close to the upper molars as possible). If you still find this difficult, try modifying the vowel so it is closer to an 'err' vowel, as Fraser does on the suggested recording.

Sheet Music

The correct sheet music for this song is available at www.musicnotes.com.

'Lost in the Wilderness'
from *Children of Eden*

Music and lyrics by Stephen Schwartz

Choose this song if: you have high pop belt voice, enjoy dynamic, high-energy songs and are suited to playing the angry, brooding outsider.

Given Circumstances

WHO ARE YOU: Cain, the Biblical figure, son of Adam and Eve. You are an argumentative and troubled seventeen-year-old who eventually murders your younger brother, Abel.

WHERE ARE YOU: In an unspecified outdoors location in the Wilderness, a short distance from the shanty in which you live with your family. The terrain would resemble something like the near-desert conditions of parts of modern Iraq.

WHEN IS IT: 9.30 a.m., a spring morning, in the time of the Book of Genesis, about eighteen years after Adam and Eve's expulsion from the Garden of Eden.

WHAT HAS HAPPENED BEFORE: At the dawn of time, God (called Father in the musical) created the universe. In six days and six nights he made the Heavens and the Earth – populating it with all living creatures. On the seventh day he made your mother and father – Adam and Eve, the first man and woman – in his own image. Father greatly loved them both as his children, and they wanted for nothing in the perfect paradise he had made for them: the Garden of Eden. The only thing denied to Adam and Eve was that Father forbade them from eating the fruit from the mysterious Tree of Knowledge.

At first your parents were content with their lives, but as she grew older your mother became restless. She began to question Father about what lay beyond the waterfall on the borders of the Garden and why she could not eat the forbidden fruit. Father did not answer her questions, instead telling her to have faith that he was doing what was in their best interests.

This did not satisfy Eve, and one day the Devil – taking the form of a serpent – tempted her to eat from the Tree of Knowledge. The strange fruit gave Eve the newfound ability to see all of the possibilities of the world: how she could invent new things, travel the Earth and bear children. She was a child herself no longer. Excited by her fresh knowledge, and comforted by a belief that Father's warnings about the danger of eating the fruit had been proved unfounded, she tricked Adam into drinking cider made from the forbidden fruit when she returned home.

Discovering that he had been disobeyed, Father was furious. Blaming Eve, he ordered her to leave this paradise forever, and told your father that he must choose to stay with him – and never see Eve again – or to leave the Garden with her and never return. Feeling that he could not be without his lover and wife, Adam decided to leave with Eve, so Father banished them both to the Wilderness.

Life in their new desert home was hard for your parents. They had to farm the arid land for food, and they experienced pain and hardship for the first time. But despite the difficulties of their new lives, Adam and Eve both found contentment in the fact that their few possessions were the fruits of their own labours. After a year in the Wilderness, Eve gave birth to you, her first child, followed two years later by your younger brother.

As a young child, Abel was very much like your father, in that he was hard-working and devout, whereas you had much more of your mother's rebellious spirit. Eve became worried when, as a child of ten, you said that you wanted to explore what lay beyond the waterfall. When you began to enquire about the world, Adam – just like Father before him – told you not to ask such questions. Feeling that your curiosity was being suppressed, your resentment towards your father began to grow over the coming years, particularly when you learned that it was his decision that had cheated you out of a life in the Garden.

In recent months your anger towards him has become increasingly violent. Last night you revealed to Abel your plan to head off in search of the Garden, and told him that you wanted him to come with you. This morning you were tending the field next to your house with your brother when your parents headed off to the nearby river to fetch water. Sensing the opportunity to escape, you ran into the house to fetch your belongings and came back to tell Abel it was your chance to leave. He told you that he had decided not to come with you. When you began to remonstrate with him, he told you that, instead of leaving, you should remain and you should put your faith in Father – that it was his will that the family lived in the Wilderness, and not in the Garden.

WHO ELSE IS THERE: Abel. In the song you refer directly to Adam and Eve. It is useful to suppose that when the song takes place they are still down by the river, which is close enough to be seen in the near distance, but far enough away that the scene takes place in complete privacy.

WHO SHOULD YOU SING TO: For most of the song you are talking to Abel. In one moment you talk directly to Father.

Textual Analysis

When the introduction begins you are bristling with a sense of rejection, as you feel your brother has chosen your father over you. During the first verse you channel your sense of resentment into your complaint that you are not living in the paradise of the Garden, and instead are banished to this barren wasteland. Your objective in this section is: to get Abel to blame your parents for the loss of the Garden. In this part of the song you are quite confrontational, even though you are trying to win your brother over. Try using actions such as: I antagonise, provoke, confront and challenge Abel. When you move into the first chorus your objective alters. You now want Abel to wake up to the bleak reality of life in the Wilderness.

Fuelled by your temper and your failure to win him over, in the second verse you personally attack your brother. Your objective in this section is: to ridicule Abel for his compliant behaviour. You can explore actions such as: I mock, humiliate, mimic, patronise and deride Abel. In the second chorus, although you continue to be somewhat sarcastic in your manner, your objective alters again and you now try to awaken Abel to the detrimental effect that the Wilderness is having on his life.

During the bridge, when you begin to talk about the eagle, your tone changes radically. Your argument at this point becomes suddenly uplifting and positive; you begin to enthuse Abel with your passion. Your objective from this point until the end of the song is: to inspire Abel to join you on your adventure – an objective in which you are ultimately successful, which thus makes the last note the event of the song.

KEY MOMENTS/TOP TIPS

1. The driving musical introduction mirrors Cain's internal rhythm: he is feeling very wound up. Your performance therefore needs to have a quick internal rhythm. To convey this, try making a dynamic physical entrance from a corner of the room into the centre of the space during those opening bars, as though you are rushing in to confront Abel.

2. As the song is mainly delivered to one person, and is quite confrontational, it is not suitable to address the panel. Fix a spot for your imaginary Abel behind their heads.

3. A tricky moment to act is the instrumental break between the first chorus and the second verse, which is not really possible to cut. Try playing this moment as though you are too exasperated to speak. You might walk away from your imaginary Abel for a moment, then return to argue with him once more.

4. It is interesting to act the bridge as though an eagle passes by at that exact moment. You can then play the section as though spotting the bird provides a spark of inspiration for your passionate argument. So that this choice reads to the panel, imagine that the bird flies across the sky – and trace its journey with your gaze until it passes out of sight.

5. At the root of this song is a primordial story of sibling rivalry, and a troubled relationship between father and son. The key to Cain's psyche is his misplaced perception that his father loves Abel more than him.

6. Remember: Cain eventually murders his brother. By exploring the extreme mood swings in the song as you oscillate between moments of great affection for Abel, and a deep anger towards him, you will be able to portray Cain's emotional volatility.

Vocal and Musical Analysis

WHO TO LISTEN TO: Darius de Haas on the American premiere cast recording (1998).

VOCAL RANGE: D3 to G4 (with a possible riff up to B4).

ORIGINAL KEY: D major.

ACCENT: The song is written to be sung in General American, and it is undoubtedly easier to sing in that accent due the higher tongue position prevalent in the dialect. However, if you are performing the song in a UK audition, there is a strong argument for delivering it in Standard English, which will sound more neutral to British ears. This can be a good choice as the location of the Wilderness is so nebulous.

STYLE OF MUSICAL: Contemporary musical (pop-based).

VOCAL SET-UP/MUSICAL TIPS

1. The set-up for the verse is a version of Speech quality. If you lift the back of the tongue a little higher than you

would do normally in this set-up and tighten the AES, you can add a little twang. This will give you a bright American Speech sound that is appropriate for the pop-based music of Schwartz. Don't add twang if you are singing in Standard English.

2. In the choruses, take the opportunity to sing with a legato line – to show the panel you have the ability to deliver long phrases. This is important as the verses are very broken and conversational so may not reveal the full potential of your voice. To achieve the legato phrasing use simultaneous onsets wherever possible and look to run the vowels together. The voice quality for the choruses is Twang.

3. In both choruses you go up to a top G. Add a little torso anchoring at these moments to make them easier to achieve.

4. During the second chorus the word 'lost' is notated to be sung over three bars. It has become an industry expectation that you would riff higher at this point up to a high B, as de Haas demonstrates on the suggested recording. If possible you should sing this riff, which should be delivered in a mixed belt (see p. 54). If this proves to be too difficult for you, you can sing the phrase notated on the music and sustain a single long note instead.

5. From the point where you sing the words 'off we go' until the end, there needs to be a gradual crescendo from an intense, hushed, excited quality to a powerful finish on the last belted note. You can affect this build in the following way. Start the section identified in a breathy Speech quality, by using lots of aspirate onsets. When you sing the lyric 'where our future', shift to a simultaneous onset to achieve a more legato line. Also tighten your AES. By doing so, you will have added a little volume and be in a Twang quality. During the next few bars release your thyroid tilt, and relax your AES so you thicken your vocal folds and transition into Speech quality. Add some torso

anchoring from the word 'there' onwards to add further resonance. Finally: lift the chin and belt the last note.

Sheet Music

The correct sheet music for this song is available at www.musicnotes.com.

'Marry Me a Little'
from *Company*

Music and lyrics by Stephen Sondheim

Choose this song if: you enjoy playing roles that have a
psychological complexity. The song requires both charm and
vulnerability. Vocally, it sits comfortably in the baritone
register.

Given Circumstances

WHO ARE YOU: Bobby, a popular, charming, single man from
New York. In your day-to-day life you are surrounded by a
large circle of married friends, yet you have always struggled
to sustain a meaningful romantic relationship. You have
reached a stage in your life when you are seriously debating
whether you want to be single any more.

WHERE ARE YOU: Notionally, you are in the main living space
of your chic, modern apartment in New York City, USA.
Much of the action in *Company* takes place in Bobby's
imagination and memory – including this number. You can
therefore decide to locate the song anywhere that an intimate
and private conversation might occur, such as the kitchen of
your friends Amy and Paul's apartment (see below).

WHEN IS IT: Early evening on your thirty-fifth birthday. When
Company was written in 1970, it was intended that the action
would be set in the present day. Although certain aspects of
the technology involved in the action (notably the answering
machine in your apartment) do date the action, for audition
purposes it still makes sense to set the song in the here-and-
now.

WHAT HAS HAPPENED BEFORE: The events in *Company* occur as
a series of vignettes that unfold in a non-linear manner, rather
than as a traditional through-narrative. The piece is about

marriage and many of the scenes depict your interactions with your married friends. In the narrative structure the individual vignettes are framed by fragments of a recurring scenario: the evening of your thirty-fifth birthday party.

This evening (at the beginning of the piece) you were surprised at your apartment by ten of your best friends, who are all married couples. They had arrived to celebrate your birthday. They offered you their congratulations and gifts, and then one of them, Amy, presented you with a birthday cake. The ladies in the group encouraged you to blow out the candles – and to make a wish. You tried to do this, but the candles remained lit. You then told them that this didn't matter, because you had not wished for anything anyway.

In the structure of show, around the vignettes, the scene with the birthday cake is returned to briefly at the end of Act One – just after you have sung 'Marry Me a Little' – and at the beginning and the end of Act Two. At the end of the show on this occasion, your friends are waiting for you at your apartment, and you have simply not shown up. So they decide to leave and, with the apartment left empty, you appear – having apparently been hiding. Finally alone, you blow out the candles – this action signifying that at last you are ready to commit to a long-term relationship. The surreal nature of the events of the birthday party suggests that the intervening vignettes all happen in Bobby's imagination or memory.

The vignette that occurs immediately before 'Marry Me a Little' is about the wedding of one the couples: Amy and Paul. On the morning of the wedding the three of you were in the kitchen of Amy and Paul's apartment. You were to be best man. Amy was suffering from a very bad attack of premarital nerves. With Amy running late, and the wedding party waiting at the church, both yourself and Paul tried to calm her. Your attempts were unsuccessful and, in her panic, Amy told Paul that she didn't love him enough to get married. Devastated that the wedding was off, Paul went outside in the rain and asked you to tell the other guests. The moment Paul had left, Amy started to worry that she had made an awful mistake. Impulsively, you then asked Amy if she would marry you instead. You argued that if the two you got married, then you would be freed from the pressure of your friends urging you to tie the knot. This jolted Amy back into reality. She thanked you for the offer, but told you that you couldn't just marry *any*body, such as yourself; it had to be *some*body special. She realised that she really loved Paul, so grabbed an umbrella and overcoat for him and ran out into the rain to save the wedding.

WHO ELSE IS THERE: You are alone.

WHO SHOULD YOU SING TO: An imaginary woman, someone who you want to marry. In some sense this imaginary woman has the qualities of Amy.

Textual Analysis

The song starts with a chorus. Your objective in this first section is: to convince your imaginary someone to marry you – but only on your terms. As you can be a charming Lothario, try using a range of actions such as: I flatter, amuse, seduce and captivate her.

In the first verse you suggest to your imaginary someone that you could be best friends. With these words you are trying to calm and comfort. Your objective here is: to convince her that having a relationship with you would protect her from the outside world. Like your attitude towards Amy in the scene that precedes the song, this sentiment shows a naivety about the realities of marriage. You are advocating that the relationship would be like a friendship, free of the troublesome demands and responsibilities that marriage places on the respective partners.

The repetition of the words 'I'm ready' suggests a different objective at the end of the verse. At this point you want your future partner to enter your life.

During the second chorus and second verse the same objectives are repeated. This textual and musical repetition is symptomatic of your increasing desperation for your imaginary someone to arrive. To portray this, explore playing more desperate actions in the second half of the lyric, for example: to implore, beg, beseech, hustle, urge, harass, provoke and compel. By the time you are repeating the words 'I'm ready' at the end of the song, we should see that you are almost tortured in your loneliness and need for love.

KEY MOMENTS/TOP TIPS

1. There are two different ways in which you might deliver this song in relation to the audition panel. Firstly, you could sing the song directly to the panel. If you choose this option, use each person on the panel as though they are someone you are trying to convince to marry you. Deliver each new thought to a different member of the casting team. Alternatively you can sing the song to an imaginary woman situated behind the table. If you choose this option, ensure you are very clear what this person looks like. Try to envisage her behaviour: see her smile, walk away from you, shrug her shoulders, etc., so you can be responsive to her imagined behaviour.

2. The text is full of contradictions and antitheses, notably in the title lyric (marriage is usually considered to be a wholehearted commitment, and therefore is not something you can do 'a little'). This exposes Bobby's confused state of mind: although he wants to be in a relationship, he is not realistic about, nor committed to, the obligations that it entails.

3. Search the lyric for the elements of a relationship that Bobby craves, and for the aspects that he dreads. For example, he wants a relationship that is passionate, yet he doesn't want to surrender control of his own feelings. Make these moments of antithesis key to your performance – they portray a man who is constantly backtracking and second-guessing himself.

4. The most important moment of the song, the event, comes on the word 'someone'. Here we understand that Bobby is desperate to meet his life partner. Although he does not quite yet fully understand the commitment involved in a marriage, he has resolved himself to the truth: that he wants to be settled with someone.

Vocal and Musical Analysis

WHO TO LISTEN TO: Adrian Lester on the Donmar Warehouse revival cast recording (1996).

VOCAL RANGE: G2 to F4.

ORIGINAL KEY: B major.

ACCENT: New York.

STYLE OF MUSICAL: Concept musical.

VOCAL SET-UP/MUSICAL TIPS

1. The two choruses of the song (which both start with the title lyric) should be very conversational, and therefore delivered in a Speech quality. It can be appropriate to half-speak some of the lyrics in these sections.

2. Observe the rests at the ends of each phrase in the verses. Don't extend the notes longer than they are written. If you make this section too lyrical, the listener can be drawn to the sound of your voice, rather than paying full attention to the complex lyric.

3. Sondheim indicates that during the long note on the word 'now' there should be a decrescendo. To achieve this, begin the note strongly in a Speech position by using a glottal onset, then gradually add thyroid tilt as you sustain the sound to affect the decrescendo.

4. Both verses should be very tender vocally. Lift your larynx at these points, tilt your thyroid and use simultaneous onsets to achieve a sweet, legato Cry quality.

5. You sing the word 'someone' on high pitches twice in the song. These moments should be the vocal climaxes of the your performance. Anchor your torso at these points to add further resonance to your Speech quality, and add a little thyroid tilt to give the sound a moaned quality, like a sound of longing.

Sheet Music

The correct sheet music for this song is available at www.musicnotes.com.

'Martin Guerre'
from *Martin Guerre*

Music by Claude-Michel Schönberg, lyrics by Alain Boublil

Choose this song if: you have a legit, high-baritone voice with
an excellent belt. The song may suit you if you enjoy playing
characters that are driven by a sense of injustice.

Given Circumstances

Note: *Martin Guerre* has been heavily rewritten several times
since its premiere in London in 1996. As a result, many
different versions of the given circumstances exist. The
authors, when revisiting the material for the 2011 production
at the Watermill Theatre, Newbury, based it heavily on the
original production. As this is the version they consider
definitive, it is the one used for the purposes of this book –
combined with some of my own judgements when there is no
clear textual evidence. The version of the lyrics recommended
is that which appears on the original London cast recording –
which is the best for audition purposes.

WHO ARE YOU: Martin Guerre, a sensitive, confused, teenage
member of the Catholic landowning aristocracy.

WHERE ARE YOU: Artigat, a small village in Southern France.

WHEN IS IT: Midday, some time in April 1558, during the years
of unrest that preceded the outbreak of the French Wars of
Religion (1562–98) between the Catholics and the Protestants
(also known as the Huguenots).

WHAT HAS HAPPENED BEFORE: Twelve months ago your uncle
Pierre forced you into an arranged marriage with Bertrande
de Rols – the teenage daughter of another Catholic
landowning family. You had been pressurised into this union
as the village yearned for a Catholic heir. They were afraid
that if you did not have a child, then your family's land could

fall into the hands of the Protestants. Your failure to consummate the marriage during the following year was seen by the superstitious community to be the cause of a flood that plagued the village and therefore the work of the Devil. In an attempt to drive out the spirits possessing you, the priest, Father Dominic, has just beaten you in the market square. You have been left alone nursing your wounds, feeling angry and humiliated.

WHO ELSE IS THERE: You are alone.

WHO SHOULD YOU SING TO: At times you are talking to yourself. At others you talk to the villagers. (This is an imaginary conversation that takes place in your head, as the villagers are not actually present. You are dreaming about the conversation you would have with them if you were able to return in a few years as a hero.)

Textual Analysis

At the start of song you are singing to yourself. Your objective in the first section is: to criticise the cruel behaviour of the villagers. In the two lines that precede the main melody you then taunt them – warning that their negative impression of you will be proved wrong on the day of your return.

In the verse that follows the first instrumental section, you make an important decision: to leave the village. Although you have already mentioned departing, this is the moment where that idea crystallises into a definite decision. Your objective is: to galvanise yourself into action.

During the first chorus you begin a fictitious conversation with the absent villagers. You start to imagine yourself returning triumphantly in ten years' time. Your objective here is: to get the villagers to take notice of the returning hero. You want them to see that they were wrong when they thought you were weak and emasculated.

Having momentarily slipped into this daydream, during the bridge you come back to reality and reflect on the behaviour

CONTEMPORARY UP-TEMPO

of your uncle Pierre. Your objective here is: to curse Pierre, and to condemn the entire village. You vent the feelings of resentment and betrayal that have been lingering inside you for months.

When the music for the second chorus begins, you once more daydream about returning to the village in triumph. Rather than singing to the absent villagers, on this occasion explore singing to yourself. Your objective here is: to indulge your fantasy of returning victorious from the war. You want to inspire and uplift yourself. By the end of the song you are completely successful in this objective; you end the scene defiant, resolute and ready to leave the village.

KEY MOMENTS/TOP TIPS

1. The song has no introduction, so it is especially important you start your performance in a charged and explosive manner. Remember: Martin has just been beaten and publicly humiliated, so he is furious when the song begins. You could imagine you have just been spat on by one of the villagers.

2. In the bridge there is a single line of singing that has no piano accompaniment, when you talk about your uncle selling you for land. That Schönberg chooses to make this line a capella is significant, as it is a key moment of discovery for Martin. He realises that until now he has been a pawn to his family and that he will no longer tolerate it. This moment is the event of the song.

3. The emotional journey of the lyric is a progression from feeling completely defeated to being proud and defiant. Explore how you might physically realise this in your performance. You could begin the song on the floor, crouched, with your head stooped, and end the piece standing upright and defiant.

Vocal and Musical Analysis

WHO TO LISTEN TO: Matt Rawle on the original London cast recording (1996).

VOCAL RANGE: D2 to A4.

ORIGINAL KEY: B♭ minor.

ACCENT: Received Pronunciation. In British productions of Boublil and Schönberg's most famous work – *Les Misérables* – the device of using English accents to denote class and geography is also used, even though both pieces are, of course, set in France.

STYLE OF MUSICAL: Contemporary musical (legit-based).

VOCAL SET–UP/MUSICAL TIPS

1. The song should begin in a very intense Speech quality. You want to give the impression that you are spitting these words in vengeance. To achieve this make use of some heavy glottal onsets. Really bite your consonants; for example, you can almost hiss the 's' sounds, as Rawle does at times on the suggested cast recording.

2. The high A on the word 'back' should be belted. Although this note is written as a crotchet (a one-beat note), in practice it is often delivered as a dotted minim (a three-beat note). This is advisable in audition, as it gives you the opportunity to showcase the highest part of the voice.

3. After the first instrumental section, try delivering the next verse in a breathy Speech quality. Think of your sound being almost whispered. This helps portray Martin's inner determination at this point.

4. Once you reach the chorus, sing in longer phrases. This is not only stylistically appropriate, but having previously delivered much of the song in a conversational fashion, this section also gives you the opportunity to show the panel you can sing with a legato line.

5. From the word 'strides' to the end of the chorus there should be a crescendo. Start the section with a tilted thyroid cartilage. Then, from the word 'laughs' begin to release the tilt to thicken your vocal folds. By the time you sing the word 'all' you should have added some torso anchoring to finish the chorus in a loud, anchored Speech quality.

6. The first two lines of the second chorus should be sung as quietly and thoughtfully as possible, as Rawle successfully demonstrates. Lift your larynx and use lots of thyroid tilt to achieve this sound.

7. On the word 'yes' you want your sound to be suddenly much louder. You can half-shout this word.

8. In the second half of the chorus, starting on the word 'he's' there is another crescendo. Achieve this in the same manner as in the previous chorus.

Sheet Music

The correct sheet music for this song is available in *Martin Guerre Vocal Selections* (it has a red front cover) from www.amazon.co.uk.

'Out There'
from *The Hunchback of Notre Dame*

Music by Alan Menken, lyrics by Stephen Schwartz

Choose this song if: you like to sing in a contemporary, Disney sound, have a strong, high belt to an A, and are able to play the emotionally intelligent, downtrodden hero.

Given Circumstances

Note: The given circumstances below are those from the Disney film version.

WHO ARE YOU: Quasimodo, a twenty-year-old, sensitive, lonely hunchback who is the bell-ringer of Notre Dame Cathedral.

WHERE ARE YOU: In the bell tower of Notre Dame, Paris, France.

WHEN IS IT: About 11.00 a.m., a bright winter's morning. It is the Feast of Fools (New Year's Day), 1482.

WHAT HAS HAPPENED BEFORE: Twenty years ago, when you were a baby, your mother tried to sneak you into Paris with a group of fellow Gypsies. The group had arrived illegally and, when they disembarked at the docks near Notre Dame, they discovered they had fallen into a trap at the hands of the wicked Judge Claude Frollo. Frollo, who longed to purge the world of vice and sin, and who considered all Gypsies to be evil and corrupt, ordered that the boatload of immigrants be arrested and taken to the Palace of Justice.

Hearing this, your mother took you in her arms and ran. She managed to reach the Cathedral and pounded on the door, pleading for sanctuary. It was the dead of night, and before anyone could answer she was caught by Frollo, who took you from her arms, then kicked her down a flight of stone steps. The fall killed her.

Frollo had assumed your mother was carrying stolen goods, but when you began to cry he realised that there was a baby wrapped inside the blanket. When he pulled aside the cloth and saw your face, he was horrified by your deformity. Denouncing you as a monster, he was about to throw you down a nearby well when he was the interrupted by the Archdeacon of Notre Dame. The Archdeacon condemned Frollo for spilling the blood of your mother, and warned him of the consequences in the eyes of God should he do the same to you. Fearing for his immortal soul, Frollo asked how he might save himself. The Archdeacon ordered Frollo to raise you as his own. Frollo reluctantly agreed, as long as he could hide you away in the bell tower so you would never be seen. With the Archdeacon's consent you were taken into the Cathedral. Not knowing your real name, Frollo named you Quasimodo, which means 'half-formed'.

Today is the Feast of Fools – an annual, popular festival that mocks the great and the good of Paris. A few minutes ago a bird that had been nesting in one of the stone gargoyles for some time, and whom you had watched grow, became old enough to take flight for the first time and flew away. Although you were pleased that the bird was now free, you were also sad as it made you reflect on your confinement in the bell tower. Three of the gargoyles – called Victor, Hugo and Laverne – then magically came to life. They were excited to be watching the festival with you, as they do every year, so were surprised to find out that today you didn't want to do so. You explained that you were tired of observing the world, and that you wanted to be an active participant in it. Hearing this, the gargoyles tried to encourage you to defy Frollo and attend the festival in disguise. You had just convinced yourself to take this risk, and sneak outside, when Frollo appeared. Guessing that you were considering attending the festival, Frollo warned you that, as you are so deformed and ugly, the world would consider you a monster, and you must stay inside for your own protection. Having gained your reluctant agreement, Frollo has just left, and you are crestfallen.

WHO ELSE IS THERE: You are alone.

WHO SHOULD YOU SING TO: Yourself and a higher power: Fate. In the audition you can use the panel as if they are Fate.

Textual Analysis

At the beginning of the song you are deflated, as Frollo has just seemingly crushed your dream of going to the festival. In the first verse your objective is: to analyse whether your years of confinement have been good for you. During the last two lines of the verse – when you wonder what it would like to be amongst the people, rather than simply observing them – you make a decision: that you will defy Frollo and go to the festival. This decision is the event of the song.

Having determined what you want, in the chorus you begin to talk to Fate. In the first half of that chorus your objective is: to get Fate's permission to attend the festival. (In the film you also talk to the gargoyles during this section, but this is not an appropriate choice in audition.) In the second half of the chorus you want to convince Fate that you would do anything for this opportunity. It is useful to explore this verse with an obstacle to your objective, so you could imagine that Fate is reluctant to give you its permission, so you must work hard to gain it.

During the second verse you once more speak to yourself. Your objective here is: to protest that the people of Paris don't appreciate their freedom. You swear that you would relish it if you had similar opportunities to them. The momentum that is leading you on this adventure builds during the second chorus, when your objective becomes: to visualise exactly what your day outside will be like. You really need to see the images at this point: of a sunny morning, of the Seine. As the song motors towards its musical climax, and you ask for 'just one day', you address Fate for a final time. You promise Fate that if you are granted permission to attend the festival – just this once – then you will be forever content. By the end of the last note, Quasimodo has therefore changed: he now feels that he has permission to attend the Feast of Fools and is ready to set off on his adventure.

1. In the musical the song begins with a short solo for Frollo then a duet section. These should both be cut. The analysis above is for Quasimodo's solo section. When cutting the music, you should start four bars before the word 'safe' to give you a suitable introduction.

2. If you were playing Quasimodo in a full production you would undertake a heightened physical transformation. That approach is not advisable in audition, as you will be singing this song for another production, rather than being cast in this particular role.

3. During the first verse Quasimodo asks himself an important question. It is probably the first time in his life that he has made a significant decision. In this section the actions you might play include: I probe, cross-examine, interrogate, query, enkindle, ignite and rouse myself.

4. From the first chorus onwards, the music is incredibly uplifting. This needs to be reflected in the choices of action. When Quasimodo is talking to himself, try choices such as: I excite, elevate, animate, thrill, galvanise and uplift myself. Equally, when you are pleading with Fate you need to be dynamic and persuasive in your argument. Try such actions as: I reassure, persuade, goad, compel, hurry and press Fate.

5. In your performance, embrace Quasimodo's characteristics. He is optimistic, empathetic, sensitive, positive and hopeful – despite all of the difficulties he has encountered up to this point.

6. Remember this is a turning point in Quasimodo's life. He has experienced many years of longing and frustration about not being able to enter the outside world. As the song grows towards its conclusion, and he realises that he

is going to attend the festival, the excitement and exhilaration he feels must be immense. Let go and enjoy that.

Vocal and Musical Analysis

WHO TO LISTEN TO: Tom Hulce on the Disney film soundtrack (1996).

VOCAL RANGE: E♭3 to A4.

ORIGINAL KEY: C major. *Note*: This is the key for Quasimodo's section, the full song begins in C♯ major.

ACCENT: General American or Received Pronunciation. The song was written to be performed in General American, and the vowel positions are easier to sing in this accent. You should certainly make that choice if you have a native North American accent. Quasimodo is, of course, French, though if you are auditioning in the UK it is probably more appropriate to choose RP as an alternative to General American, rather than a French accent.

STYLE OF MUSICAL: Contemporary musical (pop-based).

VOCAL SET-UP/MUSICAL TIPS

1. The majority of the song should be delivered in the archetypical Disney set-up, which is oral Twang, and is clearly demonstrated by Hulce on the suggested recording. In this quality remember to keep the thyroid tilted and the larynx high.

2. Create a big crescendo as you build into the opening chorus. You can achieve this by adding some torso anchoring and tightening the AES further to get even more twang.

3. Perhaps one criticism of Hulce's performance might be that there is an overuse of vibrato in the middle of phrases. Try to hold back your vibrato until the ends of sentences,

as this helps create a sense of suspense for us as the listener, as we must wait for the end of phrase before we get the satisfaction of hearing your vibrato.

4. The song has two phrases that require you to Belt: when you say 'if I was in their skin' and the final line of the song.

5. Normally it is best to avoid breathing in the middle of sentences. However, on this occasion it is advisable to breathe before the final word. The music lends itself to this – and it is very helpful as the last note is a long one!

Sheet Music

The correct sheet music for this song is available at www.musicnotes.com.

'That's What He Said'
from *Parade*

Music and lyrics by Jason Robert Brown

Choose this song if: you enjoy songs that have strong, driving
rhythm, and like playing characters that are charismatic and
manipulative. The part was written for an actor of African-
American descent and requires you to belt a top G.

Given Circumstances

Note: Although *Parade* is based on the real-life trial of Leo
Frank, many of the facts in the case were much contested –
and so the given circumstances of the musical outlined below
contain events that are either fictional, or could be disputed.

WHO ARE YOU: Jim Conley, a twenty-seven-year-old African-
American ex-convict who is a janitor in a pencil factory in
Atlanta, Georgia, USA. You are cocky, arrogant, selfish – and
in this moment being a bit of a showman.

WHERE ARE YOU: In the witness dock of the Atlanta County
Courthouse.

WHEN IS IT: About 3.00 p.m., a hot August afternoon, 1913.

WHAT HAS HAPPENED BEFORE: Two months ago, Leo Frank, a
Brooklyn-born Jewish manager of the local pencil factory, was
falsely accused of the rape and murder of thirteen-year-old
Mary Phagan – an employee of the same company. Despite no
conclusive evidence against him, Leo found himself on trial at
the hands of local prosecutor Hugh Dorsey, who was under
pressure from Jack Slaton, the Governor of Georgia, to secure
a conviction.

In the lead-up to the trial, Leo found himself to be the victim
of prejudice, not only because of the widespread anti-
Semitism but also as he is from one of the northern states,

and as such is seen as a 'Yankee'. (In the American Civil War the North triumphed over the Southern Confederacy – of which Georgia was a part – only a generation earlier.)

When the trial began, some of the factory girls and Frankie Epps, a friend of Mary, testified that Leo behaved in a creepy manner that made the young girls feel uneasy. Minnie McKnight, Leo's housemaid, exacerbated this poor impression of the defendant by providing exaggerated testimony about the extent of the marital problems between him and his wife, Lucille – saying that she forced him to sleep on the floor. She also stated that Leo acted strangely on the night of the murder. These testimonies, whilst being detrimental to Leo, still only provided circumstantial evidence. For him to be convicted, there needed to be an eyewitness to the crime. Leo is innocent, and there is therefore no such witness – but Prosecutor Dorsey approached you prior to the trial. Several years ago you were a runaway from a chain gang (a form of imprisonment). As you had not served your full term, Dorsey threatened to re-imprison you as an escaped convict unless you testified against Leo Frank. You agreed to do so and, a few weeks ago, Dorsey coached you about what to say. Judge Roan has just called you to the stand.

WHO ELSE IS THERE: There is a packed courtroom, comprised almost entirely of white people. There is a strong undercurrent of racism towards you. Key people that are present in the court include: Leo and his wife Lucille, Prosecutor Dorsey, the jury, the general public – who would be sitting in the gallery – and Judge Roan (who would likely have been the judge who presided over your original conviction).

WHO SHOULD YOU SING TO: The song is delivered to the various people in the court. In the first two-thirds of the song the majority of your testimony is directed towards Judge Roan and the jury, but with some reference to Leo, who is sitting in the dock, when you mention 'Mr Frank'. At one point you also draw attention to Leo's wife, though you are not talking directly to her. In the final third of the song (where the chorus call for Leo to be hanged on the recording) you are now grandstanding for the entire courtroom.

Textual Analysis

Note: There are two small sections of dialogue in between the verses. The first of these should be cut, but you should deliver the second. No changes to the written score are necessary to accommodate this, as the first section will become a brief instrumental.

At the beginning of your testimony it is likely that you are incredibly nervous, as you are about to lie to the court. Your body language is probably closed and defensive; you may find it hard to look people directly in the eye. (This nervousness is exposed moments later when you call the victim 'Mary Perkins' by mistake.) In the first verse your objective is: to convince the court that Frank enjoyed the company of young girls. In doing so you want to outrage the assembly and depict Leo as a sexual predator. The shocked responses you hear in response to this testimony tell you that the public gallery is beginning to believe you. This relaxes you and gives you the confidence to go on.

During the second verse you continue your fictitious account by describing how Frank supposedly told you he had punched and killed Mary Phagan. At this point your objective is: to appal the courtroom with Frank's violent behaviour. You are careful to indicate that you yourself were horrified when you saw Mary's body, so as to avoid sharing in any of the blame or scorn.

In the first chorus you then describe Frank's reactions to Phagan's death. At this point you are warming to your theme, and are going beyond what Dorsey had coached you to say. Your objective here is: to portray Frank as being wild and out of control.

When you get to the third verse you recount the key 'fact' that Dorsey has told you to convey: that Frank bribed you to help

CONTEMPORARY UP-TEMPO

him take the body down into the basement. Your objective here is: to convince the court that Leo is not only guilty, but also callous. By saying that he paid you off with a hundred dollars you are portraying Frank as a man who thinks he can buy his way out of the rape and murder of thirteen-year-old girl. This inflames the community's prejudices towards rich Jewish Yankees. In the section that then slowly builds towards the key change, your objective is: to wind the court up into a frenzy by taunting them with Leo's fictitious comments. You are totally successful in this aim, which means that in the final chorus, having brought the courtroom to uproar, you can play your ultimate objective, which is: to incite the gallery to call for the death penalty.

KEY MOMENTS/TOP TIPS

1. The music is marked to be delivered 'in strict tempo'. This is an important instruction to follow. As the chords in the piano accompaniment are very sparse at the beginning of the song, it is easy to slip into a loose, *colla voce* interpretation by mistake – but if you follow the suggested instruction, and sing resolutely in time, then the song has a natural build as the piano accompaniment develops. This mirrors Conley's growth in confidence and will help carry your performance along.

2. Conley takes great pleasure in painting Frank as a sexual deviant. For generations, black men in the South had been wrongly accused of being a sexual threat to white women. In this section Conley is able to take a measure of revenge, by using the invented words and behaviour of Frank to shock the white courtroom with the kind of sexual innuendo that he would not ordinarily be permitted to use.

3. When Conley calls the gallery 'stupid rednecks', and the crowd call for Leo's execution, it is a moment of triumph for him. He has now gone much further than Dorsey's coaching. By pretending to be articulating the words and opinions of Leo, he is able to express his own secret anger

about the white populace of Atlanta who have been racist towards him. He takes great relish in manipulating them. This moral victory is the event of the song, which is why there is a key change at this point.

4. During the song Conley is consistently trying to aggravate the court; he wants them to turn viciously on Frank. Try using actions such as: I incite, enrage, inflame, rouse, madden and incense the court.

5. It is never made explicit in the musical who actually murdered Mary Phagan. It is interesting and credible to play with the idea that Conley himself is the real murderer.

Vocal and Musical Analysis

WHO TO LISTEN TO: Shaun Escoffery on the Donmar Warehouse revival cast recording (2007).

VOCAL RANGE: D3 to G4.

ORIGINAL KEY: E minor.

ACCENT: Southern American.

STYLE OF MUSICAL: Contemporary musical (pop-based).

VOCAL SET-UP/MUSICAL TIPS

1. The song is written to be sung almost entirely in a Speech quality. As the clarity of the narrative is central to the success of the performance, it is important to make the delivery as colloquial as possible. Practise mixing all three vocal onsets (aspirate, simultaneous and glottal) to give the singing a very conversational feel.

2. The score is influenced by rhythm and blues, so stylistic devices appropriate to that genre, such as singing with pitch-glides, can be used. An example of a pitch-glide can be heard on the recording recommended above when Sean Escoffery sings about 'a hundred dollars'.

3. In the choruses, when you repeat the word 'no' the pitch moves towards the top of the male speech register, so it is necessary to move into an Advanced-Speech quality. To achieve this, add some torso anchoring and some thyroid tilt to your usual set-up for Speech.

4. As the music builds to the musical climax of the key change, there should be a crescendo. Achieve this by gradually thickening your vocal folds and then adding some torso anchoring.

5. The last long high note (on the word 'no') should be belted.

Sheet Music

The correct sheet music for this song is available at www.musicnotes.com.

'And They're Off'
from *A New Brain*

Music and lyrics by William Finn

Choose this song if: you have a contemporary pop voice, and
are suited to quirky, unconventional characters and material.
You need to have an excellent belt to a G.

Given Circumstances

Note: *A New Brain* is, in many ways, an autobiographical
piece of work, in that Finn – like the central character
Gordon – suffered from a serious condition of the brain called
an arteriovenous malformation (AVM). Some elements of the
given circumstances suggested below, which are left
unanswered by the script, are therefore derived from Finn's
own life experiences.

WHO ARE YOU: Gordon Schwinn, a frustrated, lovable,
unconventional, sarcastic and rebellious songwriter. You are
Jewish and gay. Currently you are suffering from an AVM,
which is causing you symptoms such as: headaches,
hallucinations, dizziness and partial paralysis.

WHERE ARE YOU: In reality you are in a hospital bed in New
York, but in your imagination you are at a horse-racing track.

WHEN IS IT: 9.10 p.m., September, 1992.

WHAT HAS HAPPENED BEFORE: A few days ago you had been
struggling to meet a deadline for a song about frogs called
'The Spring Song'. You were composing this number for your
employer, a children's television host called Mr Bungee, who
dresses as a frog on his show. Frustrated at your lack of
progress, you went out to meet your friend Rhoda for lunch.
Over the meal you expressed your disquiet to Rhoda that all
of your time was taken up writing songs for the television
show, rather than composing material that you were

passionate about. Whilst sat at the table you began to worry that you were hallucinating. After having a sudden and severe headache you collapsed and passed out with your head in your food. You were immediately rushed to hospital. On arrival, the doctors were at first unable to diagnose the cause of your condition.

In your hospital bed you began to descend into a state of delirium. Thinking that you might die, you began to panic about all the songs that you hadn't yet had chance to write, songs that would now never be composed or heard. Over the next few days you were subject to a series of hallucinations featuring people from your real life. At times it was hard for you to distinguish between events that were actually occurring in your hospital room and others that were only happening in your head. These hallucinations included a simultaneous visit from your mother, who assured you that everything would be alright, and Mr Bungee in his frog suit. In another, your boyfriend Roger, rather than being at your bedside in this moment of crisis, appeared to be off sailing on his boat.

When two nurses arrived to check in on you, they asked both yourself and your mother for a family medical history. Your mother responded by saying that any genetic medical issues that you may have were the fault of your estranged father. Perhaps as a result of this conversation, you have just begun to reflect upon and hallucinate about your childhood relationship with your father.

WHO ELSE IS THERE: In the musical, all of the people in your life – your friends, family and the medical professionals – are onstage. They form a backing chorus for the song. However, in an audition you should act as though you are alone.

WHO SHOULD YOU SING TO: The audience (panel).

Textual Analysis

You start the song by remembering a racetrack you visited as a child, and begin to see this memory in your imagination. Your first objective is: to get the audience to picture the scene at the racetrack. Try to conjure up the atmosphere of the event so you can tell them the story of the day your father lost the family fortune betting on horses. As the chorus begins, you behave as if one of the horse races is happening again, right in front of you. Your objective in this moment is: to get the audience to share in the exhilaration and excitement of the race.

As your father lost his bet on this particular race, during the second verse your objective becomes: to get the audience to empathise with how this felt – you want them to comprehend your family's reaction after your father lost so much money. To portray this successfully, you need to be clear about your own attitude towards both the outcome of the race and to both of your parents. The textual evidence suggests that you pitied your mother. Your reactions to your father could be played many different ways, but you appear to be incredulous that he could have been so foolish.

When you sing the chorus for the second time, the melody is identical, but this time, rather than getting the audience to imagine the race (which was exciting), you want the audience to picture your parents fighting on the floor (which must have been upsetting to see). The use of the same jaunty melody suggests your approach to the storytelling is sarcastic and ironic. Your objective here is: to mock the behaviour of your parents.

In the bridge, when you talk about how funny life is, your objective is: to get the audience to understand how ironic it is that betting – which can be so much fun in the moment – can cause so much misery. You want them to appreciate the realities of a gambling addiction.

During the final verse you offer up both positive and negative thoughts about your family relationships as a child. Your objective in this section is: to get the audience to take a balanced view of your family's history. This reveals that over the years you have perhaps developed a sense of perspective about your father's addiction. In the final chorus you reveal to the audience that your father walked out on you and your mother after this day at the races. Your final objective is: to get the audience to think he was a bad father.

KEY MOMENTS/TOP TIPS

1. There are backing vocals in the recording. For audition purposes, just ignore these and sing Gordon's line throughout.

2. At the end of the first chorus the race is lost. This is not mentioned in the lyric, so you need to make it clear in your physicality so the panel can comprehend the narrative.

3. The song is generally very light and ironic, despite discussing the break-up of a family. You need to investigate the subtext of the song very thoroughly: what effect did it have on Gordon when his father walked out on him? Look to find a deeper emotional connection underneath the jaunty music.

4. The high belt near the end (see below) is not motivated by a change in the lyric. You therefore need to find an acting reason for why you sing in this extended vocal set-up. Try exploring the idea that this is the moment where Gordon connects to his true feelings about his father abandoning him.

Vocal and Musical Analysis

WHO TO LISTEN TO: Malcolm Gets on the original Off-Broadway cast recording (1998).

VOCAL RANGE: C3 to G4.

ORIGINAL KEY: C major.

ACCENT: General American.

STYLE OF MUSICAL: Contemporary musical (pop-based).

1. The song should be delivered with a contemporary pop musical-theatre sound. To achieve this, work mainly in a Speech quality but with some twang and thyroid tilt added to effect this set-up.

2. During the song you recount conversations that your father had with you. When you sing 'he said' and 'she said', these words can almost be spoken. If you then contrast this by making the quoted text more sung and legato, it would help make the conversation clear. Gets demonstrates this admirably on the suggested recording.

3. It is a surprise to Gordon when he remembers that – as well as fighting – his family also laughed a lot. This moment feels very authentic and autobiographical. Try to highlight this moment of vulnerability by delivering the line in a different vocal set-up, such as Cry quality.

4. Finn's music often features the use of 'bent' jazz notes. This involves singing what is known a quartertone (a note that sits somewhere in between two notes on the piano). You can hear this on the suggested recording on the words 'daddy', band', 'play' and 'terrible'. Try bending the pitch of these notes slightly to highlight the jazz influence of the score.

5. At the end of the song, when you sing the high note on the word 'around', this should be in a belt position.

Sheet Music

The correct sheet music for this song is available at www.musicnotes.com.

COMEDY/CHARACTER

'The Streets of Dublin'
from *A Man of No Importance*

Music by Stephen Flaherty, lyrics by Lynn Ahrens

Choose this song if: you are an actor who likes portraying characters that are cheeky, charming and charismatic. The song suits a folk/pop voice and requires you to belt to an A. The song was originally written for an Irishman.

Given Circumstances

WHO ARE YOU: Robbie Fay, a handsome, magnetic, Irish bus driver in his late twenties. You are very masculine and self-confident, which helps mask the fact that you are a closeted homosexual.

WHERE ARE YOU: The garage of a bus depot, Dublin, Ireland.

WHEN IS IT: 6.10 p.m., a Friday evening, spring, 1964.

WHAT HAS HAPPENED BEFORE: Your colleague, Alfie Byrne – a bus conductor in his mid-forties – is the director of the St Imelda Players, an amateur-theatre group connected to a local church. Recently Alfie, who is also secretly gay, wanted to mount a production of Oscar Wilde's *The Tragedy of Salome*. The priest, Father Kenny, refused on the grounds that the play was immoral – calling it a 'dirty play'.

After the opening scene of the musical, the piece takes a theatrical twist in that the players decide to tell the story of Alfie himself, rather than a play by Wilde or Shakespeare. This shift occurs in a non-naturalistic manner, with the St Imelda Players becoming a Greek chorus that narrate the events of Alfie's life.

Yesterday, in this newly created theatrical world, the players drew together the chairs of the church hall to form the bus on which you and Alfie work. The 'play' thus began, and was entitled: *The Tragedy of Alfie Byrne, a Dublin Coachman, or A Man of No Importance.* In the first scene of this new story, Alfie recited passages by his beloved Oscar Wilde to the passengers on the bus. During the journey a new, previously unseen passenger – an attractive teenager called Adele Rice – boarded the bus. Alfie assumed you must fancy her.

At the end of the working day, after all of the passengers had disembarked, you told Alfie how much you enjoyed working with him as you drove the empty bus back to the garage. He reciprocated by telling you how much he liked you. That evening, back at the apartment he shares with his sister Lily, Alfie told her that he had met someone he liked. Assuming it was a girl, Lily was delighted, as she had been delaying her own marriage to a man named Mr Carney in order to take care of her brother.

When the St Imelda Players then re-formed their theatrical bus made of chairs, they asked Alfie what the next play would be. Alfie decided he wanted to try and mount *Salome* again. This time he hoodwinked Father Kenny, getting his agreement by telling him it was a play about John the Baptist. When he convinced Adele to play the title role, she asked him whether he would be cast as her leading man. Alfie replied that he wasn't right for the part, but that he would ask you instead.

Today after work you were both back at the bus garage. Stripped to the waist, you were changing a broken tyre when Alfie tried to convince you to join the cast of *Salome*. You refused, saying that you were not an actor. Alfie sought to change your mind by telling you that all your scenes would be with the pretty Adele. He asked if you were interested in her romantically. When you said no, he asked you whom you were attracted to. You replied: 'That's for me to know and for you to find out.' In this moment, the secret of both your sexualities was hinted at. Following this conversation you decided that you wanted to get to know the shy Alfie better. Rather than letting him go home to his sister's house, as he usually would, you have just resolved to convince him to come out drinking with you.

WHO ELSE IS THERE: Alfie.

WHO SHOULD YOU SING TO: Alfie.

Textual Analysis

The crux of this song is that Alfie has not really lived his life, whereas you lead a more vibrant and colourful existence, despite your suppressed sexuality. The main objective for the song, which you play during the opening verse, is: to get Alfie to appreciate what a wonderful city Dublin is. You try to excite and inspire him with stories of the city and the personalities of the people who live there. The way you pursue this objective should be playful and entertaining. Try the following actions on Alfie: I amuse, entertain, regale, delight, inspire, animate and embolden you. In the first chorus your objective alters slightly and becomes: to convince Alfie to come and experience Dublin. You argue that, because you are not a man of poetry, like he is, your words cannot do the city justice. He must come and see for himself.

In the second verse you return to your main objective of trying to excite Alfie about Dublin. In this section you try to appeal to his senses – you want him to see, hear and taste the atmosphere of the city. During the second chorus you play the same objective as you did in the first: to encourage Alfie to come and see Dublin for himself.

Gradually Alfie begins to give in to your infectious charm, and from the start of the bridge to the end of the song your objective becomes more specific. Rather than talking about the entire city, you focus on convincing Alfie that a night in a Dublin pub is a wonderful thing, as this is where you will lead him.

KEY MOMENTS/TOP TIPS

1. On the recording there is an introductory section of four lines of singing before the main song. I would suggest you cut these, and begin with the first verse that starts when

you talk about Tommy Flanagan, as indicated on the suggested sheet music.

2. Although the song is directed towards Alfie, in audition the song works well when you address the panel. Perform the song as though you are trying to get the entire room to come out drinking in Dublin.

3. Throughout the show Robbie frequently says that he is not a poetic man like Alfie. This is ironic, because his descriptions of Dublin are articulate and evocative. This gives an insight that, underneath his charm and bravado, Robbie lacks self-esteem.

4. After talking about 'surviving the day', there are a couple of bars of quieter, more melancholic music. This moment allows us to have an insight into Robbie's hidden feelings. Underneath his fun-loving, optimistic exterior he is carrying a secret that in 1960s Ireland he would likely have been deeply ashamed of: his sexuality. In this brief piece of music there is the opportunity for you to let the panel understand his vulnerability. This is the event of the song.

Vocal and Musical Analysis

WHO TO LISTEN TO: Steven Pasquale on the original Off-Broadway cast recording (2003).

VOCAL RANGE: E3 to A4.

ORIGINAL KEY: E major.

ACCENT: Southern Irish (Dublin).

STYLE OF MUSICAL: Contemporary musical (pop-based).

COMEDY/CHARACTER

VOCAL SET-UP/MUSICAL TIPS

1. The song should be achieved predominately in a Speech quality, and this set-up needs a huge amount of variety and play. Try mixing up your use of onsets – don't be afraid to speak or shout occasional words and play with dynamics.

214

2. When you get to the choruses, although the set-up remains in Speech, make the phrases longer and more legato. Link the vowels together and make more use of simultaneous onsets.

3. On the line identified above about 'surviving the day', you should decrescendo by gradually tilting the thyroid and raising the larynx so you end up in Cry quality. This will help give the section the required sense of sensitivity. Stay in this quality after the brief instrumental until the word 'wives', when you should suddenly crescendo by reversing the described process.

4. The last time you sing the word 'Dublin' should be in a belt position.

Sheet Music

The correct sheet music for this song is available at www.musicnotes.com.

'To Excess'
from *Out of Our Heads*

Music by Michael Kooman, lyrics by Christopher Dimond

Choose this song if: you suit quirky, offbeat, comedic roles, and have an excellent contemporary pop voice. The song gives you the opportunity to show off a Falsetto quality.

Disclaimer: Although this song is written to be comedic, the given circumstances – which relate to a stalker – may be distressing for some, and so where and when to perform this material is something you should consider with care.

Given Circumstances

Note: This piece is from a song-cycle album, rather than a musical, so all of the information available relating to the character and situation are contained within the lyric. The given circumstances outlined below are therefore to a large degree invented and can be adjusted to suit your own interpretation.

WHO ARE YOU: Randy, a sweaty, unattractive, mentally disturbed stalker in his late twenties with obsessive and psychotic tendencies.

WHERE ARE YOU: In the bedroom of Claire, a girl you have been stalking, in her house in a suburb of Newark, New Jersey, USA.

WHEN IS IT: 5.30 p.m., a Friday, summer, present day.

WHAT HAS HAPPENED BEFORE: A few months ago you met a girl called Claire, a pretty but feisty student in her early twenties. You saw her for the first time in a Stop and Go grocery store on the local high street. When you caught her eye, she smiled at you in a polite but awkward manner, as she sensed you were attracted to her, a feeling she didn't reciprocate. To try to gain her attention you deliberately bumped into her leg with your shopping trolley. She responded by shouting 'What the hell?' at you, which you inexplicably took to be a moment of romance. When Claire left the store you secretly followed her home and then memorised her address.

Since that first meeting you have been constantly stalking Claire, which has been frightening her immensely. A few weeks ago she spotted you on the street outside her apartment. She pulled down the living-room blind so you couldn't see her. Unbeknown to Claire, you responded to this by climbing a tree on the opposite side of her street. From the vantage point of the treetop you took pictures of her getting changed in her bedroom and watched her sleeping.

With your obsession growing, a couple of days later you stole a mannequin from a clothing shop in the local shopping mall. You then took it home and dressed it up to look like Claire. Over the next couple of weeks you took your Claire mannequin out with you around town and behaved as if it was her. One day you were in the park and you became convinced the doll was looking at other men, so you punched it in the face. To make amends for this 'fight', you took the mannequin to a public bathroom and masturbated over it.

Events with the real Claire came to a crisis point last Saturday when you followed her to Chili's, where she was on a first date with a muscular guy named Dan. At the end of the evening, after the pair parted at the door, you followed Dan down a side street in your car and ran him over. You found this episode particularly unsettling to your mental equilibrium, so when you arrived home you carved Claire's name into your thigh with a penknife and wrote a haiku (a Japanese poem) using the blood you spilt.

This morning Claire visited her grandmother's house. You followed her there, waited around the corner in your car, and then, after she'd left, you kidnapped her grandmother. Taking the old lady back to your house you tied her up in a secret underground bunker you had built some years earlier. After you had completed the kidnapping you made the short journey to Claire's apartment. About twenty minutes ago you climbed the fire escape and broke in. Completely unaware of this, Claire returned home a few moments ago. When she walked into the bedroom she found you lying on her bed sniffing some of her underwear. Frightened by your intrusion, she has just picked up a baseball bat and begun to threaten you – telling you to leave immediately.

WHO ELSE IS THERE: Claire.

WHO SHOULD YOU SING TO: Claire.

Textual Analysis

The action of the song begins before you first speak when Claire walks into the bedroom. In actuality you would have her underwear pressed to your face at this moment, so it is sensible to play the opening lyrics as though you have been caught doing something you shouldn't, and are trying to cover it up. (It's not necessary to bring a pair of ladies' underwear to the audition, though you could make this choice if you were feeling brave!) After a few lines Claire picks up a baseball bat to defend herself. Your objective then becomes: to get Claire to put down the bat down. You want her to listen, and to understand why you broke in to her house.

Your objective changes when you get to the first verse. At this point you want Claire to understand how much your first meeting in the supermarket meant to you. In the last line of this verse, when you liken your behaviour to a crime, you confess that your love is excessive. Your objective in this moment is: to take responsibility for your extreme behaviour. You play this same objective repeatedly throughout the song, on the repeated lyric that occurs at the end of each verse.

In the second verse, beginning with you telling Claire that you are not in very good shape, you list a series of behaviours you have engaged in whilst stalking her. Because of your warped perspective – even though what you're telling Claire is appalling – you see it as an affirmation of how much you care for her. Your objective when making this list is: to get Claire's approval for the attention you lavish on her.

As the song moves into the bridge you notice Claire glancing towards the window, as she is trying to figure out how to escape from the bedroom. This should add a sense of time pressure to the scene at this point – you feel you need to urgently make your point of view whilst you still have Claire's attention. Your objective at this moment is: to convince Claire that you are not a psychopath. It will help you to remember the obstacle to this objective: it is difficult for you to convince Claire because the memory of you attacking her date is still very fresh in her mind.

There are further new objectives in the remaining two verses. In the third verse your objective is: to convince Claire that you are a romantic guy. This is despite the fact that your attempts to prove this – such as writing a poem in your own blood – are very strange, to say the least. During the fourth verse, which occurs after the key change, your final objective is: to get Claire to agree to marry you. You want to envisage the wonderful life you could share together.

KEY MOMENTS/TOP TIPS

1. The song is obviously very silly and funny, and the lyrics are so exaggerated that the scenario quickly becomes ridiculous. However, when performing it, try to deliver the material as 'straight' as possible, i.e. don't strive to be comedic. If you play the song as if Randy is trying to be honest and sincere – and is completely unaware of how strange his behaviour is – then the song becomes much funnier to watch.

2. A key to acting the song successfully is to be clear what your imaginary Claire is doing at each moment in the song. You need to imagine her picking up the bat, looking nervously for a possible exit, beginning to cry, edging towards the door, etc.

3. This is the first time Randy would have had the chance to have a protracted conversation with Claire. Use this aspect of the given circumstances to inform your performance. The song should feel like a stream of consciousness. Having stalked Claire for months, finally you have the chance to unload the thoughts and feelings that you have bottled up inside. To portray this, try performing the song with a quick inner tempo.

4. The use of extreme physical stillness when approaching a characterisation can help create an unsettling quality in performance. Explore using a sense of strange, creepy stillness at times in your portrayal of Randy.

Vocal and Musical Analysis

WHO TO LISTEN TO: Christopher Sieber on the *Out of Our Heads* studio album (2011).

VOCAL RANGE: B2 to G♯4.

ORIGINAL KEY: B♭ major.

ACCENT: General American.

STYLE OF MUSICAL: Contemporary musical (pop-based).

COMEDY/CHARACTER

VOCAL SET-UP/MUSICAL TIPS

1. The opening section is written to be spoken. (In musical notation all notes with an 'x' as the note-head should be spoken rather than pitched.) A rhythm for these lines is indicated in the score, but the music is also marked 'freely' so you should speak the words in a way that feels natural, as there is room for a degree of rhythmical interpretation.

2. When you sing the line about Claire's panties being pressed to your face, try singing as quietly and sweetly as possible. This romantic vocal choice helps bring out the irony and humour of this particular lyric.

3. When you sing about your mother near the end of the lyric, this is the event of the song and should be the loudest vocal moment. To achieve this, start a crescendo on the word 'champagne' by gradually taking the thyroid tilt out of your voice from this point until you end up in a Speech quality. As the melody becomes higher on the words 'you and me', add some torso anchoring to find additional resonance. Then when you descend the phrase and confess to your final crime, reintroduce the thyroid tilt once more to return to a sweet, quiet, romantic Cry quality.

4. When you sing about being sentenced for life it can be funny to flip into a comedic Falsetto quality (think John Travolta singing the end of 'Summer Nights' in the film of *Grease*).

Sheet Music

The correct sheet music for this song is available at www.scribd.com.

'Try Me'
from *She Loves Me*

Music by Jerry Bock, lyrics by Sheldon Harnick

Choose this song if: you would suit playing a bookish, enthusiastic, lovable young lad. The song sits in a very comfortable range for baritones, so suits both actors who sing as well as performers who enjoy singing in a legit sound.

Given Circumstances

WHO ARE YOU: Arpad Laszlo, a clumsy, overkeen, put-upon, sixteen-year-old delivery boy.

WHERE ARE YOU: Mr Maraczek's private hospital room, Budapest, Hungary.

WHEN IS IT: Breakfast time, 8.30 a.m., mid-December, some time in the early 1930s.

WHAT HAS HAPPENED BEFORE: For a frustrating period of nearly a year you have been employed as a delivery boy in Mr Maraczek's parfumerie (a shop that sells perfume). Although well liked, you tend to be the focus of your colleagues' mirth. Ilona Ritter, an attractive colleague, often teases you about marrying her, even though she is having an affair with the handsome Steven Kodaly. Several months ago you were busy stacking the shelves with a new product – a leather musical cigarette case – when Maraczek insisted that one would be purchased within the hour. When a young woman named Amalia Balash came into the shop to ask for a job, the assistant manager Georg Nowack told her that they were not hiring. When Amalia managed to sell one of the cigarette cases to a customer, she impressed Maraczek enough to be offered a job.

Over the next few months, tensions began to develop between the staff at the parfumerie. Ilona and Steven were constantly arguing, as were Georg and Amalia, who were unwittingly anonymous romantic penpals – they didn't realise the other's secret identity. When you noticed their squabbling, your colleague Ladislav Sipos explained that this was because they secretly liked each other. As someone who was inexperienced in the ways of love, this was something you failed to understand.

Yesterday at the shop Maraczek threatened to fire Georg, after complaining that he was not dedicated enough to his job. Incensed, Georg resigned. In reality this was because Maraczek suspected Georg was having an affair with his wife. Maraczek learned shortly afterwards from a private investigator that it was actually Steven Kodaly with whom she was having the affair. Once the investigator had left, Maraczek received a phone call from his wife. During the phone call she lied, saying she would be late home because she was out with a female friend – when actually she was meeting Kodaly. Hearing this, Maraczek made his way to his office to collect his revolver. Just at this moment you came out of the stockroom. As Maraczek raised the gun to his forehead you called out, which distracted Maraczek enough for him to botch his suicide attempt.

First thing this morning you came to visit Maraczek in the hospital. With him feeling down on his luck, and having a need to replace Georg, you felt it would help you both if you convinced him to make you a salesman.

WHO ELSE IS THERE: Mr Maraczek, your difficult, prickly, sixty-year-old boss.

WHO SHOULD YOU SING TO: Mr Maraczek.

Textual Analysis

Note: Only the first section of this song is appropriate for audition. You should therefore end the song just before Mr Maraczek interjects with his first line of dialogue, which is at the end of bar 46 in the score. This makes for a short, snappy audition piece. The recommendations outlined below explore this suggested cut.

Immediately prior to the song, Maraczek rejects your suggestion that he promote you to the position of sales clerk. You should start with an impulse to respond to this rejection; you need to urgently change his mind. In the short pre-chorus your objective is: to convince Maraczek that you thoroughly understand the requirements of the job. You seek to reassure him that you would know exactly what is required if he made you a clerk in the parfumerie.

Once the main melody begins your objective is encapsulated in the title of the song. Very directly, you implore Maraczek to give you an opportunity, to give you a try. To persuade him, explore actions such as: I beseech, urge, enthuse and electrify. In your argument you should be an excited bundle of persuasive energy.

As you move into the bridge you have two different, clear objectives. The first is: to convince Maraczek that he needs you. You want him to believe that he wouldn't be able to get by without promoting you. The second is: to persuade him to give you the job, rather than someone new. You attempt to do this by amusing him with a joke at your own expense.

During the second verse, having been so far unsuccessful, you change tactic and now aim to reassure Mr Maraczek. You want to assure him that if he were to give you the job, he wouldn't regret his decision. By the end of the song your argument should be inspiring, infectious and uplifting. This is thus the event of the song, as you feel that you have emphatically made your case.

KEY MOMENTS/TOP TIPS

1. The fast, rhythmic accompaniment of the song reflects Arpad's sparky personality and rapid internal rhythm. This should be reflected in an energised, punchy physicality and dynamic use of gesture.

2. It is very important to imagine Maraczek's responses when you are acting. The lyric indicates at one point that he is

COMEDY/CHARACTER

frowning as he is doubtful about what you're suggesting. During your performance, picture him ignoring you, or smirking at you, or attempting to dismiss you. By imagining these moments of rejection, it will give you the impulses you need to try harder to persuade him.

3. There is a clear musical build towards the end of the song. This reflects Arpad's growth in confidence. By the end of the number he feels that he has made a good case, and that he will get the job. This transformation, from nervous and desperate at the beginning of the song, to confident and self-assured by the conclusion, gives the audition piece an engaging journey.

Vocal and Musical Analysis

WHO TO LISTEN TO: Brad Kane on the Broadway revival cast recording (1993).

VOCAL RANGE: B2 to D4.

ORIGINAL KEY: C major.

ACCENT: As an American show, this song is most usually performed in General American. However, if you have a native Eastern European accent, it would be highly appropriate to use your own voice.

STYLE OF MUSICAL: Book musical.

VOCAL SET-UP/MUSICAL TIPS

1. The song should sound very conversational, so begin your performance in a Speech quality. To maintain this conversational quality, keep your thyroid cartilage in a horizontal position even on the higher pitches that occur in the first few phrases. Don't let the sound become too pretty or beautiful.

2. When the main melody begins, the accompaniment slips into a rhythmic, driving pulse. Vocally, you need to match

this with an added sense of urgency and intensity. Try using some aspirate onsets to achieve a breathy, excitable sound at this point.

3. In the next section – where you tell Maraczek that he needs help – you should make your phrasing more legato. Use simultaneous onsets and work for long phrases.

4. The last two held notes should be sonorous and rich. These notes are too low to belt, so to achieve this fullness of sound, anchor your back, sing with thick vocal folds and lower the larynx a little to achieve a rich legit sound.

Sheet Music

The correct sheet music for this song is available at www.musicnotes.com.

COMEDY/CHARACTER

'When I Find My Baby' from *Sister Act*

Music by Alan Menken, lyrics by Glenn Slater

Choose this song if: you are a confident, comedic actor with a soulful, baritone Motown voice who can belt to a top A. The part was originally written for a African–American actor.

Given Circumstances

Note: The following given circumstances are for the 2011 Broadway version of the show. In the earlier London version of the show this character had a different surname.

WHO ARE YOU: Curtis Jackson, a smarmy, manipulative, small-time gangster and club owner.

WHERE ARE YOU: In an interrogation room in a police station, Philadelphia, USA.

WHEN IS IT: 11.00 a.m., early January 1978.

WHAT HAS HAPPENED BEFORE: On Christmas Eve last year your girlfriend Deloris Van Cartier auditioned for the chance to sing in your club. You refused, saying she wasn't ready for stardom. Deloris, feeling trapped by the relationship and held back in her career, decided to leave you.

A short while later in the alley outside, Deloris saw you shoot dead one of your gang, Ernie Williams, as she was trying to leave the club. You'd decided to kill Ernie after you'd discovered he had snitched on you to the police. Having witnessed the murder, Deloris ran away. Afraid that she might go to the police, you sent some of your gang members after her, but she escaped.

At the local police station Deloris relayed what had happened to an officer she knew from school, named Eddie. Eddie told her that as a key witness to the crime she needed to be protected. To ensure her safety he decided to enroll her in the witness protection programme and hide her away for a month in a convent called The Holy Order of the Little Sisters of Our Mother of Perpetual Faith.

Whilst Deloris was settling in at the convent, Eddie arrested you. A few minutes ago, in the interrogation room, in front of your lawyer Tony and three of your thugs, Joe, Pablo and TJ, Eddie informed you that the police had found Ernie Williams' body in the dumpster behind your club. When you dismissed this as circumstantial evidence, Eddie revealed that the police also had a witness to the crime. He then stormed out of the room followed by Tony.

After they had gone you discovered Deloris's fur coat, which she had left behind in the interrogation room. As soon as they realised that Deloris was the witness, Joe, Pablo and TJ began to panic – wondering how they would ever find her. Responding to their jitters, you have just decided to settle their nerves.

WHO ELSE IS THERE: Joe, Pablo and TJ.

WHO SHOULD YOU SING TO: Joe, Pablo, TJ and yourself.

Textual Analysis

Responding to the nervousness of your gang, in the first verse your objective is: to reassure them that you know Deloris inside out. You want to instil confidence that you will find her again. On the last line of that verse is the event of the song. At this point you swear that you will get her back – no matter what. Once that decision is made, your vivid imagination is released. During the first chorus your objective becomes: to imagine what you will do to Deloris when you find her. This involves you indulging yourself in the fantasy of killing her.

During the second verse your attention turns to how Deloris must be feeling at this moment. Your objective here is: to convince the gang that Deloris is feeling trapped and under pressure in her hiding place. You find this idea reassuring, because if she is feeling afraid, then she is less likely to come forward and provide testimony against you. You go on to reassure yourself during the second chorus, when you sing a countermelody, that everything will be all right because Deloris cannot hide her true feelings from you. Warming to your theme, your next objective is: to imagine the bloody revenge you will take upon her. In the last few lines you turn your attention squarely on the gang once more. Your objective in this final section is: to get them to go and find Deloris.

KEY MOMENTS/TOP TIPS

1. There are backing vocals in the recording. For audition purposes you should ignore these and sing Curtis's line throughout, which means switching to the countermelody instead of the melody at the second chorus.

2. During the song there are some instrumental breaks for dialogue. These should be cut.

3. The song is a pastiche of some the Motown hits of singers like Lionel Richie and Marvin Gaye. The comedy comes from performing the song very straight – like an entertaining upbeat disco number – which then contrasts humorously with Curtis stating in the lyrics that he wants to murder and disembowel Deloris.

4. The vocal line contains many exclamations on words like 'yeah' and 'who'. Think of these moments as a gift – they are a chance to indulge in moments of pure emotional connection. They are joyful, celebratory releases for Curtis.

5. With Curtis's delivery it is fun to explore the idea that his murderous intentions have an almost sexual quality to them. You can play with this idea in a very silly and ironic manner.

Vocal and Musical Analysis

WHO TO LISTEN TO: Chris Jarman on the original London cast recording (2009).

VOCAL RANGE: C3 to A4.

ORIGINAL KEY: F major.

ACCENT: General American.

STYLE OF MUSICAL: Contemporary musical (pop-based).

VOCAL SET-UP/MUSICAL TIPS

1. To achieve that distinctive Motown sound, you need to lower your larynx, use smooth onsets and maintain a modicum of twang. You can also afford to use pitch-slides between notes.

2. You can try add some 'growl' to your voice during the first verse, as Jarman demonstrates on the suggested recording. This is achieved by adding some false vocal-fold constriction.

3. It is valid to half-speak some words for comedic effect. Jarman does this clearly on words such as 'kill' and 'wham bam' on the suggested recording.

4. As the song progresses into the key changes and the pitch rises, add slightly more twang to the sound to achieve a fuller resonance.

5. The song lends itself to some vocal improvisations and riffing after the first key change. If this is something you are not used to, then you are advised to explore them in a singing lesson and fix your choices in advance. Don't try to improvise the riffs in the audition room.

6. The last two words – 'oh no' – should be belted.

Sheet Music

The correct sheet music for this song is available at www.musicnotes.com.

COMEDY/CHARACTER

Baritone/Bass

'Lonely Room'
from *Oklahoma!*

Music by Richard Rodgers, lyrics by Oscar Hammerstein II

Choose this song if: you have a rich bass-baritone voice and suit roles that are menacing, sinister and violent. The song has a limited range and does not require you to access the upper register, so can suit actors who sing.

Given Circumstances

WHO ARE YOU: Jud Fry, a hired farmhand. You are an intimidating, short-tempered man with a strong physical presence. A little slow-witted, you display a propensity for violence.

WHERE ARE YOU: In the smokehouse that serves as your living quarters. The smokehouse sits on an outlying part of a farm in Oklahoma territory (it had yet to become a state) in the USA. Your dwelling is cramped and dilapidated, with low ceilings, squeaky floorboards and mice running around. On the walls are pinned some pornographic images of women.

WHEN IS IT: 4.30 p.m., summer, 1906.

WHAT HAS HAPPENED BEFORE: For some months you have been obsessed with Laurey Williams, the attractive niece of Aunt Eller, who owns the farm on which you are an employee. Despite your attempts to win her affections, she has shown no interest in your advances.

Today has been a day of much activity because everyone in the locality has been preparing for the Box Social – a dance that is to happen this evening. The high point of the event will be an auction of the lunch baskets prepared by the local girls, with the highest bidder for each basket getting to share the meal with the girl who prepared it. It is your plan to win Laurey's basket and use the opportunity of time alone with her to gain her heart. Earlier that morning, unbeknownst to you, Laurey had been asked to the dance by Curly McLain – a handsome cowboy to whom she is secretly attracted. With both of them too proud to reveal their true feelings, they had teased each other. When Laurey mocked Curly's efforts to court her he stormed off. Shortly after this you asked Laurey to the dance yourself and, out of spite towards Curly, she accepted. About fifteen minutes ago, when Curly discovered that Laurey is to go to the Box Social with you, he tried to persuade her to change her mind. Even though Laurey is sometimes afraid of you, she felt she could not go back on her word. This put Curly in a temper and, about thirty minutes ago, he stormed over to the smokehouse to see you. He took the opportunity to mock you by suggesting that you should hang yourself – to make everyone realise how much they would miss you. This led to an angry altercation between the two of you. He left moments ago, leaving you alone, feeling vengeful and angry.

WHO ELSE IS THERE: You are alone.

WHO SHOULD YOU SING TO: Yourself.

Textual Analysis

The song begins with you looking round the smokehouse, stewing on the fact you are stuck in this inhospitable environment. You complain about your miserable living space, vent your frustration and criticise yourself for having ended up living in such a place. Your objective in this first verse is: to bemoan your lonely existence. When the music changes, and the first chorus begins, you start to remember how differently you feel when the moonlight appears through the window and you dream of Laurey. Your objective in this chorus is: to excite yourself about the possibility of an alternative future for yourself, a future in which you are married to Laurey. This dream becomes so vivid that by the end of the chorus you abandon yourself completely to the fantasy of Laurey's hair falling across your chest.

234

After pulling yourself out of this daydream you return to describing your unhappy surroundings – but this time your attitude has shifted. Rather than simply complaining, your objective in the second verse is: to convince yourself that your current life can no longer to be tolerated. When the music changes once more into the dramatic final section, your resolve strengthens. Your objective from this point until the end of the song is: to resolve to make Laurey your own, no matter the cost.

KEY MOMENTS/TOP TIPS

1. You might want to consider sitting down to begin this song, as it will help convey the sense of brooding reflection that is needed. A good time to stand might be as you begin to daydream of the moonlight and how it makes you feel about Laurey.

2. The song begins with you commenting on your surroundings (the floorboards, the door, the field mouse, the broom and the window), so you will need to see these in your imagination. In your rehearsals decide where each object is situated in your imaginary smokehouse. When you mention them, look in the direction they are located and ensure you are genuinely visualising them. Of course, the choices need to be logical (don't put the window on the floor!), but do try to ensure that objects you mention are in noticeably different places so it is clear to those watching. For example, the door might be on an angle to your right, the field mouse and broom over to your left.

3. Using your body, try to wring every last drop of water out of an imaginary towel. In this exercise you are using one of movement analyst's Rudolph Laban's 'efforts of movement': wringing. This exercise works in a psychophysical way – by changing the way you are moving your body, an emotional response can be provoked. When you then act the song, you no longer need to externalise this movement, but a sense of inner frustration will persist. This is really helpful to access Jud's frustration at the beginning of the song.

4. Remember the smokehouse is very small, so don't move too much in the space. Your performance will benefit from the feeling that Jud is like a beast trapped in a cage.

5. The event of the song occurs when you decide that you are not simply going to dream about Laurey any more – you are going to make her your bride. This moment wants to be very dynamic physically, with a strong sense of inner action. It requires a sense of danger from you as an actor, as you realise you are prepared to murder Curly if necessary to make Laurey your own – which is what you attempt to do later in the show.

Vocal and Musical Analysis

WHO TO LISTEN TO: Shuler Hensley on the National Theatre cast recording (1998).

VOCAL RANGE: D3 to C♯4.

ORIGINAL KEY: D major.

ACCENT: Oklahoma (a southern American state).

STYLE OF MUSICAL: Book musical.

VOCAL SET-UP/MUSICAL TIPS

1. In the verses there is a great deal of inner tension and frustration felt by Jud – which is reflected in the persistent, discordant accompaniment. This might be reflected in your performance through a repetitive physical tic, such as drumming your fingers on your thigh, or tapping your foot.

2. In the opening section (and when the same music returns later) a Speech quality is appropriate – though perhaps modified slightly from Estill's pure definition of a Speech quality to include a degree of laryngeal lowering. This will make your sound a little more classical, which is appropriate for the score. The set-up is wonderfully demonstrated by Hensley on the suggested recording.

3. The songs in *Oklahoma!* should be delivered in a legit style. So, in the section you begin to dream of Laurey, you should maintain the laryngeal lowering to keep a dark tonal quality but introduce more thyroid tilt so this section sounds more 'sung'. This is Sob quality.

4. Throughout you should use strong biting consonants, which will help to convey the anger and frustration that pervades the material.

Sheet Music

The correct sheet music for this song is available at www.scribd.com.

'Man of La Mancha'
from *Man of La Mancha*

Music by Mitch Leigh, lyrics by Joe Darion

Choose this song if: you have deep baritone voice. This song
will particularly suit you if you are a middle-aged actor, but
also works for younger actors who can play roles that require
weight and authority.

Given Circumstances

WHO ARE YOU: Miguel de Cervantes, a man who has failed as an
author, soldier, actor and tax collector. By this point of the
musical you are pretending to be a mad old gentleman named
Alonso Quijano, who in turn has named himself Don Quixote
de La Mancha. Despite the convoluted play-within-a-play
structure of *Man of La Mancha*, for the purposes of audition
you need only think of yourself as Don Quixote, a heroic knight.

WHERE ARE YOU: In a literal sense you are in the common room
of a stone prison vault in Seville, Spain, but the scene takes
place in a fictional world from the imagination of Miguel de
Cervantes.

WHEN IS IT: 10.00 a.m., autumn, late-sixteenth century.

WHAT HAS HAPPENED BEFORE: You (Cervantes) and your
manservant have just been put in prison at the hands of the
Spanish Inquisition (the court of this period responsible for
maintaining Catholic orthodoxy). On your arrival, your fellow
prisoners decided to put you on mock trial, where you were
accused of the absurd crimes of being an idealist, a bad poet
and an honest man. In response to these allegations you asked
to deliver your defence in the form of a charade, an
entertainment. In that charade you would impersonate an old
country squire named Alonso Quijano. As they might derive
some pleasure from your performance, the prisoners agreed.

CLASSICAL

When you began your charade you explained to them that the character Alonso, having read book after book since his retirement, had become indignant at man's murderous ways towards his fellow man. Having brooded for a long time on this melancholy burden, he had therefore decided to transform himself into a knight-errant named Don Quixote and to go forth into the world to right all wrongs. Whilst offering up this prologue to your fellow prisoners, and with the help of your manservant, you began to dress in a costume and apply make-up fitting for a knight. Once this transformation was complete you began to perform the role of Don Quixote.

WHO ELSE IS THERE: In the world of the play, other prisoners would be present, but for the purposes of an audition you should behave as if you are alone.

WHO SHOULD YOU SING TO: The bleak and sinful world.

Textual Analysis

The driving introduction reflects the narrative at this moment of the story – it is the beginning of an adventure. Use the momentum of this introductory music to help you prepare yourself for the objective of the opening two lines which is: to get the world to pay attention, so you can denounce it as wicked and debauched. In the third line this objective changes slightly, and you now want: to challenge the world. In the chorus, having thrown down that gauntlet, your objective becomes: to now announce yourself and to glorify your imminent journey.

In the second verse your focus becomes more particular, as you begin to address specific enemies. Your objective here is: to warn your foes of their imminent downfall. When you return to the chorus the lyric is repeated, so the objective is the same as the previous chorus. In order to make this section interesting for the audition panel, ensure you play different actions second time around. Although the objective is the same, one particular moment should be quite different in the second chorus. When you say that you will follow the winds of fortune whithersoever they blow, you have a momentary premonition that this quest could lead you to your death – which turns out to be true at the end of the story.

KEY MOMENTS/TOP TIPS

1. It is hugely egotistical to keep repeating your own name as Don Quixote does. Explore what this might mean as a character choice and how you might choose to sing the name. (To more fully understand this note, try listening to Philip Quast's performance of Javert – another character who constantly repeats his own name – in the tenth-anniversary concert recording of *Les Misérables*.)

2. Make strong, defined physical choices for this role. Don Quixote should be imposing. Ensure that you are always grounded, with your weight evenly distributed through both feet. Use your full height by lengthening the spine and engage your torso anchoring (which will help with your singing) to make you look physically imposing. When you make gestures let them be crisp and authoritative.

3. Your choice of actions should convey a character who is feeling inspired, who has the chutzpah to challenge his enemies and who is filled with a sense of mission. Try playing choices such as: I challenge, goad, confront, hound, electrify, hurry, warn, prepare and caution the world.

4. To convey the impression that you are speaking to the entire world you should behave as if you are addressing a large crowd. For example, locate your 'heathens' and 'wizards' as imaginary people placed beyond the audition table. You can also include the panel at times, by addressing them as though they are also part of the sinful world. Don't deliver too many of the challenging actions to the audition panel, as it can be uncomfortable for them if they feel obliged to maintain sustained eye contact with an aggressive or confrontational character.

CLASSICAL

Vocal and Musical Analysis

WHO TO LISTEN TO: Brian Stokes Mitchell on the Broadway revival cast recording (2002).

VOCAL RANGE: B♭2 to D4.

ORIGINAL KEY: C minor.

ACCENT: Of course, Don Quixote would have a Spanish accent. If you are from any part of Spain, or indeed even from Latin America, then this song would work well in your own voice. If you are performing this material in the UK, and are not from one of those countries, then perform the song in Received Pronunciation.

STYLE OF MUSICAL: Concept musical.

VOCAL SET-UP/MUSICAL TIPS

1. In the middle of the song there is a section sung by your manservant, who takes on the role of Don Quixote's sidekick, Sancho. In audition this should be cut in its entirety. At the end of the first chorus, jump to the beginning of the second verse (where you speak to the heathens and wizards). In the score Sancho also has a countermelody during the second chorus. Again, this should be cut. Continue singing the main melody at this point, ignoring Sancho's lyrics.

2. The style of this song should be quite classical in nature, almost operatic. To achieve this sound sing with a lowered laryngeal position, a tilted thyroid and an anchored torso. Try to achieve efficient vowel production in the song by keeping the tongue from moving unnecessarily by aiming to keep the sides of the tongue as close to your upper molars as possible.

3. In the verses Don Quixote should sound driven and determined. One way to achieve this is to mix in some aspirate onsets to your sound to achieve a breathy Speech quality.

4. The choruses should be louder than the verses. To achieve this, take some of thyroid tilt out of your sound to achieve a thicker vocal-fold mass whilst keeping the larynx lowered.

Sheet Music

The correct sheet music for this song is available at www.musicnotes.com.

CLASSICAL

'So in Love'
from *Kiss Me, Kate*

Music and lyrics by Cole Porter

Choose this song if: you have a rich, classical baritone voice
and enjoy playing the ultra-masculine leading man. This role
is normally played by an actor who is physically imposing.

Given Circumstances

Note: The given circumstances outlined here are for the
reprise version of the song.

WHO ARE YOU: Fred Graham, a thirty-one-year-old, egotistical,
self-absorbed producer, director and leading man of a musical
version of Shakespeare's *The Taming of the Shrew*.

WHERE ARE YOU: Backstage at Ford's Theatre, Baltimore.

WHEN IS IT: About 9.00 p.m., during the second act of the
opening night of the show, June 1948. (It is also the first
anniversary of your divorce.)

WHAT HAS HAPPENED BEFORE: Today the cast has been engaged
in final rehearsals for the show. You are playing the role of
Petruchio, opposite your ex-wife Lilli Vanessi, a movie star,
who is playing Katherine. Tensions have been rising, not only
because it is unseasonably hot, but because Katherine called
you a bastard onstage during the dress rehearsal. At the half-
hour call for the first performance you went to Lilli's dressing
room to complain about her behaviour. She taunted you by
showing off her new engagement ring from the wealthy
Harrison Howell, who not only has the ear of the US President,
but who has financed the show with $200,000 of his own
money. Your humiliation was exacerbated when she compared
your careers since your divorce. Whilst she had been successful
in Hollywood, your production of *Cyrano de Bergerac* – a labour
of love – had closed in Paris after only four nights. After your

bickering, the pair of you began to reminisce about the first night you met. For a moment you both were laughing and dancing – revealing that you still had feelings for each other.

This serenity didn't last for long. Straight afterwards you went into your adjacent dressing room, to be met by two gangsters. They had come to collect $10,000 that they mistakenly believed you owed them. In fact, Bill, who is playing Lucentio in the show, lost the money gambling and signed an IOU in your name. When you denied the debt, they said they would return later. Matters became worse when Lilli accidentally received a bunch of flowers you had sent. They were an exact copy of her wedding bouquet. Believing that you had remembered your anniversary, and still had feelings for her, Lilli confessed to herself she was still in love with you. The flowers were actually meant for Lois Lane, the beautiful young actress playing Bianca and the girlfriend of Bill. With Lilli delighted about your 'gift', you tried to recover the card that came with the flowers before she could read it, but she put the unopened envelope down her bosom and went onstage – promising to open it later.

A few scenes into the first act – after she'd had the opportunity to read the card – Lilli slapped you on stage. You responded by spanking her in front of the audience. After you had come offstage, Lilli, who was furious about being publicly humiliated, told you she was quitting on the spot and would not complete the performance. She then got on the phone to Harrison and told him that he should come and collect her, because she wanted to marry him that evening. The two gangsters, who had by now seen the show and were highly impressed, were not pleased when you told them that Lilli was intending to quit the show, as you could only repay your 'debt' if the show was to enjoy a successful run at the box office. So they threatened Lilli, telling her that they wouldn't allow her to leave and that she must complete the show.

During the second act of the performance Howell arrived. In her dressing room Lilli tried to convince him that she was being held hostage, but he didn't believe her. With Lilli intent on marrying Howell, you tried to make her realise that life with him would be dull and unfulfilling, but she stubbornly refused to change her mind. A few moments ago the two gangsters revealed that their boss had just died, which meant your debt was cancelled and Lilli was free. You made a final plea for Lilli to stay, but she ignored you and has just walked out through the stage door to join Harrison in the cab to take them to the airport.

WHO ELSE IS THERE: You are alone.

WHO SHOULD YOU SING TO: The absent Lilli.

Textual Analysis

The beginning of the song is incredibly romantic. Your objective in this first verse is: to make Lilli understand how much she means to you. In the second verse you then confess to Lilli how you behave when she is not around, when you are alone and thinking of her. Your objective at this point is: to convince Lilli that you need her. To open up in this way is something you have always found difficult due to your stubbornness and pride.

During the bridge you want Lilli to remember the night you first met, and how special it was. Your objective in this section is: to warm Lilli with the memory of your first meeting. At the start of the final verse your objective changes, you now wish: to get Lilli to take out her anger on you. This objective may seem perverse, but you are inviting Lilli to test you, so she can understand the depth of the love you feel for her. When you say ultimately that you are hers until you die – which is the event of the song – you are making a promise. From that point until the end of the song your objective is: to convince Lilli that you will love her forever. This objective, like all those before it, is doomed to fail, because Lilli is not present and in reality you are talking to yourself.

KEY MOMENTS/TOP TIPS

1. It is useful to direct much of the song in the direction that Lilli just exited. To portray this, imagine the stage door is somewhere behind the panel on a slight angle.

2. Even though is Lilli not present, you should play the
   objectives as though she might still be convinced by your
   words, even though she can't hear them. This helps keep
   the intentions of the song active. The song is the imaginary
   conversation you wish you'd had with someone, something
   we often do in life.

3. This is perhaps the first time in his life that Fred has
   allowed himself to be vulnerable in love. Faced with the
   likelihood of losing Lilli forever, he finally realises how
   much she means to him.

4. You should play the song as though you believe you will
   never see Lilli again (although your relationship is
   eventually repaired at the end of the show). This will make
   the stakes incredibly high, as you believe you are about to
   lose the woman you love.

5. The relationship between Fred and Lilli closely resembles
   that of Petruchio and Katherine in *The Taming of the
   Shrew*, so it useful to have at least a general understanding
   of Shakespeare's play.

Vocal and Musical Analysis

WHO TO LISTEN TO: Ben Davis performing at the BBC Proms
(2014).

VOCAL RANGE: C3 to F4.

ORIGINAL KEY: F minor.

ACCENT: General American.

STYLE OF MUSICAL: Book musical.

VOCAL SET-UP/MUSICAL TIPS

1. The beginning of this song should be delivered in a Sob
   quality. Work for a lowered larynx, use simultaneous onsets
   and a good deal of thyroid tilt. This is the set-up Davis
   uses in the suggested version.

2. When you sing about stars filling the sky, you should effect a crescendo. Do this by gradually releasing your thyroid tilt so you end in a horizontal position, and add some torso anchoring. You should reverse this process as you decrescendo on the next line.

3. The second verse should again begin in a Sob quality. When you sing 'you know darling why', you once again crescendo, then decrescendo on the next line (achieve this by using the process described in point 2).

4. In the bridge the sound should be richer and fuller. To realise this, add some torso anchoring to your Sob quality, particularly on the highest notes.

5. The final verse, in which you ask Lilli to taunt you, should be louder than the previous repetitions. To achieve this use a thick vocal fold, as you would in a Speech quality. You should continue to lower your larynx to keep the legit quality to the sound, and add a degree of torso anchoring and thyroid tilt on the higher phrases.

6. During the last phrase, when you repeat the words 'so in love', you should gradually decrescendo, until you end in a Cry quality. To achieve this, slowly remove your torso anchoring, tilt the thyroid cartilage and raise the larynx.

7. The sheet music is written for the whole piece of music to be repeated. This is not necessary in an audition, and you should sing the song once through only. To mark this on your music you should cross out the first time bars (the four bars on the last page which are marked with a number 1 and a bracket above them).

Sheet Music

The correct sheet music for this song is available at www.musicnotes.com.

'They Can't Take That Away from Me' from *Crazy for You*

Music by George Gershwin, lyrics by Ira Gershwin

Choose this song if: you enjoy music with a jazz influence and playing stylish, romantic roles. The song sits comfortably with a baritone register so is suitable for an actor who sings.

Given Circumstances

Note: This song was originally from another show by the Gershwins called *Shall We Dance*. The given circumstances below are those from *Crazy for You*.

WHO ARE YOU: Bobby Child, the son of a rich banking family, who longs to work in musical theatre. A bit of a dreamer, Bobby is enthusiastic, optimistic and passionate and has a never-say-die attitude.

WHERE ARE YOU: On the stage of the Gaiety Theatre, Deadrock, Nevada.

WHEN IS IT: 10.30 a.m., a summer's morning, early 1930s.

WHAT HAS HAPPENED BEFORE: A few weeks ago you turned up – uninvited – to audition for Bela Zangler, a great theatre impresario in New York. You wanted to be cast in the next *Zangler Follies*, but unfortunately he was not impressed by your appeals. After being rejected, you made your way out into the street where you bumped into your fiancée of five years, Irene Roth, and your mother. Irene, whom you don't truly love, tried to pressurise you into going ahead with the marriage. Your mother, who doesn't like Irene, instead tried to coerce you into undertaking some business for the bank. She wanted you to visit Deadrock, a former gold-mining town in Nevada. Your business there would involve tricking the proprietors of the local Gaiety Theatre into signing a property deed, in order to save money for the bank on their foreclosure costs. Faced with the choice of marrying Irene, or going to Nevada, you chose Nevada.

In Deadrock a few days later, Everett Baker, the owner of the theatre, and his daughter, Polly, received a letter from the bank forewarning them of your imminent arrival and the bank's intention to repossess the theatre if the mortgage was not paid. Shortly after they received the letter, you arrived. When you first met, Polly and yourself were instantly attracted to each other – though Polly did not realise you were working for the bank. You became worried that if you followed your mother's instructions, and closed the theatre, you would lose this girl you were falling for – so you came up with the idea of putting on a show to help pay off the mortgage and save the theatre. Polly initially agreed, but later was heartbroken and furious when she discovered who you really were.

Believing that you must save the theatre to win Polly's heart, you decided to disguise yourself as Mr Zangler and to put on the show regardless. In your new guise you trained some of the local cowboys into song-and-dance performers in preparation for the show. This new company was swelled by the fortuitous and highly coincidental arrival of ten Zangler Follies Girls who happened to be on vacation in Nevada. With rehearsals progressing well, Polly began to fall for you again, but only because she believed you were Zangler.

Yesterday the performance took place. Despite the success of the rehearsals, the show itself was a disappointment, in that only two British tourists – Eugene and Patricia – turned up to watch. Although it wasn't a financial success, it did help bring the whole town together. In the saloon after the show, now out of your disguise, you professed your love for Polly and tried to convince her that you had been impersonating Zangler. At that very moment the real Zangler turned up – making you seem like a liar. Polly kissed the dumbfounded new arrival and then left. Shortly afterwards you returned in your Zangler clothes to convince Polly of the truth, but she had now gone. You and Zangler then got incredibly drunk together, ending up asleep under the table.

This morning, about twenty minutes ago, Polly discovered you both asleep where you had collapsed. Seeing you together, with you still in dressed as Zangler, she realised the truth. Feeling that you had made a jackass out of her, Polly slapped you. After she left, Irene, who had arrived to take you back to New York, put pressure on you to leave immediately.

Back at the theatre, a few minutes ago, a company meeting was held about the show. With only two weeks to go before the mortgage must be paid, you tried to encourage everyone to mount the show one more time (this does eventually transpire later in the story and is what saves the theatre). Polly, who was feeling deflated and being obstinate, initially disagreed. Eugene and Patricia then urged everyone to show some fight, and after their encouragement Polly and a few others changed their minds and agreed, but the majority of the company were still set against it. With the show seemingly destined to never happen, and with Polly apparently out of reach, you have just told her that you are going to return to New York. Unbeknown to you, she has just begun to realise that she really is in love with you.

WHO ELSE IS THERE: Polly.

WHO SHOULD YOU SING TO: Polly.

Textual Analysis

During the introduction it is important to generate the melancholic atmosphere of your parting with Polly, as both of you are regretful that you are leaving. To achieve this, ensure you prepare yourself imaginatively by focusing on the previous circumstances before you start singing. In the first few lines of the song you should then attempt to lighten that downhearted mood. Your objective here is: to cheer Polly up. You try to do so by reminding her of some happy and amusing memories.

In musical theatre the title of the song is often the most important idea of the lyric, and that is the case here. After trying to make Polly smile at the beginning of the song, when you sing the title lyric your objective becomes: to convince Polly that you won't forget her. You want her to understand that the time you spent together meant something. Try making your delivery of this particular lyric heartfelt and direct.

Throughout the first two verses, and indeed later in the song, you need to be very specific about the memories of your relationship with Polly. Many are amusing, shared reminiscences. But some are very private, that you have never shared with anyone before, such as when you tell Polly about your dreams.

In the bridge your feelings are more raw. This should be the moment in the song of the greatest emotional release. Allow yourself to be physically free and brave at this point because the stakes are high – you are about to lose the person you truly love. Your objective in this section is: to make Polly face the reality of your parting.

In the final verse you return to the objective of trying to cheer Polly up with your shared memories. Some of the lyrics at this point can seem slight, but these memories (like the recollection of the way that Polly holds her knife) should be endearing, as small idiosyncrasies often are when people are in love. Let these affect you as much as, if not more than, the more overtly romantic moments, such as remembering dancing together in the early hours.

The last lyrics need to be informed by the fact that you are about to leave for New York. Deliver the last lines as if this is goodbye; as if you think this is the last thing you will ever say to Polly.

KEY MOMENTS/TOP TIPS

1. The song is an intimate conversation with one person. In audition it is preferable to deliver this to an imaginary partner situated behind the audition table, rather than singing directly to the panel.

2. The key to acting this material is memory – as discussed, Bobby constantly refers to the memories he has of his time with Polly. Spend time preparing detailed images for each of these memories. For example, when you remember Polly singing off-key, you might visualise an image of her rehearsing for the show. Be clear about what your Polly looks like, see the stage of the theatre where that rehearsal took place, envisage her behaviour (she might have been laughing at her mistake). The more nuanced and well-prepared your memory/images are, the more they will affect you during your performance.

3. In the title lyric you should be clear in your mind who you are referring to when you say 'they': you are talking about Irene and your mother, and perhaps in a wider sense a rich society that expects you to follow a certain life path rather than pursue your dreams of working in musical theatre and being with Polly.

4. Although Bobby is wistful about leaving Polly behind, the song is nearly entirely positive. Your choice of actions should reflect this. Try playing the following choices on Polly: I charm, entertain, tickle, amuse, console, comfort, hearten and cheer you.

5. Bobby is an aspiring musical-theatre performer. At points in this song he is fooling around to amuse Polly. In order to do this, you might reference a little of Bobby's physical language as a song-and-dance man.

6. As you part company with Polly at the end of the song, explore taking a few steps towards the door during the play-out of the music to complete the scene.

Vocal and Musical Analysis

WHO TO LISTEN TO: Kirby Ward on the original London cast recording (1993).

VOCAL RANGE: B♭2 to E♭4.

ORIGINAL KEY: E♭ major.

ACCENT: General American. (Bobby is from New York but, as he is rich and from a well-educated background, in this period it is unlikely that he would have a distinguishable New York accent.)

STYLE OF MUSICAL: Musical comedy.

VOCAL SET-UP/MUSICAL TIPS

1. The song should feel very easy and conversational. To achieve this, work predominately in a Speech quality and keep the last words of the majority of phrases very short.

2. A good way to highlight the more emotive phrases of the song is to make them more legato and sustained. This will make them stand out from the conversational tone of the rest of the song. You can hear Ward demonstrate this on the suggested recording, for example when he sings about how Polly has changed his life.

3. The tempo in the bridge (which begins when Bobby says they will never meet again) should be quicker. Lead the pianist during this section, as the music benefits from a feeling of increased momentum at this point.

4. The last line should be delivered in a sweet and quiet Cry quality with a high larynx. This will help portray how Bobby really feels to be leaving Polly.

Sheet Music

The correct sheet music for this song is available at www.musicnotes.com.

'Young and Healthy'
from *42nd Street*

Music by Harry Warren, lyrics by Al Dubin

Choose this song if: you enjoy playing the charming, flirtatious juvenile lead. The song is upbeat, fun, relatively short and sits within a comfortable vocal range.

Given Circumstances

WHO ARE YOU: Billy Lawlor, a dashing, confident actor who has been cast as the young romantic lead in *Pretty Lady*, a new Broadway show.

WHERE ARE YOU: In the midst of a dance audition on the stage of the 42nd Street Theatre, Broadway, New York, USA.

WHEN IS IT: about 11.10 a.m., a spring morning, 1933.

WHAT HAS HAPPENED BEFORE: The USA is in the grip of the Great Depression following the Wall Street Crash of 1929. Julian Marsh, with a long history of success as a Broadway producer, was hit hard financially by the crash, but is now hoping that his new production of *Pretty Lady* will put him back on top. You have been pre-cast as the leading male role in the show.

This morning the auditions for the chorus are being held. There has been a huge amount of excitement leading up to the auditions because of Marsh's reputation and because jobs have been so hard to come by in the current economic climate. Peggy Sawyer, a teenage actress, had come straight off the bus from Allentown, Pennsylvania, hoping to try out, but when she arrived outside the theatre for the audition – where hundreds of performers were already learning a tap sequence – she was too frightened to come through the stage door.

Peggy arrived on the stage a few moments ago with the audition just having finished and with the chorus already

C L A S S I C A L

chosen. She had been outside for an hour. When she came in you spotted her and found her instantly attractive. You went over to her and asked her who she was looking for. She told you she was trying to find the dance director, Andy Lee, and confessed to you that she has never worked in show business before. (Peggy goes on to become a star later in story by taking the title role of *Pretty Lady* when the original leading lady, the ageing Dorothy Brock, has to withdraw due to a broken ankle.) Despite her inexperience, Peggy was not impressed by your brag that you are one of the best juvenile leads on Broadway. You have just asked if she will go out to lunch with you but she has declined, saying she really must find the dance director.

WHO ELSE IS THERE: Peggy and Oscar (the rehearsal pianist). The newly auditioned chorus are also on the stage but they are busy handing over their addresses to Andy and the writers (Maggie and Bert), so are not aware of this conversation.

WHO SHOULD YOU SING TO: Peggy.

Textual Analysis

You first saw Peggy only moments before, so at the beginning of the song you are still operating on the rush of adrenaline that comes from asking a complete stranger on a date. In your self-confident manner you are teasing and mocking her. Your objective in this first verse is simply: to win Peggy's attention. You try to do so by making her laugh.

When the chorus begins you become much more direct. Your objective here is: to convince Peggy that it would be a great idea if you were to go out with each other. On the final line of this chorus you attempt to get Peggy to feel sorry for you. You jokingly complain that now you have met her you don't know what to do with yourself.

In the bridge, you start to play a new objective: to convince Peggy that it is impossible for you to stay away from her, because she is too beautiful and you are too full of 'vitamin A', i.e. energy. This last line can perhaps have a playful sense of double entendre.

In the final chorus, having been so far unsuccessful, you try posing a new argument to win your date. Your objective in this section is: to convince Peggy to take a risk by going out with you, because in a few years you will both be too old. This is, of course, a particularly fun and playful argument – because you are both so young.

KEY MOMENTS/TOP TIPS

1. During the verse of the song you talk about Peggy. As discussed above, you are playing with her, pretending you are almost talking about another person, even though you're referring to her. You can sing this section to an imaginary Peggy situated behind the audition table. Alternatively you can try playing this section to different members of the panel, as though you are sharing a piece of gossip with them.

2. In many book musicals the conceit is that the characters are not aware that they are singing; stylistically the songs are an extension of the spoken dialogue. That is not the case with this song. Billy has encouraged Oscar to play a well-known song at the piano that he can sing in order to charm and impress Peggy. It just so happens that the lyrics of this song happen to mirror how he feels about Peggy. In terms of your performance, this means that there should be a sense of showmanship – of a talented young performer knowingly showing off in order to seduce a beautiful young girl. Although you might refer to him in the musical, it is not advisable to acknowledge an imaginary Oscar in the audition room.

3. It is instructive to remember how Peggy would be behaving during the scene. In the musical, at this point she would be running around, desperate to locate Andy. In your audition you will, of course, not have an actor playing Peggy. Therefore you should direct the song to an imaginary

Peggy located behind the audition table. You don't need to behave as though Peggy is moving about (locate her in one place), but it is useful to imagine that she is distracted, so you have to work very hard to win her attention. This is a great obstacle to play with, as it will make you try harder to succeed in your objective.

4. The type of actions Billy plays are those you might use in many upbeat romantic songs: to charm, tease, seduce, amuse, exhilarate, enchant and spellbind. What makes the performance fun and individual is if you play those actions with Billy's characteristics in mind, which are: self-confident, brave, positive and enthusiastic. In other words, how does a self-confident person amuse? How might an enthusiastic person spellbind?

5. Remember that Billy has already been cast in the show, he knows the people on the stage, whereas Peggy is new here. This gives him the upper hand – this is his world.

6. When you are listening to the recommended version of this song you will hear that there is some dialogue and a duet section with Peggy. These should both be ignored, instead follow the structure of the published solo version (see below).

Vocal and Musical Analysis

WHO TO LISTEN TO: David Elder on the Broadway revival cast recording (2001).

VOCAL RANGE: D3 to E♭4 (E♭ major version).

ORIGINAL KEY: F major (show version) – though it is recommended that you use the solo version published in E♭ major which goes straight through, without the underscore for dialogue or the duet section with Peggy.

ACCENT: General American.

STYLE OF MUSICAL: Musical comedy.

VOCAL SET-UP/MUSICAL TIPS

1. The verse should be in a Speech quality, but with some twang added to the set-up by slightly tightening the AES (aryepiglottic sphincter).

2. In the 1930s it was commonplace for singers to insert grace notes (short additional notes, added as an embellishments to the melody) in their vocal performance. It is useful to add this to your performance in order to capture the period style. You can hear this in Elder's performance; for example, on the words 'passes', 'to do' and 'away'.

3. Billy is a romantic singer by profession, and in this period he would most likely have sung in the style of a crooner (think Frank Sinatra or Gene Kelly). To work for this sound, sing with a legato line once the main melody starts, make use of simultaneous onsets with no glottals, lower the larynx slightly, and play with grace notes as previously suggested.

Sheet Music

The correct sheet music for this song is available at www.musicnotes.com.

CLASSICAL

'A Bit of Earth'
from *The Secret Garden*

Music by Lucy Simon, lyrics by Marsha Norman

Choose this song if: you have bass-baritone voice with a rich lower register and are able to successfully access a Falsetto quality. This song may suit you if you are a slightly older performer, or have a similar gravitas.

Given Circumstances

WHO ARE YOU: Archibald Craven, a middle-aged English aristocrat who suffers from a kyphosis, or hunchback. You have been mourning for the death of your wife for many years and as a result have a tendency to be a recluse. You can be cold, withdrawn and morose – though this is far from your true nature. When your wife was alive you were warm, caring and fun-loving.

WHERE ARE YOU: In your library in Misselthwaite Manor, North Yorkshire, England.

WHEN IS IT: 10.30 a.m., a rainy spring morning, 1906.

WHAT HAS HAPPENED BEFORE: Your wife, Lily, whom you loved greatly, died several years ago. Since that time you have become increasingly withdrawn, and have allowed your brother, Dr Neville Craven, to manage Misselthwaite. (Unbeknown to you, Neville covets the estate for himself.) The house is full of memories for you and is haunted by Lily's ghost, which appears to you at times.

You have a ten-year-old son, Colin, whom you have confined to bed since his mother's death, as you fear that he will suffer from the same spinal condition as yourself. (In fact, you discover later in the story that Colin's spine is completely healthy. The ailments that confine him to his room are purely psychosomatic, induced by your own overprotectiveness, and

encouraged by Dr Craven, who is happy to see the rightful
heir of Misselthwaite deteriorate through being unnecessarily
bedridden.)

A few days ago, Mary Lennox, your ten-year-old niece,
arrived from India. Her mother Rose (Lily's sister) and father
had died of cholera, so she was sent to live with you, as you
are now her legal guardian. Since her arrival you have been
avoiding Mary as she reminds you of Lily, which you find
incredibly painful. Despite her loss, and your coldness, Mary
is full of spirit and brings a new life and energy to the house.

Encouraged by the housemaid, Martha, Mary went off
exploring the grounds of Misselthwaite. Whilst doing so she
discovered a walled, secret garden that she could not find the
entrance to. Ben Weatherstaff, an old gardener, revealed to her
that the garden has been locked since Lily's death because it
reminds you of your late wife. Martha's brother Dickon, who
is also a gardener, then taught Mary to speak to the animals,
notably a robin, by using a Yorkshire dialect. The bird
consequently led Mary to the hiding place of the key for the
secret garden, though she still did not know the whereabouts
of the door. Alongside her adventures in the grounds, Mary
had also been exploring the house. In doing so she heard some
mysterious crying sounds, which she believed to be a ghost
(but she will later in the story discover to be Colin).

Moments ago you had a conversation with your brother in the
library. He tried to convince you to send Mary away to
boarding school and to stop sitting by Colin's bed, night after
night, hoping for a miracle. Neville was trying to negate the
reasons that make you feel obligated to stay, as he wanted to
encourage you to move to Paris so he could take the house for
himself. You were unaware of his motives and were close to
falling for this trap, but just as you are beginning to acquiesce,
the housekeeper, Mrs Wedlock, brought in Mary, whom you
had asked to see. Following your brother's lead, you told Mary
that you were considering sending her away to boarding
school as you were worried that there was so little for her to
do here. She protested strongly against this, saying how much

there was to engage her in the garden. You agreed to let her stay, her interest in gardens particularly catching your attention. You then asked if she wanted any books, toys or dolls, but Mary replied that she only desired 'a bit of earth': a garden. You replied that she could have as much garden as she wished before dismissing her from the library.

As soon as she was out of the door, Neville, who was concerned that Mary might reignite your love for both the garden and for Misselthwaite – and therefore ruin his plans – tried to warn you to stay away from Mary. He said she was causing you too much pain. Noticing you were distracted by your previous conversation with Mary, your brother tried to get you to sign over the lease to the house. When you failed to do so, he left.

WHO ELSE IS THERE: You are alone. (In the musical Neville interjects with spoken dialogue – his request to sign the lease – during the first verse. However, as you don't reply to any of these lines, and are oblivious to what he is saying, for audition purposes it is easier to perform the entire song as if no one else is there.)

WHO SHOULD YOU SING TO: Yourself, though in this situation you can share many of your thoughts with the panel as though they are your inner-consciousness.

Textual Analysis

The song starts with you feeling confused. Your objective in the first verse is: to understand why young Mary is asking for a garden. You struggle to comprehend this request, when you could give her anything she desires. To understand why this question matters so much to you, it is important to realise the significance of the garden. In a garden plants take root, bloom for a time, and then die. The life contained within them is therefore transient. Lily tended the secret garden when she was alive, and as both she and the garden eventually died, you see it as a metaphor for the futility of life. So when you ask why Mary wants 'a bit of earth', you are really asking: how can this child believe in life rather than death?

In the second verse (that begins with your conclusion that Mary needs a friend), your objective is: to convince yourself that neither you, nor the garden, can give Mary what she really needs. So during the first half of the bridge, where the music increases in intensity, your objective becomes: to convince yourself that Mary should be like other children. You think she should desire the gifts that other little girls covet, such as a pony, or a doll's house. As you realise that such gifts are the last thing that Mary wants, your objective in the second half of the bridge is: to understand why Mary doesn't want material belongings. At this point you discover that your feelings for Mary are developing – you want to provide for her and care for her as if she were your own daughter.

In the final verse, when the lyric returns to an analysis of Mary's desire for 'a bit of earth', you are for a moment more hopeful. Perhaps for the first time since Lily's death you imagine how the garden might bring someone joy, rather than the despair it has provoked in you these last few years. Your objective in this moment is: to convince yourself that the garden will make Mary happy. This moment of hope proves to be fragile. When you think of autumn your mind returns to the death of Lily, and negativity creeps back in. But perhaps, in the last high notes of the song, there is a sense that you believe, by allowing Mary to tend the garden, that a sense of new life might indeed enter Misselthwaite Manor. This proves to be the event of the song.

KEY MOMENTS/TOP TIPS

1. Although Archie is a hunchback, it is not advisable to work for this physical transformation in the audition room, as you will be using this song to audition for a different show or purpose.

2. The heart of the song is: should I carry on wanting to be alive, like Mary does? This is obviously a huge, existential question for someone grappling with grief, and is ferociously difficult for Archie to answer. So play strong

actions on yourself such as: I interrogate, question, scrutinise and provoke myself.

3. A moment of musical lyricism in the second verse indicates that, of the long list of Mary's needs that you feel cannot be fulfilled, the most important is the comfort of a mother's arms. You can hear this clearly in Quast's performance on the suggested recording (see below).

4. During the course of the song you should gradually, piece by piece, let the warmth of Mary's enthusiasm begin to melt your hardened feelings towards the world, so the song has an emotional journey. We see how Mary is helping Archie become the man he used to be.

Vocal and Musical Analysis

WHO TO LISTEN TO: Philip Quast on the original London cast recording (2001).

VOCAL RANGE: D♭3 to A5.

ORIGINAL KEY: A major.

ACCENT: Received Pronunciation.

STYLE OF MUSICAL: Contemporary musical (legit-based).

VOCAL SET-UP/MUSICAL TIPS

1. The opening line is written to be spoken in rhythm rather than sung – in the show the song emerges out of a scene – but in audition it is advisable to ask for a 'bell note' and sing from the very first word. You should ask the pianist to play an E.

2. Explore singing the first verse in a Cry quality, mixed with aspirate onsets, to make your sound thoughtful and inquisitive.

3. As you approach the second verse, start to use only simultaneous onsets, and gradually take the thyroid tilt out

of your voice to transition into a Speech quality. This will provide a sense of vocal progression as you can then sing the second verse with thicker vocal folds.

4. The vocal quality in the bridge should be strong and athletic. At this point use a modified Speech quality, by lowering the larynx slightly and adding some torso anchoring to make the sound rich and resonant.

5. After the bridge return to a Cry set-up. Lift the larynx as high as possible to make the sound very light and reflective.

6. The last note should be delivered in a quiet, vulnerable Falsetto quality.

Sheet Music

The correct sheet music for this song is available at www.musicnotes.com.

'Different'
from *Honk!*

Music by George Stiles, lyrics by Anthony Drewe

Choose this song if: you have a contemporary musical-theatre voice and enjoy playing the nerdish, lovable outsider.

Given Circumstances

Note: *Honk!* is a musical version of the famous children's story *The Ugly Duckling*.

WHO ARE YOU: Ugly, a sensitive, awkward and shy young cygnet.

WHERE ARE YOU: By the lake on a ramshackle country farm in a backwater of England.

WHEN IS IT: 11.10 a.m., a bright spring morning, present day.

WHAT HAS HAPPENED BEFORE: Ida, a duck, had been sitting for several weeks on a clutch of five eggs, keeping them warm until it was time for them to hatch, but they were overdue. Today Ida complained to her husband, Drake, that she was concerned that one of the eggs was unusually large. Drake teased Ida that the egg might belong to the turkey, before disappearing off to the lake.

Whilst he was gone, the four regularly sized eggs hatched into healthy ducklings. Seeing them on his return, Drake felt very proud and decided to take his new offspring for a swim. He encouraged Ida to abandon the remaining egg – which had failed to hatch – and join her new family. Ida declined, deciding to sit for a while longer.

A few minutes after the others had gone, the larger egg hatched, and you were born. Your egg had been bigger because you were, in fact, a cygnet (a young swan) not a duckling at all. Unaware that you were a different species, Ida was at first concerned about your unusual appearance. Her motherly instincts kicked in regardless, and she told you not to worry about what others might think of you and to hold your head up high. She then took you for a swim, something you were surprisingly good at for one so young.

When you returned to the nest a few minutes ago, Drake and your adoptive siblings were already there. Drake was afraid when Ida mistakenly explained to him that you were his son, as he thought he had fathered a monster. Your siblings called you names and mocked you for your appearance, as did your neighbours, who had come round to see what the fuss was about. A family photograph was taken of you all, but when your siblings saw it they complained that you had ruined the picture.

Moments ago, when one of your neighbours, Maureen the moorhen, brought some French bread for the new arrivals, the other ducklings pecked and bullied you. Even though you were hungry, you couldn't get to the bread and had to go without. As the others left one of your siblings, Beaky, threw the family photograph at you, which was now torn. Feeling unloved and abandoned, you have just tried to practise your duck's 'quack', which came out as the ugly 'honk' of a swan.

WHO ELSE IS THERE: You are alone.

WHO SHOULD YOU SING TO: At times you speak to yourself, at others to your absent siblings. In audition it is useful to share some of the thoughts that are addressed to yourself to the panel, as if they are your inner-consciousness. When you address your siblings, talk towards the place they just exited, which should be situated somewhere behind the audition table.

Textual Analysis

The song starts with a short pre-chorus. Having attempted and failed to quack like a duck (which is a metaphor for trying to fit in), you fall into despair, hating everything about yourself. In the first line your objective is: to wish that you were the same as your siblings.

CONTEMPORARY BALLADS

The main melody then begins. During the first half of the opening verse you take pity on yourself. Your objective here is: to accept your lot. But in the last few lines of the first verse your objective becomes: to understand why you are the recipient of prejudice. It is a struggle to understand why you are made to feel sad, just because you are different. You might play actions such as: I interrogate, cross-examine and search myself in trying to find the answer to this question. In the second verse the objective could be interpreted in several ways, but try playing the following: to convince yourself that you are not to blame for your situation.

During the bridge, rather than talking to yourself, you now begin to address your absent siblings. Your objective in this section is: to get your siblings to empathise with you. You want them to understand it is not easy to be different from everyone else. Try playing actions such as: to shake, challenge and confront them.

Gradually your attitude to being an insider starts to change. In the third verse you begin to pull yourself together and find an inner strength. Your objective here is: to convince yourself that you shouldn't blame yourself. In this objective you prove to be successful, and by the last three lines you have undergone a moment of catharsis: and have learned to embrace your individuality. This is the event of the song.

KEY MOMENTS/TOP TIPS

1. If you were involved in a production of *Honk!*, you might be asked by the director to include elements of a swan's physicality in your performance. This is not appropriate in an audition. If you wish to transform physically you might instead explore the body language and behaviour of a human being who is shy and awkward.

2. Self-pity is often not an engaging quality to watch on stage. In order to prevent your performance becoming downbeat or self-absorbed, seek to find the positive choices

in the song, places you might uplift, cheer or amuse yourself. The song benefits greatly if you find a sense of irony and your performance of Ugly is not defeatist.

3. A key moment is the last line of the bridge, when you talk about your ego taking a knock. This should be the most earnest, exposing moment of the song. Try to connect to Ugly's vulnerability at this point.

4. The heart of the song is about feeling excluded. If you are able to empathise with this situation, you might be able to relate the song to times you have felt rejected, or been prejudiced against, in your own life.

Vocal and Musical Analysis

WHO TO LISTEN TO: George Stiles on the original demo recording (released 2008). This version recorded by the composer is helpful with regards to vocal interpretation. Musically it corresponds to the original vocal score. Alternatively listen to Arthur W. Marks on the Music Theatre of Wichita cast recording (2001), which corresponds to the music in the vocal selections.

VOCAL RANGE: *Note*: As indicated above there are two versions of the song, with slightly different vocal ranges: D♭3 to E♭4 (original vocal score), and D♭ to F5 (vocal selections). You could choose to sing either version.

ORIGINAL KEY: D♭ major.

ACCENT: A regional British accent that suggests a rural setting is appropriate for this song, so Yorkshire, Lancashire, West Country, Irish, Welsh and Scottish accents work well. If your native accent is a rural one, then I would advise you to use your own voice when singing this song, but try turning up the strength a little. It is generally good practice when singing to ensure the choice is clearly perceived by the audience, and particularly in a stylised musical such as *Honk!* Accents that stereotypically denote upper class (i.e. Received Pronunciation)

268

or city accents (such as Cockney, Liverpool, Mancunian) are not appropriate.

STYLE OF MUSICAL: Contemporary musical (pop-based).

VOCAL SET-UP/MUSICAL TIPS

1. The pre-chorus should be delivered in a Speech quality. This is a good opportunity to make the regional accent you have chosen especially clear.

2. Although the choruses remain in a Speech position, they require more of a legato phrasing. Make greater use of simultaneous onsets at these points to help you achieve this.

3. When you arrive at the bridge, this section needs to have a feeling of musical momentum, which works well with Ugly's desire to protest with his siblings. Push the tempo forward a little in this section.

4. At the end of the bridge, when you talk about your ego taking a knock, deliver those two lines as quietly as you can in a Cry position. Use as much thyroid tilt as possible and raise your larynx.

5. If you are singing the version from the vocal selections, the high F you sing immediately prior to the instrumental break (on the second syllable of the word 'along') should be belted.

6. The final few lines, which are quiet and reflective should be sung in a Cry position – this highlights that this is the event.

Sheet Music

The correct sheet music for this song is available at www.scribd.com.

'I Chose Right'
from *Baby*

Music by David Shire, lyrics by Richard Maltby Jr.

Choose this song if: you are drawn to playing emotionally honest, sensitive characters. The song has a gentle Country feel, and the published version sits comfortably in the male baritone register, so suits actors who have a limited vocal range.

Given Circumstances

WHO ARE YOU: Danny, an open-hearted, optimistic and romantic twenty-year-old final-year music student who is opinionated, but who can feel lost and emasculated at times.

WHERE ARE YOU: At the bus station in an unspecified small university town in the USA.

WHEN IS IT: 10.55 a.m. mid-May 1983.

WHAT HAS HAPPENED BEFORE: In March you moved into a basement apartment with your girlfriend Lizzie. You both were feeling buoyant about your relationship and your future career as musicians. Lizzie had been feeling unwell, and when she went to the doctor she received the shock news that she was pregnant. Initially you felt traumatised at this news, but when you both began to think through the prospect of having a child you knew it was something you wanted to do. With this decision made, as you loved Lizzie very much, you suggested that the two of you should get married. Although she reciprocated your feelings of love, Lizzie was dead set against this suggestion.

Over the next month your plans about how to handle the pregnancy began to diverge from Lizzie's. She decided that she would get a job over the summer recess to allow you the space to pursue your dream of writing music. Despite her best intentions, this idea concerned you. You were worried that she wasn't demanding a serious level of commitment from you. You also struggled with the prospect of not providing for your child, as it made you feel that you weren't fulfilling your duties as a father.

A couple of weeks ago you tried to propose, but Lizzie stopped you before you could get down on one knee. She was afraid that marriage would lead to you both sacrificing your aspirations and career prospects. Later you told her you had decided to take a gig playing for a rip-off punk band called The Magnets over the summer to make money to provide for the baby, and so that Lizzie didn't have to take a job. As The Magnets are a band you both despise, the decision confirmed her fears about you being forced to sell out due to the pregnancy.

This morning you arrived at the bus station together. With your bus due to leave for New Orleans in ten minutes, Lizzie confessed that she was very worried about you being separated for three months. In response, you took an engagement ring from your pocket and slipped it on her finger. She realised at that moment that she did want to marry you, she had just been worried about you both feeling trapped. An announcement over the loudspeaker has just said that the bus is leaving in five minutes. In response you have just taken a cassette tape out of your pocket, put it in your cassette player, and pressed play. Recorded is the accompaniment of a song you have written for Lizzie. You begin to sing to her.

WHO ELSE IS THERE: Lizzie. You are at a bus station so there would be other passengers nearby, but either they are far enough away not to be able to hear you, or if they can, you don't really care.

WHO SHOULD YOU SING TO: Lizzie.

Textual Analysis

You start the song with a desire to be completely candid. In the first two lines, your objective is: to admit that it has been difficult to leave your single life behind. During the opening verse you confess that you have been taken aback by the speed with which the relationship has progressed, and how quickly the feelings between the pair of you have grown. But despite these concerns having given you a sleepless night, your objective is: to convince Lizzie that you have made the right decision. You are glad to have chosen her.

In the second verse you reveal that, as Lizzie had been worrying about, you had indeed been considering alternative life choices, such as putting your career first. But although those others paths had been tempting, when you look at her you know you have made the right choice. Again your objective is to convince her of this fact.

During the bridge you are honest in saying that there is a real possibility that the relationship between yourself and Lizzie may not ultimately work out. Your objective at this point is: to be realistic about the future. But despite your pragmatism, you also assure Lizzie that you fully intend to make good on the promises that you are giving her.

You want to to leave Lizzie fully reassured before you get on the bus, so in the final verse your objective is: to convince Lizzie that you are not like your friends. They are still immature in their relationships, whereas you are fully committed both to her, and to bringing up your child.

KEY MOMENTS/TOP TIPS

1. The song is a gentle, romantic conversation. Lizzie, although she did not explicitly say so, accepted your proposal only moments before. So although your objective (to reassure her that you are committed to relationship) is a very important one, it is delivered in an atmosphere of loving acceptance, rather than through urgent argument.

The actions you choose should therefore reflect this intimacy of tone, and not be too strident. Try playing choices such as: to calm, reassure, warm, strengthen, comfort, tickle, soothe, protect and insulate her.

2. Although Danny is being totally honest in his intentions, and truly believes that this is a lifetime commitment, it is worth remembering that he is only twenty. Find the romantic openness and freedom of a man who can make heartfelt promises with the good fortune never to have suffered any real heartbreak.

3. The bridge of the song is more rhythmic and bouncy. Allied with some flippant lyrics, this suggests that at this point Danny's choices are more humorous. Try playing: to amuse, cheer, entertain, enliven, vitalise and brighten Lizzie.

4. The event of the song is near the end of the lyric when Danny says that he will be true and follow through on his commitment. This should be the most focused, heartfelt moment. Work to find a genuine emotional connection at this point.

Vocal and Musical Analysis

WHO TO LISTEN TO: Todd Graff on the Broadway revival cast recording (1983).

VOCAL RANGE: B♭2 to E♭4 (E♭ major version).

ORIGINAL KEY: G major (show version) – though I would recommend you use the version published in E♭ major.

ACCENT: General American

STYLE OF MUSICAL: Contemporary musical (pop-based).

VOCAL SET-UP/MUSICAL TIPS

1. Embrace the Country style of the music by using a simultaneous onset, a slightly raised larynx, a little bit of

twang and a consistent use of vibrato. A good example of this style of singing is John Denver's famous performance of 'Annie's Song'.

2. Try both the opening two lines and the first verse in a Cry position, with a tiny amount of twang added. Increase the amount of twang in the second verse by tightening your AES to gain slightly more volume. This will help achieve a feeling of musical development.

3. During the title lyric that occurs at the end of second verse, slowly remove your thyroid tilt so that you can transition into a Speech set-up for the bridge.

4. Deliver the two lines after the word 'might' in a very quiet and sweet Cry quality – this helps clarify the event of song. Raise the AES as much as possible at this point to remove any twang.

5. Near the end of the song there is an ascending phrase on the word 'you'. Ideally this should remain in this Cry set-up. You can practise this by repeatedly sirening the phrase. If you still find the phrase difficult, an alternative solution is to deliver the top note in Falsetto. If you make this choice, make the preceding notes as quiet as possible to help disguise the transition between voice qualities.

Sheet Music

The correct sheet music for this song is available at www.musicnotes.com.

'If I Can't Love Her'
from *Beauty and the Beast*

Music by Alan Menken, lyrics by Howard Ashman and Tim Rice

Choose this song if: you have a powerful bass-baritone voice and excel at singing with a legit musical-theatre sound. If you enjoy performing tragic, emotive material, then this song might be for you.

Given Circumstances

WHO ARE YOU: A handsome young prince who has been turned into a beast. You can be melancholy and self-absorbed. As someone with a quick temper, you are also prone to self-pity.

WHERE ARE YOU: In the West Wing of the Prince's castle in a faraway magical kingdom.

WHEN IS IT: 9.30 p.m., after dinner on a winter's evening, once upon a time. (From an aesthetic perspective, fairytales that begin with the line 'Once upon a time' often contain elements that are a fantasised and romanticised version of the European medieval period.)

WHAT HAS HAPPENED BEFORE: Ten years ago, an old beggar woman visited your castle. She offered you a single red rose in return for shelter from the bitter winter cold. As a prince you were spoilt and selfish, and repulsed by her haggard appearance, so you dismissed her gift and tried to send her away. The beggar woman warned you not to be fooled by outward appearances, telling you that true beauty was found within. When you dismissed her for a second time she revealed herself in her true form: a beautiful and powerful enchantress. You begged the enchantress for her forgiveness, but it was too late. As she sensed no love in your heart, she placed a spell on the castle, transforming you into a monstrous beast and all of your servants into furniture.

As you were ashamed of your new physical from, you concealed yourself within the castle, with a magic mirror being your only window into the world. The sorceress left behind the rose. It too was enchanted and she told you it would continue to bloom for many years. She said that if you learned to love another before the last petal fell – and earned that person's love in return – then you would be transformed back into a prince. If not, you would remain a beast forever. For the past decade you have been shut away in the castle, growing more and more despondent.

This morning, Maurice, an eccentric inventor who lives in the nearest town, became lost in the woods and stumbled upon your castle. Despite being welcomed by your servants, when you discovered his presence you locked him away in the dungeon for trespassing.

Back in the town, Maurice's daughter, the beautiful Belle, became worried when another man, called LeFou, returned from the woods wearing her father's scarf. She decided to go searching for her father and discovered him locked away in the castle. When you trapped and caught her, she told you that her father was unwell and begged for his freedom. You agreed that you would release him, if in return she would remain imprisoned in the castle. When she agreed, her generosity towards her father moved you, but still you insisted that she remain in the castle. With her fate decided, you then released Belle from the dungeon, taking her to one of the bedrooms instead. You told her that she could go anywhere in the castle, except the West Wing (where the rose is kept) and then ordered her to have dinner with you that evening.

A couple of hours ago, Belle refused to come down for her meal. You responded by saying that if she wouldn't eat with you, then she wouldn't eat at all. Despite this, your servants entertained Belle with a huge feast. A few minutes ago two of your servants, Cogsworth and Lumière, took Belle on a tour of the castle. Slipping away from them, she ventured into the West Wing. Fascinated by the mysterious rose she discovered there, and unaware of your presence, she reached out to touch it. Seeing this, you were afraid that she might damage the precious rose, and consign you to being a beast forever. You revealed yourself and Belle tried to run away. In your anger you accidentally knocked her over. Fearing for her life, Belle renounced her promise and fled the castle, leaving you alone, fearing that now the spell would never be broken.

WHO ELSE IS THERE: You are alone.

WHO SHOULD YOU SING TO: Yourself, though in audition you can share many of your thoughts with the panel as though they are your inner-consciousness.

Textual Analysis

The song begins with you at your lowest. Your objective when you start singing is: to wallow in self-loathing. At this point you not only have contempt for your physical appearance, you also believe you are a bad person. After the first couple of lines, your objective shifts to the main aim of the song: to stop yourself hoping. You want to make yourself accept that there is no escape from the enchantress's curse. Although this objective seems perverse, you are acting out of self-preservation. By constantly hoping to reverse the spell you had been torturing yourself, and with the departure of Belle this has now become unbearable. During the chorus this same objective continues, but it now becomes harder to achieve because you are battling with the fact that having Belle in the castle for a brief time raised your hopes.

In the bridge your objective changes. You now want to punish yourself for your foolishness when you were a prince. At this point you are incredibly hard on yourself, and take all the blame for your situation upon yourself. After this section, when the chorus returns, you pursue this harsh objective to its ultimate conclusion: by forcing yourself to give up on any hope of salvation, by the last line you are contemplating your own suicide.

KEY MOMENTS/TOP TIPS

1. As you begin the song talking about your appearance, you can perform the opening section as if you are looking in an imaginary mirror (perhaps located behind the audition table). If you decide to take this approach, then do some practice in front of a real mirror so you can replicate the behaviours you undertake when looking at your reflection. When performing the song you will need to imagine the Beast's reflection in your imagination. This is skilled piece of storytelling – it must be immediately apparent to the panel that you are looking in a mirror, or the choice won't make sense. It is a good idea to get a friend or colleague to observe your rehearsals to see if this part of your performance is clear. If it is not, an alternative approach to the opening section is to talk directly to the panel instead.

2. If you were playing the Beast in a full production you would undertake a heightened physical transformation. That approach is not advisable in audition, as you will be singing this song for another production or for entry to drama school, rather to be cast as the Beast.

3. The overall objective (to make yourself give up hope) is a difficult one to play. To realise this, you first need to understand the obstacle to you achieving your objective – that, deep within, the Beast *does* still harbour a hope that Belle will be his salvation. The objective therefore involves an internal battle between the head and the heart. During your performance, allow yourself to see positive memories of Belle – such as her beautiful face, or her kindness towards her father – then use the lyrics to dismiss these from your mind.

4. During the song the Beast constantly criticises himself, and is full of self-contempt. It is worth remembering that he was placed under this spell because of his faults, and so it is likely he will have spent many years blaming himself for his fate, assuming that he deserved it. In this darkest of moments that long-held guilt floods easily to the surface.

5. The actions in this song are played on yourself and are mainly negative. Try such choices as: I punish, chastise, torture, criticise, discipline, crush, interrogate and flog myself. The moments of joy and hope you feel when you see the images of Belle will balance the performance and add some lightness and humanity to the work.

6. There is an instrumental section in the song that should be shortened. After the word 'onward' make a cut so that you re-enter with the vocal line on the word 'no'. (In total you are cutting the eight bars that begin at the key change into D major.)

Vocal and Musical Analysis

WHO TO LISTEN TO: Alasdair Harvey on the original London cast recording (1997).

VOCAL RANGE: B2 to F4.

ORIGINAL KEY: C major.

ACCENT: General American or Received Pronunciation. The song was written to be performed in General American, and you should certainly take that approach if you have a North American accent yourself, and could also do so if General American is an accent you do well. Equally, the song can work successfully in Received Pronunciation if that accent suits you better.

STYLE OF MUSICAL: Contemporary musical (legit-based).

VOCAL SET-UP/MUSICAL TIPS

1. The correct vocal set-up for this style of musical theatre is sometimes unkindly called 'poperetta', and is a mix between a pop sound and operatic set-up. (Many singers have used a similar vocal style in productions of *Les Misérables* and *The Phantom of the Opera*.) The fundamental colour of the sound is achieved through a

lowered laryngeal position. The set-up also contains thyroid tilt, some twang and an anchored torso. Use a simultaneous onset wherever possible.

2. The beginning of the song is very reflective. A good way to achieve this is to use a Speech quality, but with the use of some aspirate onsets to make it sound thoughtful and introspective.

3. The chorus should be delivered in a very pure, quiet Cry quality (almost as quiet as you sing). You will need to sing with a raised larynx, so ensure you lengthen your neck to sustain the laryngeal position. You should also sing in a very legato fashion and run the vowels together as much as possible.

4. In the bridge, use a Speech quality but modified to include a lowered larynx and an anchored torso. This will give you a rich, powerful sound.

5. The last high note on the word 'me' is challenging. It is very hard to belt because of the vowel and because the pitch is bit lower than is ideal for Belt quality. Because the song reaches a climactic quality, and a belt is not an easy option, it can be difficult to get the volume and resonance you desire. A solution is to remain in a tilted thyroid position, add twang, add torso anchoring and focus on the tongue position (with the tip being behind the lower front teeth and the sides being in contact with the upper molars). If you avoid driving for volume, this set-up should be successful (Alasdair Harvey is adopting something similar on the recording). If you do want to belt, try modifying the vowel sound on the word 'me' so it sounds more like 'may'. You will then find it easier to get into the set-up, though modifying the vowel is not to everyone's taste.

Sheet Music

The correct sheet music for this song is available at www.musicnotes.com.

'If I Didn't Believe in You' from *The Last Five Years*

Music and lyrics by Jason Robert Brown

Choose this song if: you have an excellent pop-based musical-theatre voice, and like to explore characters who have the capacity to be cruel, hurtful and sarcastic.

Given Circumstances

Note: *The Last Five Years* is notable in its construction in that the stories of the two protagonists are told from different chronological perspectives. Jamie's story is told in the order the events occurred, whilst Cathy's is delivered in a reverse chronology. In the musical the only time the two characters interact directly is when the two timelines intersect in the middle of the story and they get married to each other. For ease of understanding, though, the events below are outlined sequentially.

WHO ARE YOU: Jamie Wellerstein, a twenty-seven-year-old successful young novelist. Whilst you are supremely talented, and can be caring and romantic, you are prone to be arrogant, selfish, self-absorbed and spiteful at times.

WHERE ARE YOU: The apartment you share with your wife Cathy on 73rd Street in Manhattan, New York City, USA.

WHEN IS IT: 7.10 p.m., a Tuesday, autumn, 2012.

WHAT HAS HAPPENED BEFORE: Four years ago you began dating an young aspiring actress named Cathy. After years of trying to please your mother by dating Jewish girls, you were delighted to have met this sexy, vibrant woman who you described as a 'shiksa goddess'.

Following a hectic and exhilarating few months, Cathy, who had been hurt in a previous relationship, convinced you to move in with her. Cathy was ambitious and swore she would never return to a small town like the one she grew up in.

Shortly after you moved in together, your career as a novelist rapidly took off when you were signed by a top literary agent. Several publishers soon became involved in a bidding war for your first novel. Whilst your career was taking a steep upward turn, Cathy was struggling with her own. Constantly attending auditions, she was failing to get cast and began to become a little despondent. Her disappointment was balanced by the joy she felt when the two of you became married.

Despite the happiness you both felt in your personal lives, after the wedding your careers continued to head in opposite directions and this began to put a strain on the relationship. In the year that followed, whilst you became one of the most sought-after novelists in the country, Cathy continued to find acting work hard to come by, and became ever more frustrated at her lack of success. Now something of a celebrity in the literary world, you started to become tempted by other women who were attracted to your success. Although Cathy was constantly attending the parties and functions connected with your writing, you did not always give her much attention, and she began to doubt how much she really meant to you.

That summer Cathy accepted a part in a small show in Ohio, which was not the calibre of production she had been hoping for. A lingering feeling began to grow between you both that she was taking a backwards step into a small-town existence. You began to resent taking the trip to Ohio to visit, as it took you away from your exciting metropolitan life.

Recently, whilst you were working to finish a new novel, Cathy came close to landing a show in New York. When she failed to get the role she reluctantly accepted another summer season in Ohio. She was due to leave this week, so was anxious to spend time with you, however, you were incredibly busy as your next book was soon to be published. This evening you were due to attend a party for the book launch, but a few moments ago, as you were getting ready, Cathy refused to go. She cited the many parties at which she felt abandoned and ignored as a reason.

WHO ELSE IS THERE: Cathy.

WHO SHOULD YOU SING TO: Cathy.

Textual Analysis

The song begins in the middle of an argument, so it is important that you start the song with a high degree of intensity. With the conversation already unreasonable from both sides, your first objective is to make Cathy accept – in no uncertain terms – that you will be going to the party. This should be done in a harsh and sarcastic manner. Try playing actions such as: I denigrate, mock, humiliate and dismiss Cathy. As is sometimes the case in arguments with the one you love, in the song you flip very quickly between extremes of anger and a desire to comfort and protect. One such change occurs when you ask Cathy what her behaviour is really about. Your objective in this moment is: to find out the real reason for Cathy not wanting to attend the party. Here try playing actions such as: I implore, question, beseech and comfort Cathy. You suspect that the real problem is her disappointment with her own career, and you try to encourage her to share this with you.

When you get to the first chorus (that begins with the title lyric) your motives become entirely positive. Your objective is: to reassure Cathy about your feelings towards her. You want to convince her that you wouldn't be in this marriage if you didn't believe in her. In the second chorus you warm to this theme, and the choice of actions should reflect this. Try to charm, warm, reassure and comfort Cathy.

At the bridge, when you ask Cathy whether you get to be happy, there is a fundamental shift. Suddenly you are on the attack again. Your objective here is: to punish Cathy for her part in putting the relationship under strain. Another abrupt change comes soon after – when you tell Cathy you don't want her to be hurt. For a few lines your objective becomes: to comfort her, but this doesn't last long and your anger quickly gets the best of you once more. After you shout at Cathy, and tell her to listen to you, your objective becomes: to force Cathy to accept she is a failure as an actress. This is an incredibly cruel moment. After you have said the word 'win' the atmosphere in the room should be toxic.

You actually become very tender in the final chorus that follows, but now you are expressing regret and longing rather than actively seeking to salvage the relationship. Irrevocable damage has been done. In this section your objective is: to tell Cathy how much you loved her when you got married. You want to convince her that you really did believe in her back then. But this should feel like a moment of catharsis for you, a letting go of a love you once felt, rather than words of comfort for your wife. It is ultimately an act of selfishness.

KEY MOMENTS/TOP TIPS

1. Elements of this song are particularly aggressive and confrontational. For that reason it is strongly suggested you sing to an imaginary person located behind the audition table, rather than use someone on the panel as Cathy.

2. This is the argument that finally breaks the marriage. The things that are said in this room are so hurtful that there can be no going back from this point. For this to be credible, the harshest moments – such as when you tell Cathy that you can't fail in order to make her feel comfortable (which is the event of the song) – should be delivered with real anger and venom. They are fuelled by resentments that have been building for years.

3. Some of the flips in the song, from outright cruelty and anger, to attempts to be tender and comforting, are acute. This quite accurately reflects the tone of arguments that occur when a relationship is breaking down, and both great

love and tremendous pain are involved. To make these notable shifts feel authentic, it is useful to imagine how Cathy's behaviour prompts these changes. For example, if you try to comfort her and she then rejects you, or turns her back on you, this may help give you the impulse to suddenly become confrontational or aggressive.

4. A key moment in the lyric is near the end when you use the words 'hadn't believed' instead of 'didn't believe'. For the first time you talk in the past tense about your faith in Cathy's abilities. This reveals that, in the moment that you shouted at her, some fundamental doubts you had been feeling about Cathy became crystallised – and now the relationship is broken.

Vocal and Musical Analysis

WHO TO LISTEN TO: Jeremy Jordan on the film soundtrack (2015).

VOCAL RANGE: B♭2 to G5.

ORIGINAL KEY: F major.

ACCENT: General American.

STYLE OF MUSICAL: Contemporary musical (pop-based).

VOCAL SET-UP/MUSICAL TIPS

1. The beginning of the song should feel very conversational, so deliver this section in a Speech quality. It is appropriate to half-speak some words, to avoid extending the note-lengths and to give as much weight to the consonants as the vowels. The use of vibrato should also be minimal. This is clearly demonstrated in Jordan's exceptional vocal performance.

2. When you ask Cathy if she is disappointed about returning to Ohio, try raising your larynx, as this will help these lines feel much more gentle.

3. After the bitter opening, the first chorus is tender and romantic. To portray this change vocally add thyroid tilt and a little twang. In the second chorus, also work for a legato line in your phrasing.

4. During the bridge, the pitch rises above a normal Speech register, so you should now work in an Advanced-Speech quality. Add some torso anchoring and thyroid tilt to realise this position successfully.

5. The high point of the song vocally is the section that begins with you telling Cathy to listen to you. If you were to act these moments as spoken dialogue, you would be shouting. So don't be afraid to make ugly sounds in this part of the song. Again Jordan demonstrates this remarkably well on the suggested recording.

6. In the last chorus try raising your larynx and sing in a Cry position with a little twang added. This will help create a very vulnerable vocal choice.

Sheet Music

The correct sheet music for this song is available at www.musicnotes.com.

'If I Sing'
from *Closer Than Ever*

Music by David Shire, lyrics by Richard Maltby Jr.

Choose this song if: you are an accomplished actor who can connect to deeply emotive material and who is comfortable singing directly to the audition panel when required. The song sits within a comfortable baritone register.

Given Circumstances

Note: *Closer Than Ever* is a revue show, rather than a musical with a through-narrative. The given circumstances below, though derived from the lyric, are therefore meant as a suggestion, and could be altered to suit your needs.

WHO ARE YOU: David, a humble, sensitive, renowned rock-and-roll songwriter in his mid-thirties.

WHERE ARE YOU: A lecture hall in the Juilliard School, New York City, USA.

WHEN IS IT: 10.30 a.m., a Wednesday, October, present day.

WHAT HAS HAPPENED BEFORE: When you were growing up, you and your father were very close. He was an inspiration to you as a child, supporting and encouraging you in pursing your ambitions to be a musician. Some of your most vivid and happy memories were watching him play show tunes at the piano when you were a small child.

This early musical education that he gave you became formalised when you went on to study as a composer at the prestigious Juilliard School. Upon graduating, you forged a highly successful career writing pop and rock-and-roll songs for some of the greatest artists in the world.

Over the past five years your father, who is now in his mid-seventies, became increasingly frail. Eighteen months ago he was diagnosed with Alzheimer's. The disease progressed aggressively, causing him to rapidly lose his memory. Unable to look after himself, and with your mother no longer alive, he moved into a care home. Through a combination of arthritis in his fingers and dementia caused by the Alzheimer's, your father was no longer able to play the piano. You knew how this saddened him, so six months ago you composed him a song and visited the care home to play it to him. It was a moving event for you both.

You visited your father for the last time three months ago and his condition had deteriorated markedly. He was suffering from severe memory loss and could no longer recognise you at all. This was a great shock to you, as your busy work schedule meant you hadn't found the time to see him in the past few months. The next day your father died.

A few weeks ago an old professor who trained you at Juilliard, and who still teaches there to this day, invited you to speak to the freshman year as one of the most successful graduates of the institution. You arrived this morning and were led to a lecture hall full of eager young musicians. After a lot of other questions, one of the students has just asked: 'Why did you become a musician?'

WHO ELSE IS THERE: The freshman students at Juilliard.

WHO SHOULD YOU SING TO: To the freshman music students at points, and at others to your absent father.

Textual Analysis

In the first verse your opening lyrics are a response to the freshman's question about why you became a musician. During the introduction, in trying to formulate an answer, search your memory and remember watching your father play the piano when you were a child. Your objective in this verse is: to get the lecture hall to picture your father's piano-playing. You want them to understand how inspirational it was to you.

During the first chorus your focus shifts. Your mind drifts into your own thoughts and you begin to talk to your absent father. Your objective here is: to thank your father for the positive effect he has had on your music.

Having been lost in your own world, you then come back to reality, and in the second verse you recount the story of visiting the care home to the students. You explain how, although you could not find the right words to comfort him about the effects of his illness, you did manage to communicate how much you loved him through the music you played for him. Your objective in this section is: to get the students to understand what the visit meant to you and your father.

In the second chorus you once more try to convince your father of how much of an inspiration he was to you. This time you want him to understand that his influence was greater than the effect it had on you as a composer – the way he raised you fundamentally shaped you as a man.

The climax that occurs at the key change is the event of this song; you should strive for an emotional release at this point. It is the moment you finally voice all of the guilt that you have been feeling since your father died – guilt caused by the fact that you never told your father how important he was to you whilst he was still alive. Your objective at this point is: to apologise to your father for not being there for him in the weeks before his death. The event of the song is thus a catharsis. When you are able to say that your father will live on in you, you are in some measure coming to terms with his passing.

KEY MOMENTS/TOP TIPS

1. There is a single-line melody played in the right hand of the piano part at the start of the introduction. These opening bars should be cut and the pianist should begin from where the main accompaniment starts.

2. When you are addressing the music students (during the two verses) sing directly to the panel as if they are the freshmen in the lecture hall. In the remainder of the song, when you are talking to your father, address a point behind the table to show that you are talking to someone who is not present.

3. In the bar that precedes each chorus there are a few high notes in the piano accompaniment. Imagine these are fragments of the melody you played for your father at the care home. At these moments, recall that memory and the pleasure it gave to you both.

4. In the second verse, immediately after you have said that your father can no longer play, there is a momentary break in the piano accompaniment. Try exploring in this moment of silence a connection to the death of your father.

Vocal and Musical Analysis

WHO TO LISTEN TO: Richard Muenz on the original Off-Broadway cast recording (1990).

VOCAL RANGE: A2 to F4.

ORIGINAL KEY: A major.

ACCENT: General American.

STYLE OF MUSICAL: Contemporary musical (pop-based).

VOCAL SET-UP/MUSICAL TIPS

1. The verses of the song should feel very conversational indeed. Deliver them in a Speech quality. It is appropriate to half-speak some words, to avoid extending the note-lengths and to give as much weight to the consonants as the vowels. The use of vibrato should be minimal.

2. The first two choruses require a completely different vocal set-up. This helps clarify that you are now talking to your

dead father and that your mood is more sombre and reflective. Add a great deal of thyroid tilt and thin your vocal folds to make the sound much quieter and sweeter. Make your phrasing more legato and sustained.

3. In choruses one and two there is a crescendo that begins in the middle of the chorus and a decrescendo that happens on the last line. Achieve these dynamics by either removing, or introducing, thyroid tilt as applicable.

4. In the third chorus, after the key change, the song should become very passionate and emotive vocally. To achieve the necessary volume you should remain in a Speech quality, but add some torso anchoring and a little thyroid tilt to achieve the sound of someone singing with great passion and emotion.

5. To reflect the importance of the discovery you make on the very last line, try making a sudden change in your vocal set-up. Lift the larynx, thin your vocal folds and add thyroid tilt to make the delivery very contemplative and vulnerable.

Sheet Music

The correct sheet music for this song is available at www.onlinesheetmusic.com.

'It's Hard to Speak My Heart' from *Parade*

Music and lyrics by Jason Robert Brown

Choose this song if: you enjoy songs with substantial, detailed acting content, and suit playing introverted, conflicted and intellectual characters.

Given Circumstances

Note: Although *Parade* is based is based on the real-life trial of Leo Frank, many of the facts in the case were much contested and so the given circumstances of the musical outlined below contain events that are either fictional, or could be disputed.

WHO ARE YOU: Leo Frank, a twenty-nine-year-old, Jewish, Brooklyn-born manager of a pencil factory in Atlanta, Georgia, USA. You are often shy, defensive, sarcastic and cold. You can think yourself superior to others, though in this moment your pride has been stripped away by your present circumstances. For perhaps the first time you are learning to be emotionally honest.

WHERE ARE YOU: In the dock of the Fulton County Courthouse.

WHEN IS IT: Afternoon, August 1913 (historically the trial began on 28th July, and Leo's statement would have been towards the end of the trial, just before the jury retired to make their decision). It is a hot time of the year in this part of the world.

WHAT HAS HAPPENED BEFORE: In May you were falsely accused and indicted for the rape and murder of thirteen-year-old Mary Phagan, a junior employee at the pencil factory. Unbeknown to you, the local prosecutor, Hugh Dorsey, had been put under pressure from the state governor, John Slaton, to secure a conviction. Unwilling to pursue the predictable course in this part of America during the period, and 'convict another negro', he decided to prosecute you instead.

In the run-up to the trial, a great degree of anti-Semitism emerged in the attitude of both the press and the public towards you. False stories about you having been a paedophile were published. This prejudice towards you was amplified as you were portrayed as a rich and arrogant 'Yankee' (someone from one of the northern states of the USA). In Georgia, which was part of the defeated Confederacy in the American Civil War a generation before, there was still a lot of anger towards people from the victorious north, particularly those seen as rich capitalists.

During the trial, you were shocked because witness after witness bore false testimony against you (they had all been coached by Dorsey). Frankie Epps, a friend of Mary, testified that she had told him that you used to leer at her in a sexual manner, making her feel uncomfortable. Three other factory girls also testified that you made them feel uneasy with similar behaviour. Your maid, Minnie McKnight, then exaggerated the marital problems between yourself and your wife Lucille, and stated that you behaved strangely around the time of the murder. All of this (false) circumstantial evidence was brought into sharp focus when Jim Conley, a janitor at the pencil factory, testified that he was an accomplice to the murder, and that you paid him one hundred dollars to help dispose of the body. (In fact, Dorsey had blackmailed Conley into giving this false testimony, by threatening to convict him as he was an escaped convict.) With all of the evidence pointing towards a guilty verdict, Judge Roan has just asked your lawyer, Luther Rosser, if you wish to give a statement and he has declined. Upon hearing this, you contradicted him and said that you would indeed like to speak to the court.

WHO ELSE IS THERE: The courtroom is full and is incredibly hostile towards you, though your statement is received in silence. Lucille is present, as are some of those who testified against you (though most likely not Conley).

WHO SHOULD YOU SING TO: You are appealing directly to the jury, as they are the only people who now have the power to save your life.

Textual Analysis

This is the first time you have ever spoken in public, and as a shy man you find this very difficult indeed. In the first verse your objective is: to get the jury to understand how hard you find it to express your emotions. Showing more self-awareness than you have in the past, you acknowledge that this reticence to open up might make you seem hard and cold.

You sense that these initial pleas for empathy are having no impact, so in the second verse your arguments become much more direct. You challenge some of the key assumptions of the court: you say that you barely knew the victim, you accuse the witnesses of fabricating evidence, and promise that you never touched Mary. Your objective here is: to convince the jury that that the witnesses bore false testimony against you. To reflect your impassioned argument, your choice of actions should become more forthright, so you might try to: awaken, implore, shake, provoke and antagonise the jury.

After protesting that every single one of the witnesses is lying, you hear how incredible that argument sounds. So you then appeal in the only way that remains open to you: you ask the jury to look at you and to see, in the face of all this evidence, that you are, in fact, telling the truth. Having uncharacteristically shown your vulnerability, by the end of your statement you admit openly that you are afraid.

CONTEMPORARY BALLADS

KEY MOMENTS/TOP TIPS

1. It is a good suggestion to start and end your performance sitting on a chair. Although you will deliver the entire lyric standing up, getting to your feet during the introduction, and sitting down again once you have finished, helps portray that Leo is standing up to address the court. This is a good acting opportunity for you to show how hard he finds it to make this statement.

2. The key to the performance of this song lies in the title. Because Leo is so emotionally honest in the song, it is easy

to fall into the trap of portraying him as a great orator, when actually, as the lyric suggests, this public display of intimacy is completely out of character. When we see Leo battling through his shyness to try and save his life, then the song really begins to work.

3. It is mentioned in the script that Leo has the habit of wringing his hands in a nervous manner. The use of this repetitive gesture can be useful at the beginning of the song to highlight his nervousness.

4. The accompaniment changes significantly when Leo states that he never touched Mary – from being very still and sustained there is suddenly much more movement in the piano. This reflects a change in Leo's inner tempo and is the event of the song. Having been very inhibited up to this point, he realises his words are having no effect. So on this change of music Leo decides he must be brave as this is his last chance. At this point you may benefit from becoming physically freer and playing stronger, more desperate actions. The fact that the music returns to the stiller accompaniment at the end suggests that, after this emotional outburst, Leo somewhat goes back into his shell.

5. If there is a panel of several people in the audition, then it is very helpful to address them as if they are the jury.

Vocal and Musical Analysis

WHO TO LISTEN TO: Bertie Carvel on the Donmar Warehouse revival cast recording (2007).

VOCAL RANGE: B2 to E4.

ORIGINAL KEY: E major.

ACCENT: Southern American.

STYLE OF MUSICAL: Contemporary musical (pop-based).

VOCAL SET-UP/MUSICAL TIPS

1. The opening verse should be delivered in a quiet Cry quality to help portray Leo's vulnerability at this point. Bear in mind that you want the sound to be as colloquial as possible, so mix all three vocal onsets (aspirate, simultaneous and glottal) to give the singing a conversational feel.

2. The composer indicates that the words 'say' and 'said' that are sung on a high E should be delivered in a Falsetto quality. This again helps to portray vulnerability. If you find this a difficult position to flip into, alternatively you can remain in Cry for these moments.

3. For the second verse and during the bridge, when Leo becomes more direct and desperate, try singing in a Speech quality.

4. The high note on the word 'hand' should be the loudest of the song. To achieve this, gradually add some torso anchoring during the phrase that precedes this moment.

5. The last couple of lines should be the most quiet and vulnerable of the entire song. To realise this, after the musical climax that was previously mentioned, gradually release your torso anchoring, then introduce some thyroid tilt and then finally lift the larynx. This will allow you to decrescendo so that you finish singing very quietly and sweetly.

Sheet Music

The correct sheet music for this song is available at www.musicnotes.com.

CONTEMPORARY BALLADS

'Johanna'
from *Sweeney Todd*

Music and lyrics by Stephen Sondheim

Choose this song if: you are baritone with a classical, legit voice. This song suits actors who can play the naive, idealistic romantic lead. It has a relatively narrow vocal range, so can also work for actors who sing.

Given Circumstances

WHO ARE YOU: Anthony Hope, a cheerful, optimistic young sailor who is first mate of a ship called *The Bountiful*.

WHERE ARE YOU: In Victorian London, on the street outside Judge Turpin's house on Kearney's Lane. You are beneath the window of the bedroom of his ward, Johanna.

WHEN IS IT: 11.00 a.m., a bright spring morning, 1846.

WHAT HAS HAPPENED BEFORE: Early this morning you arrived back in London after many months at sea. At the docks you said farewell to a man known as Sweeney Todd (whose real name is Benjamin Barker). You had befriended Todd onboard having saved him from drowning at sea when you discovered him floating on a raft. As you disembarked, the secretive Todd revealed a fragment of his tragic past: that decades ago he used to be a barber, and that another man desired his wife, Lucy. After being told these few, tantalising facts, you asked Todd to tell you more of his story, but he refused. What Todd didn't tell you was that the other man who coveted Lucy was Judge Turpin. Years ago the Judge had Todd transported to Australia so he could take Lucy for his own. With Todd gone, the Judge raped the unfortunate Lucy and took Todd's one-year-old daughter, Johanna, as his ward. Lucy – who afterwards became half-mad, having drunk poison – was left to wander the streets as an unidentifiable beggar woman.

You have been strolling the streets of London for the past couple of hours. A few minutes ago you happened upon a bird-seller who was standing in the street with a cage full of birds. He was showing them to a strange but striking young woman in the first-floor window of the house nearby. The woman, Johanna, was fascinated by the captive birds. You were immediately struck by her beauty and longed for her to look down at you. For a moment your eyes met – there was a connection between you both – and then the girl disappeared inside.

After Johanna had retired from the window, the beggar woman (whom you don't know to be Lucy) appeared from behind a nearby pile of rubbish. You asked her if she knew about the girl at the window. She told you that the girl's name was Johanna and that this was the house of her guardian, Judge Turpin. After warning you not to trespass there, she tried to make a grotesque sexual advance on you, before you chased her away.

After Lucy had gone, you awoke the bird-seller who had fallen asleep on a nearby bench. You bought one of his caged birds, the one that sang the sweetest. After he'd left, Johanna returned to the window. You held up the cage to indicate it was a gift for her. Seeing this she came down to the street to accept the gift. In the musical the first verse is then sung at this stage (see point 1 below). You were then interrupted by the Beadle and an angry Judge Turpin. Despite protesting your noble intentions, the Judge warned you that if you ever came near the house again it would cost you your life. The Beadle threatened you with a truncheon before wringing the bird's neck. The pair of men then escorted Johanna into the house, leaving you alone on the pavement.

WHO ELSE IS THERE: You are alone.

WHO SHOULD YOU SING TO: Johanna.

Textual Analysis

Note: In the musical, the verses of the song are interspersed with spoken dialogue. This structure is not ideal for an audition, and in the suggested sheet music this dialogue is cut. You should therefore perform the song as though all of the described given circumstances have occurred, i.e. you have already spoken to Johanna in the street, the argument with the Judge and the Beadle has taken place, and Johanna has been returned to her private prison and is back sitting at the window.

In the first couple of lines your objective is: to convince Johanna that you empathise with her. You want her to know that you understand how she must feel being imprisoned and alone. You then tell her about your experience of meeting her in the street. Your objective at this point is: to convince Johanna that you thought you were dreaming, but are overjoyed that you were not. When you first talk about stealing Johanna, it is the event in the song: at this point you decide that you will help her escape from that prison. Your objective here is: to assure Johanna that you will be successful in freeing her.

In the next unit you begin to address the absent Judge and Beadle. Your objective now becomes: to defy their authority. In your daring attitude towards them you display the fearlessness of youth. An important, and somewhat unsettling, moment then follows when you imagine being buried in Johanna's yellow hair. The moment should be both intimate and sexual. Your objective here is: to indulge your fantasy of being intimate with Johanna.

In the second verse you return to your opening objective. You want to convince Johanna that you understand her. You then make a vow that one day you will free her, and until then you will be thinking of her. Your objective in this final section is: to promise Johanna that you will return.

KEY MOMENTS/TOP TIPS

1. As Johanna is in her bedroom, a good way to stage the song is to deliver the lyric to an imaginary first-floor window situated above the panel's heads. As discussed, in the musical the first verse is sung to Johanna, and the second to her window after she has gone. It is not feasible or desirable to try make this clear in audition, so deliver the entire song to the window, as if Johanna is visible.

2. At this time London was the largest and greatest city in the world. Having returned to the metropolis after a long voyage, Anthony is full of excitement, and – as a young man – is likely full of pent-up sexual desire. Use this idea to help fuel his adventurous demeanour.

3. There is a popularly held theory about the characters in *Sweeney Todd* that they are all in some way insane. In this song, explore the idea that Anthony's feelings towards Johanna border on the obsessive.

4. After this scene Anthony is inspired to action and sets off to find Todd to tell him about Johanna. To portray this sense of urgency, when you have finished singing, during the last few bars of the music, try running off to the back corner of the room, as if heading off to Fleet Street.

Vocal and Musical Analysis

WHO TO LISTEN TO: Victor Garber on the original Broadway cast recording (1979).

VOCAL RANGE: C3 to Eb4.

ORIGINAL KEY: Eb major.

ACCENT: Anthony is most usually played with Received Pronunciation though, as he is a sailor, he could easily be of a lower class – which would mean in this period that a wide variety of regional British accents could be appropriate.

STYLE OF MUSICAL: Contemporary musical (legit-based).

VOCAL SET-UP/MUSICAL TIPS

1. *Sweeney Todd* is performed in both opera houses and in musical theatre venues, and is often seen as being a piece that stylistically crosses both art forms. When performing this song you therefore want to lean towards an operatic sound. To achieve this, ensure you lower your larynx, use a great deal of thyroid tilt and anchor your torso whenever you are not in a Sob quality.

2. The first few lines should be intensely quiet and sweet, but still with a lowered laryngeal position. So try delivering this section in a Sob quality, making consistent use of simultaneous onsets.

3. When you reach the third line, and you talk about waking, you should sing slightly louder. Thicken your vocal folds at this point to achieve a form of Speech quality, but slightly modified to include a lowered larynx, rather than a neutral laryngeal position, and some torso anchoring.

4. The first time you sing the words 'I'll steal you' it should be the loudest moment of the song so far. Remove some more thyroid tilt as you approach this line to effect a crescendo and anchor your torso to a greater degree. When you repeat the lyric, make your sound much quieter by thinning your vocal folds and returning to a Sob quality.

5. When you begin to challenge the Judge and Beadle, and taunt them about how useless hiding behind walls will be, you should return to the set-up suggested in point 2: a modified Speech quality with a lowered larynx.

6. The second time you sing 'I feel you' it should be loud and triumphant. Use a great deal of torso anchoring and don't be afraid to use some glottal onsets to achieve a thick vocal fold.

7. When you sing that one day you will steal Johanna, you should flip suddenly back into a Sob position, to reflect the sudden shift to a quiet dynamic (marked '*mp*' or *mezzo-piano* – medium quiet – on the music). There is then a

gradual crescendo to the end of the song, so slowly remove your thyroid tilt, thicken your vocal folds, and reintroduce your torso anchoring.

8. All of the above vocal shifts are suggested by Sondheim's detailed dynamic markings, so take careful notice of when he indicates on the music that you should become louder or softer.

Sheet Music

The correct sheet music for this song is available at www.musicnotes.com.

'Blackrock (What Would You Say to Your Son?)' from *The Hired Man*

Music and lyrics by Howard Goodall

Choose this song if: you have baritone voice and like songs with an underlying political context. You may particularly want to choose this song if you are a working-class actor-singer with a native Northern accent.

Given Circumstances

WHO ARE YOU: John Tallentire, a young father in his mid- to late thirties. Formerly you were a hired farmhand, but now you are a coal miner.

WHERE ARE YOU: In the kitchen of your family home, a small miner's cottage in Whitehaven, Cumbria, England.

WHEN IS IT: 6.00 p.m., dinnertime, early summer, 1914.

WHAT HAS HAPPENED BEFORE: You married your wife, Emily, in 1898 in the rural village of Crossbridge. At this time you worked as a hired farmhand. Although you loved this work, it was hard to find regular employment and earn a decent living. Shortly after the wedding you managed to find a job working on the farm of a landowner named Mr Pennington.

Soon afterwards Emily became pregnant with your first child, a daughter, May. But despite the birth, she quickly became dissatisfied with married life. You were always working long hours and she felt trapped by the narrowness of village life.

One day you were encouraged to take a fox-hunting trip by your brother, Isaac, and decided to stay away overnight. In this moment, Emily yielded to a temptation she had been feeling for some time and slept with Jackson, the handsome son of Pennington.

After this, the relationship between you and your wife began
to deteriorate. You sensed the growing distance, though you
didn't know about the affair. Even though her feelings for
Jackson remained strong, Emily refused his requests to
abandon the marriage. Losing patience, Jackson decided to
join the army and leave for India. Emily was distraught and
begged him not to go. In the midst of this commotion you
discovered the truth about the affair and beat Jackson up in a
fight outside of the local pub. After this, Jackson left.

It is now sixteen years later and you and Emily have remained
together. You are now living in the town of Whitehaven with
May and her younger brother, your son, Harry, who is
thirteen. Having left farm work, you took a job in the local pit.
This work is incredibly dangerous and five hundred men died
recently in a fire.

You have just had dinner with the whole family. Whilst
discussing the fact that Emily and May both now have jobs,
which you don't approve of, you complained to your wife that
the family home was now more like a factory. Following this
conversation, Emily revealed she had arranged for Harry to
start work with Mr Forrester at the stables, because she didn't
want him to work down the pit like his father. She said that
she thought you should never have given up your career as a
farm labourer (a sentiment you are beginning to agree with, as
at the end of the story you eventually return to working on
the land).

At the table, Harry has just argued that he didn't want to
work with horses, that he preferred to work down the pit with
his friends and relatives. He resented that the decision had
been made for him. You tried to explain to him about the
terrible working conditions in the pit: lying on your back in a
two-foot seam with the danger of the rock collapsing from
above as the mine runs under the sea. But Harry can only see
the positive side of being miner, the better wages and the
promise of improved working conditions after the fire. He has
just revealed that he had been to see Mr Stephens, a manager
at the pit, that very afternoon. Stephens had told Harry he

could start work on Monday. You had anticipated this, but Emily, who had not, responded by warning Harry that you would be telling Mr Stephens that this would not happen. Harry has just turned to you and said: 'You wouldn't do that, would you, Dad?'

WHO ELSE IS THERE: In the musical the rest of the cast would freeze at this point and they would not be able to hear you – so for the purposes of audition you should behave as if you are alone.

WHO SHOULD YOU SING TO: This song is written to be delivered in direct address, i.e. it is sung to the audience. So in audition you should deliver it entirely to the panel.

Textual Analysis

You start the song having been put in a very difficult situation by Harry – he is asking you to choose between what Emily has decreed and his own wishes. This choice is to be made in front of them both, so the stakes are high and the need for an answer is pressing. The song is epic, rather than realistic – so all of this inner conflict is shared with the audience. Your objective in the first verse is: to get the audience to advise you. You want them to tell you what you should you say to Harry.

In the second verse, rather than asking for advice, you are going on the attack with your argument. Your objective at this point is: to get the audience to comprehend the awful consequences of Harry becoming a miner. You want them to understand the responsibility involved in such a decision.

The repetition of the word 'under' is very important. In this moment you are reliving some of your worst experiences as a miner. You are venting the frustration and fear you feel on a daily basis, a feeling that you never want Harry to endure. Your objective in the first chorus thus becomes: to make the panel take responsibility for putting Harry in a situation that would 'break him'. This works especially well if you imagine the panel are the mine-owners at this point (see point 2 below). During this argument the panel should begin to understand that working in the mines has broken you as a man.

From here to the end of the song your objective remains unchanged, until the very final line: you want the panel to decide if they would make this terrible choice. In this closing section be careful that the song doesn't become an angry rant. Find some positive choices to keep the audience engaged. Try using irony, rather than aggression, to make your point.

On the last line, when John makes his final decision (see point 4 below) – which is the event of the song – try working for complete stillness, as this will help make this conclusive moment very effective after the outburst of the two choruses.

KEY MOMENTS/TOP TIPS

1. As the song is sung in direct address, it requires a great deal of eye contact with the panel. Try to deliver a whole thought (a sentence) to a single member of the panel, before changing your focus to another person.

2. The song has a political message underpinning it: it asks the audiences to reflect on the appalling conditions of workers under the Edwardian capitalist system. The delivery can therefore be fuelled by a righteous anger. Try to make the panel feel guilty about the situation, almost imagining they are the capitalist mine-owners responsible for the miners' situation.

3. As the song is political, the actions played on the panel can be strong and direct. Try playing to provoke, shake, exasperate, bait, hector, antagonise, and needle them.

4. The song begins and ends with the same lyric, the same question. To show a development in the narrative we should see through your performance that John has made his decision. The script is ambiguous at this point, so choose whether he decides to refuse Harry's request – or to let his son make his own decision.

CONTEMPORARY UP-TEMPO

Vocal and Musical Analysis

WHO TO LISTEN TO: Paul Clarkson on the London concert recording (1992).

VOCAL RANGE: A2 to F♯4.

ORIGINAL KEY: B minor.

ACCENT: Ideally you should work for a Cumbrian accent, though this song can be delivered in most Northern accents.

STYLE OF MUSICAL: Contemporary musical (pop-based).

VOCAL SET-UP/MUSICAL TIPS

1. The dialect is an important feature of the delivery of this song. When you sing any song in an accent, you need to think of the dialect being even stronger than when you speak in that accent, as elements of the dialect are softened when singing. To make the accent apparent, don't lift the middle of the tongue towards the molars, let the tongue be in a neutral position instead, and place the vowels as you would do when speaking in a heavy version of that dialect.

2. Try the first verse of the song in a breathy Speech quality (Speech with an aspirate onset). This can help give a sense that John is struggling internally with how best to advise Harry.

3. In the second verse, lose the aspirate onset and move into a normal Speech quality. This will make your sound louder, and the vocal development will reflect John's growing passion and frustration.

4. When you get to the chorus, you are moving into an Advanced-Speech set-up, as the song is now quite high. To make this safe and healthy, introduce some torso anchoring and a little thyroid tilt on the higher notes.

5. For the final question of the song, finish in a Cry quality, with a really high larynx and a perfect simultaneous onset to give the ending an intense thoughtfulness.

Sheet Music

The correct sheet music for this song is available at
www.scribd.com.

'Everybody Says Don't'
from *Anyone Can Whistle*

Music and lyrics by Stephen Sondheim

Choose this song if: you have a strong baritone voice and like to play upbeat, inspirational and heroic characters. As this song sits comfortably in a Speech register, it can work well for actors who sing.

Given Circumstances

WHO ARE YOU: J. Bowden Hapgood, an idealist who was once a Professor of Statistical Philosophy, but who is now masquerading as a medical doctor.

WHERE ARE YOU: A hotel room in a bankrupt, imaginary American town.

WHEN IS IT: 11.45 a.m., spring, an undefined historical period but with some of the revolutionary ideals of the 1960s.

WHAT HAS HAPPENED BEFORE: The town has recently been suffering from a period of severe economic depression. As a result, its starving, miserable inhabitants had grown resentful of the Mayoress, Cora Hoover Hooper, who seemed to be the only person with any money. (Secretly she is the owner of Dr Detmold's Sanitarium for the Socially Pressured, better known to the townsfolk as 'The Cookie Jar'.) Depressed by her unpopularity in the town, Hooper decided to make a pilgrimage to a local landmark – a huge rock – on the edge of town. On her arrival, a local child, Baby Joan Schroeder, licked the rock, which instantly began to pour forth water. Mayoress Hooper instantly declared it to be a miraculous spring; a latter-day Lourdes. Claiming the spring as her own, she declared that for a small fee anyone could taste its waters – and then they would be the recipient of a miracle. Hooper was delighted that the advent of 'Miracle Rock' brought her a newfound popularity in the town, even though she soon found out the spring was actually a fake.

Hearing of the events at Miracle Rock, Nurse Fay Apple, who worked at The Cookie Jar, decided to take her patients (the 'Cookies') to visit, not because she believed in the miracle – she didn't – but because she felt they should be afforded the same opportunity as everyone else. Chaos ensued at the shrine when the Cookies arrived, as they became mixed up with the other pilgrims, with no one being able to tell the difference. The Mayoress's subordinate, Comptroller Schub, became worried that if the Cookies tasted the water – and were not cured – it would be discovered that the miracle is a fake. But despite his insistence, Apple refused to help identify the Cookies.

Shortly afterwards you arrived in the town, asking for directions to The Cookie Jar. The town authorities mistook you as Dr Detmold's new assistant, when, in fact, you were an escaped Cookie yourself. You didn't dissuade them of their error. When Hooper and Schub then appealed to you to separate your supposed patients from the other pilgrims, you confounded matters further by mixing the two groups so they became even more indistinguishable. By breaking the authority of the Mayoress you became a hero in the town, amongst Cookies and pilgrims alike.

In the chaos that followed, Apple disguised herself as 'Ze Lady from Lourdes': a fictional investigator from the famous French shrine on a mission to discover whether this new miracle was true. When you tried to seduce this gorgeous redhead, Apple revealed her true identity. She told you she had been disguising herself because she was concealing medical records from the Mayoress, records that would reveal the true identities of the Cookies. More importantly, she confessed that she felt that only by wearing a costume could she reveal her true inner feelings. With the town authorities plotting against you both, you have just divulged that you are a Cookie yourself, and encouraged Apple to let her real personality out and free herself of her responsibilities – by tearing up the records for The Cookie Jar.

CONTEMPORARY UP-TEMPO

WHO ELSE IS THERE: Nurse Fay Apple.

WHO SHOULD YOU SING TO: Nurse Fay Apple.

Textual Analysis

With a sense of revolution and rebellion in the air, your opening objective during the first verse is: to mock those in society who try to make you obey the rules. In this section you can play choices such as: to mimic, deride, parody, ridicule, satirise and dismiss both the rule-makers and rule-followers of the world. When you get to the first chorus your objective becomes more positive and uplifting. You aim is: to inspire Apple to be revolutionary. You want her to be brave and take risks, even if that might mean failure. With Apple starting to be persuaded, when you move into the second verse, your objective evolves. You do not simply mock the rule-followers, instead you seek to convince Apple that when people warn her not to break the rules, that is a sign that she is actually following the correct course.

Sensing that you are winning the argument, in the bridge your objective is: to encourage Nurse Apple to take one small step towards rebellion. You try to convince her that if she is able make a minor transgression to start with, then next time she can be truly revolutionary. In the next verse (that follows the word 'all') your objective is similar to the opening section: to ridicule those who throw up rules and barriers. You do this in order to empower Apple. Finally, from the second chorus onwards until the end of the song, your words are a rallying call to action: you want to convince Apple that if she can be brave enough to act, then she is capable of miracles.

KEY MOMENTS/TOP TIPS

1. Hapgood is an anarchic character and throughout the song is encouraging disorder. You can therefore be physically playful and anarchic. Don't hold back from making unusual and daring choices in the space.

2. The driving rhythm of the music is suggestive of Hapgood's quick internal tempo. Explore using fast, dynamic physical gestures.

3. If you were performing this song within the context of the show, your performance would be greatly influenced by the behaviour of the actress playing Nurse Fay Apple. You would respond to whether she was being changed by your attempts to lead her to revolution. In audition this is clearly not possible, so you can therefore approach the task in two ways. During the performance you can picture Apple's responses in your imagination – see her doubt you, turn away, begin to smile, or leap to her feet. Alternatively you can sing in direct address and try to inspire the panel to action. Of course, those auditioning you will not leap up in revolution! But that inactivity – their lack of response – can be incredibly useful to you as an actor. You can use it to prompt your actions, as it will make you try even harder to achieve your objectives.

Vocal and Musical Analysis

WHO TO LISTEN TO: Harry Guardino on the original Broadway cast recording (1964).

VOCAL RANGE: G2 to E4.

ORIGINAL KEY: C major.

ACCENT: General American.

STYLE OF MUSICAL: Book musical.

VOCAL SET–UP/MUSICAL TIPS

1. As a patter song, it is a challenge to make the lyrics clear. The majority of this song should therefore be delivered in a Speech quality. By singing in a Speech position, and not tilting the thyroid, it helps the panel to understand the lyric. You can also improve clarity by making the notes a

little bit staccato and by ensuring you use clear, well-articulated consonants.

2. In the first chorus – each time you sing the phrases that contain the words 'I say' – your singing should be legato. Use simultaneous onsets at this point and think of linking one vowel to the next.

3. When you reach the bridge (when you sing about making ripples) you should start in an intensely quiet Cry position, with lots of thyroid tilt and a lifted larynx. After the word 'brave' gradually release your thyroid cartilage from a tilted to a horizontal position, and lower your larynx to a neutral position to effect a crescendo – so that you have arrived in a definite Speech quality by the word 'wave'.

4. Stay in a Speech position after the word 'all' until the end of song. During the second half of the song you can afford to use more glottal onsets to achieve greater emphasis and keep your vocal folds thick. For example, this time you can glottal the word 'I' in the 'I say' phrases, as this will make them louder and stronger than the first time around.

5. In the final few lyrics, when you sing about miracles, make the phrases more legato.

6. The final note is not a belt, as it is too low a pitch for this set-up. Instead, it should be delivered in a modified Speech quality: add some torso anchoring and raise the sides of the tongue so they are touching your molars.

Sheet Music

The correct sheet music for this song is available at www.musicnotes.com.

'Giants in the Sky'
from *Into the Woods*

Music and lyrics by Stephen Sondheim

Choose this song if: you are an actor who is able to deliver songs with complex thoughts, and enjoy portraying playful, vibrant and exuberant roles.

Given Circumstances

WHO ARE YOU: Jack, a simple, naive, fourteen-year-old peasant boy. Growing up in a small village, you have lived a sheltered life, with only your mother and your best friend – Milky White, the cow – for company.

WHERE ARE YOU: In a clearing in the woods. The woods are a magical and mysterious place. Its trees are perhaps gnarled and strange, like you might see in a fantasy film by Hollywood director Tim Burton.

WHEN IS IT: 7.30 a.m., an autumn morning. (As *Into the Woods* is set in a fairytale kingdom, establishing a year in which the piece is set is both problematic and unnecessary. Because of the feudal nature of the social hierarchy, it is sensible to assume that the story is set in a world with similarities to the European Middle Ages.)

WHAT HAS HAPPENED BEFORE: Yesterday morning your mother told you that, as you were both destitute, you must go to market and sell Milky White. She told you to accept no less than five pounds as a price. You were reluctant, but set off as instructed through the woods.

Whilst in the forest you encountered a strange fellow known as the Mysterious Man (who is the absent father of the village Baker), who whimsically suggested that you would be lucky to exchange the cow for a sack of beans. Heading further into the wood you then became lost. Shortly afterwards you encountered the Baker and his wife, who tried to convince you to sell Milky White to them. Unbeknown to you, they were desperate for a white cow because it was one of the ingredients they needed for a potion. This potion would lift the spell of infertility that their next-door neighbour – the Witch – had placed on their house, and allow them to have the child they craved. Without the money to pay you, the Baker and his wife convinced you to part with the cow in exchange for five magic beans. Reluctantly you agreed, after the Baker vaguely promised that you would be able to buy back the cow one day if you had enough money.

When you returned home that afternoon you presented the prized beans to your mother. Furious with you for not returning with any money, she threw them into the garden.

That night, on the stroke of midnight, the magic beans grew into a mighty beanstalk that rose high up into the clouds. Discovering the beanstalk outside your bedroom window, you decided to climb it all the way up into the sky. At the top of the beanstalk you discovered a kingdom amongst the clouds. Filled with excitement, and some trepidation, you began to explore this new world and came across a giant's castle. Venturing inside the castle you came across a female giant who, against all your expectations, was very kind to you. Treating you like her own, she fed you, tucked you up in bed, and hugged you to her breast. When her husband returned home it was a very different matter – he wanted to eat you for lunch. Terrified, you grabbed as much gold as you could from the wealthy giants and escaped down the beanstalk.

When you arrived back home early this morning your mother was delighted, not only because you had returned with untold riches, but because she had feared for your life. Not trusting you with the gold, she took most of it from you for safekeeping, but allowed you to have five gold pieces to buy back Milky White from the Baker. You set off into the woods to find the Baker. Still full of adrenaline from your adventure, you have just decided to tell the audience of your experiences.

WHO ELSE IS THERE: You are alone. (In the musical the Baker is asleep on the floor, but this is neither useful nor relevant in an audition scenario.)

WHO SHOULD YOU SING TO: The audience (in this case, the panel).

Textual Analysis

When you first talk to the audience you are bursting with excitement and your objective is simple: to convince a skeptical audience that giants actually exist. The gap between the first and second line is important here. Imagine that when you first tell the audience this news that their reaction is one of disbelief. This will then give you the impulse to try and convince them further.

In the two-bar instrumental that precede the first verse you decide that, if the audience are going to understand you fully, you will need to go back to the beginning of the story. Your objective in the verse therefore becomes: to get the audience to understand how small you feel when you look down on the world from a great height. In the second half of the verse you then want them to appreciate how liberating it is to be free to do what you want. You are, of course, speaking from experience, as this is exactly how you felt when you arrived in the kingdom of the giants.

In the first chorus you share the experiences you had with the female giant. Your objective is: to impress the audience with your exploits – particularly that you got near to her giant breasts. You are like a teenager showing off about a first sexual conquest. In the second verse you recount the story of the arrival of the male giant. Your objective at this point is: to terrify the audience with your experiences. You do this in order to impress them with your bravery and to get them to empathise with your fears.

The key discoveries that you make during the song occur in the second chorus when you describe seeing your mother and your house again whilst climbing back down the beanstalk. At this point you discover a universal truth that is expressed in many great stories: that when a hero returns home from an adventure they are changed forever. This is the event of the song. Your objective in this section is: to make sense of your escapade. You want to understand how that experience has altered your relationship to the world you grew up in. What is fun about the way Sondheim structures the song is that, after you've made this momentous discovery, because you are just a teenager, you immediately forget it and return in the last few lines to an objective that is much more important to you right now: to boast about meeting a giant.

KEY MOMENTS/TOP TIPS

1. When working in direct address it can be helpful to make a decision about who the audience represents for the character. Jack is showing off about his adventures in the castle, so it is useful to imagine that the audience/panel are other teenage boys that he can boast to about his newfound knowledge and riches.

2. The accompaniment of this song tells you a great deal about Jack's changes of internal rhythm. For example, in the verses the busy piano part reflects Jack's excitement, whereas the lyrical verses reveal something about his sense of awe. Spend some time listening to a recording of accompaniment, which is available online. It will help you uncover the shifts and changes in Jack's mood.

3. The song is a metaphor for sexual awakening. Jack's experience with the giant's wife – being hugged to her giant breast – means that he is not a boy any more, he has taken the first steps towards being a man. He enjoys bragging about these experiences to his audience of imagined teenage boys.

4. You see many performances of this song that only depict an excitable Jack. It is worth remembering that he has had a near-death experience, and although he is exhilarated to

have escaped with the gold, he also felt very frightened
and alone.

5. The songs in *Into the Woods* are full of accented chords.
Sondheim uses these musical stabs to emphasise moments
where the characters have moments of realisation. Such
chords appear in this song after the words 'door', 'explore',
'before' and the phrase 'after the sky'. Explore these chords
as moments when Jack has epiphanies, perhaps marking
them with the a moment of stillness or physical
punctuation.

Vocal and Musical Analysis

WHO TO LISTEN TO: Ben Stott in the Regent's Park Open Air
Theatre production (2010).

VOCAL RANGE: C3 to F♯4.

ORIGINAL KEY: A♭ major.

ACCENT: When performed in the UK, *Into the Woods* is usually
delivered with British accents. As Jack is from a village in the
countryside, it makes sense to use a regional, rural accent, so
Yorkshire, Lancashire, West Country, Irish, Welsh and
Scottish accents work well. If your native accent is a rural one,
then I would advise you to use your own voice when singing
this song – but try turning up the strength a little. This is
generally good practice when singing to ensure the choice is
clearly perceived by the audience. Accents that stereotypically
denote upper class (i.e. Received Pronunciation) or very
specific city accents (such as Cockney, Liverpool, Mancunian)
are less appropriate.

STYLE OF MUSICAL: Concept musical.

VOCAL SET-UP/MUSICAL TIPS

1. This song should be delivered almost entirely in a Speech
quality. Because there are so many words in the verses, it

can be hard for the audience to comprehend some of the complex ideas you are saying. By minimising the amount of thyroid tilt you use, and staying in a horizontal position, you will find that the sense of the lyric becomes clearer for the audience.

2. In the verses you can add variety to the Speech set-up by making use of aspirate onsets. This will help give these sections a breathy, excited quality, which reflects Jack's mood when describing his adventure.

3. During the choruses your singing should be more legato to reflect the sweeping melody. Remain in a Speech quality for these sections but run the vowels together and sing longer phrases.

4. When you get to each of the top notes of the choruses, try delivering them in an Advanced-Speech quality. Use torso anchoring for these moments rather than adding too much thyroid tilt, as this will keep the conversational quality of the song in the upper register rather than allowing it to sound too 'sung' and beautiful, which is not appropriate.

5. Sondheim, more than any other musical-theatre composer (with the possible exception of Bernstein), provides great detail in terms of dynamics. Search the score for all of the changes in volume, the crescendos, etc. These provide great clues to aid your interpretation.

Sheet Music

The correct sheet music for this song is available at www.musicnotes.com.

'I Don't Remember Christmas' from *Starting Here, Starting Now*

Music by David Shire, lyrics by Richard Maltby Jr.

Choose this song if: you are an actor who can connect to emotive and confrontational material. Because the song sits in a comfortable Speech register, it suits actors who sing.

Given Circumstances

Note: As *Starting Here, Starting Now* is a revue show, rather than a musical, it does not have a through-narrative. The given circumstances below, though derived from the lyric, are therefore meant as a suggestion and could be altered to suit your needs.

WHO ARE YOU: Mark, an angry, heartbroken young professional in your early thirties.

WHERE ARE YOU: In the kitchen of your apartment in New York City, USA.

WHEN IS IT: 8.00 p.m., a Monday, March, after a long day in the office, present day.

WHAT HAS HAPPENED BEFORE: Just over a year ago you meant a girl named Emily on a rainy day in Central Park. There was a strong initial mutual attraction, you got chatting to each other and you asked her to go on a date with you. Soon you became involved in a whirlwind love affair. The relationship progressed very quickly and last Easter you introduced Emily to your family. Shortly afterwards she moved in to your apartment. During the summer months the relationship was all you had ever hoped for, you felt happy, content and hopeful for the future. During this period you went on a two-week holiday in Bermuda, which was perhaps the most joyful period in your relationship.

In the autumn, your relationship settled into more of a regular, mundane routine after the romantic highs of the first few months. Even though Emily was still happy, you worried that the loss of intensity in the relationship meant that there was something wrong. You began to put too much pressure on her and tensions between you became apparent. At Thanksgiving this reached a crisis point and you broke down. You confided that you were feeling insecure and that you were afraid of losing her. After opening up – and receiving reassurances from her – you felt more certain about the future of the relationship, though some doubts still lingered in the back of your mind.

On Christmas Eve you proposed and Emily accepted. That night you made love on the sheepskin rug in the living room. You were delighted, but what you were unaware of was that your new fiancée was already having an affair with your best friend, Jack.

It is now early January and last Tuesday you were feeling sick, so returned home early from work. To your great shock you walked in on Emily and Jack having sex on the same sheepskin rug. There was an altercation between you and Jack, which ended with you punching him. Emily moved out that evening.

Over the past week there have been several painful conversations between you and Emily. At times you have been aggressive and insulting towards her, at others you begged her to come back. Yesterday she messaged you to say she would be coming to collect the last of her belongings tonight. She arrived at the flat about thirty minutes ago, since when she has been packing. You have been trying to control your temper and be calm and reasonable in your behaviour towards her, but now you are longing to pick an argument.

WHO ELSE IS THERE: Emily.

WHO SHOULD YOU SING TO: Emily.

Textual Analysis

At the beginning of the song you walk in from the bedroom. You had previously gone in there to try to calm down, but your anger boiled up and you came back into the kitchen to confront Emily. In the first verse your objective is: to convince Emily that you have moved on. You want her to believe that you are no longer hurting. You tell her that over the last few days you had been haunted by her moving out but now, for the first time, you are over the break-up.

In the first chorus your objective is to remind Emily of the intimate times you have shared together during summer, autumn and particularly Christmas. Throughout the song you say repeatedly that you don't remember any of these past events. In actuality, you clearly recall each of these moments – in great detail. By saying that these memories have been wiped from your recollection you are, in a perverse manner, forcing Emily to recall them. You want her to feel guilty for being false in love, as you believe she made an unspoken promise of commitment in each of these moments, which she has now broken. You want her to recall the intimate moments you shared, in order to make her feel bad.

In the second verse, you return to your theme of telling Emily that for the first time you feel you have moved on. Again, this is incredibly sarcastic, and reveals that you haven't let go of your anger towards her at all. By referring to the sheepskin rug you draw her attention to the scene of her ultimate betrayal of your relationship. Your objective here is: to make her feel ashamed. In the second chorus you force her to recall some of your most romantic moments: meeting her for first time in Central Park, introducing her to your family. You do this in order to make her suffer.

In the bridge you reveal the internal struggles you have been having since the break-up. Your objective in this section is: to reveal that a part of you wants to let her go without being difficult. This attempt to be reasonable soon dissipates and after the bridge you return to the objective of trying to force

Emily to recall all the romantic moments you shared. As these become more and more personal, private and painful, you are increasing the pressure on her to feel ashamed. You are taking revenge.

1. The song is dependent on you having identified the memories of the character. Ensure you have a defined image for each of the past events you mention, for example: meeting on a rainy day in Central Park.

2. The hard, samba bassline of the verses and chorus is a reflection of your inner tempo – you are wound up and agitated.

3. The song is very intense and quite aggressive. Because of the confrontational choices required, it is therefore not a song that works well when delivered directly to the panel. Instead, sing to an imaginary Emily situated behind the audition table.

4. To avoid the song becoming one-dimensional, ensure you find actions that aren't simply attacking. Try playing: to mock, patronise, ridicule and satirise.

Vocal and Musical Analysis

WHO TO LISTEN TO: George Lee Andrews on the original New York cast recording (1977).

VOCAL RANGE: C3 to E4.

ORIGINAL KEY: A minor.

ACCENT: General American.

STYLE OF MUSICAL: Contemporary musical (pop-based).

VOCAL SET-UP/MUSICAL TIPS

1. This song is written to be delivered for the most part in a Speech quality. You should aim to make your vocal performance as conversational as possible. To achieve this, use a mix of glottal, aspirate and simultaneous onsets and avoid too much thyroid tilt.

2. In the bridge make your phrasing more legato. To achieve this, use simultaneous onsets and try to run the vowels together. This helps reflect the calmer, more reasonable lyric. As you approach the end of the bridge, and you begin to become confrontational once more, gradually take the thyroid tilt out to effect a crescendo (as you repeat the words 'forget her').

3. At the start of the chorus that follows the bridge (when you say you don't remember crying), you should suddenly sing much quieter. This is the most vulnerable lyric, so try raising the larynx and using thin vocal folds to produce a Cry quality at this point.

4. In the final section, that begins with you saying you don't remember laughing, you need to gradually grow in vocal intensity until you reach a peak on the last line. Begin this segment by using Speech with an aspirate onset and clipping the notes very short. This will make your delivery very quiet and intense. As you begin to crescendo, change to a simultaneous onset and then gradually take out the thyroid tilt. This will take you into a Speech quality and you will now be singing quite loudly. Finally, add torso anchoring on the last line to provide a final lift in volume.

Sheet Music

The correct sheet music for this song is available at www.sheetmusicdirect.com.

'If You Can Find Me, I'm Here'
from *Evening Primrose*

Music and lyrics by Stephen Sondheim

Choose this song if: you have a rich baritone voice and want to explore an excited, quirky, offbeat character.

Given Circumstances

WHO ARE YOU: Charles Snell, a brave, romantic and idealistic poet.

WHERE ARE YOU: Inside a large, strange, magical Manhattan department store inhabited by a group of mysterious people who only come out once the doors are closed and all of the customers have left.

WHEN IS IT: 9.05 p.m., winter, 1966.

WHAT HAS HAPPENED BEFORE: For many years, a mysterious group of hideaways have been living in secret in the department store. The eldest, Mrs Monday, has dwelt there since the financial crash of 1897, though most of the inhabitants moved into the store following the Wall Street Crash of 1929. For various reasons they all wanted to escape from the outside world. The only way the group can remain in the store is if their existence remains a total secret. If anyone threatens to reveal the group's existence – like a night-time burglar, for example – then that person is visited by group of sinister apparitions known as the Dark Men, who turn them into a mannequin. (This will eventually be your fate when you try to escape with a member of the group, Ella, with whom you fall in love and who wants to abscond to the outside world.)

Today you slipped into the department store just before closing time. Despairing at the constant interruptions to your writing by unwanted acquaintances and annoying neighbours, you had burnt all your existing poetry and decided you would live secretly in the department store, where you feel you will be able to write new work as you think you will be inspired and free from distractions. You feel you have been waiting all your life for an adventure, and this could be it.

A few moments ago the last of the customers left and the doors of the department store were shut. You stepped out from your hiding place to check that you were indeed alone.

WHO ELSE IS THERE: You are alone.

WHO SHOULD YOU SING TO: In the verses you sing to the people who have been previously disturbing your creativity – your unwanted friends, neighbours and landlords. In the choruses you should sing to yourself.

Textual Analysis

Note: The beginning of this song is spoken in rhythm, and though it is very well written it is not really appropriate for audition, as it takes too long before the panel get to hear you sing. Therefore this section should be cut and you should start from the point that you sing the word 'goodbye' in the lyric, using the preceding four bars of instrumental music as an introduction. The description below assumes you have made that cut.

During the musical introduction you are simmering with excitement as you realise that your plan to move into the store has been successful. Thinking of the life you have left behind, you start to address the people in the outside world that you have managed to flee. Your objective in this first verse is: to taunt them with the success of your escape. Appropriate actions might include: to tease, ridicule, heckle, provoke and torment them.

In the first chorus you now talk to yourself for the first time. Your objective in this section is: to indulge yourself in the fantasy of your new life. You revel in the freedom that you will now have to write, and in the great assortment of products from the store that will now be your possessions.

Your objective in the second verse is similar to the first: to bid farewell to those who have been disturbing your creative processes. This prompts feelings of revelry and abandon. In the second chorus your objective is once again to delight in your newfound freedom and the wonderful products at your disposal.

In the third and final verse your attention turns for the last time to the outside world. Your objective here is a harsh one: to let those outside the department store suffer the barbarity of the real world. In the last few lines you taunt those people, by inviting them to come and visit you in the department store once their suffering is over, as long as they can find you first.

KEY MOMENTS/TOP TIPS

1. In the verses, you speak to a selection of people who are not present. To make this clear, it is possible to approach the acting task in two ways. You can address a number of points in the third circle of attention to portray the sense of talking to lots of different people; as though addressing a crowd. Alternatively you can sing different thoughts to the various members of the panel, as though they are the unwanted distractions to your writing process. It is valid to use either or both options in your performance.

2. The song requires a very quick internal tempo. Give yourself permission to move freely and joyously in the space if and when you feel such an impulse.

3. There are many references to the merchandise in the shop. Have a clear understanding of the layout of the shop. You must see the shelves of books, the shoe department, etc., in your imagination so you can refer to them.

4. The music indicates where the peaks of excitement that Charles is feeling occur. Embrace what the score is revealing, so, for example, the wonderful release that occurs when you sing about pianos and shoes must be matched with a great sense of freedom and playfulness in your acting choices.

5. It is crucial to understand the metaphor of the piece, that at times as artists we have a desire to escape from the harsh realities of the outside world, but to be truly creative you must be a part of the world, not apart from it.

Vocal and Musical Analysis

WHO TO LISTEN TO: Neil Patrick Harris on the Nonesuch Studio recording (2001).

VOCAL RANGE: A2 to F♯4.

ORIGINAL KEY: F major.

ACCENT: General American.

STYLE OF MUSICAL: Concept musical.

VOCAL SET-UP/MUSICAL TIPS

1. The fundamental vocal set-up for this song is a Speech quality, with a little twang added to the sound.

2. Even though the song has a conversational feel, you should look to observe the long legato phrases. To achieve this, use simultaneous, rather than glottal, onsets wherever possible to avoid breaking up the musical sentences.

3. With the repeated top notes on the word 'here' near the end of the song, it can be tricky to achieve the desired volume to give the song its suitable final crescendo. This is because these notes (E5) are too low to belt in the male voice. To therefore achieve the required volume, avoid pushing the sound. Instead keep the tip of the tongue behind the bottom front teeth, the sides of the tongue against the upper molars, and tighten the AES to add twang to the sound.

Sheet Music

The correct sheet music for this song is available at www.musicnotes.com.

'The Kite'
from *You're a Good Man, Charlie Brown*

Music and lyrics by Clark Gesner

Choose this song if: you are interested in playing youthful roles, and excel at physical and comedic storytelling. The song sits comfortably in a baritone register.

Given Circumstances

WHO ARE YOU: Charlie Brown, a shy, nervous, underconfident five-year-old schoolboy, who always seems to be prone to failure and misfortune.

WHERE ARE YOU: A local playing field.

WHEN IS IT: 4.45 p.m., April Fool's Day, present day.

WHAT HAS HAPPENED BEFORE: This morning you were running late. On your way to school, your friends and peers were debating your various qualities and attributes. Although they agreed you were 'a good man', they noted your various faults, such as your clumsiness and lack of confidence. Your bossy schoolmate, Lucy van Pelt, described you as having a 'failure face'. You decided that you were sick of feeling like a loser and that you wanted your life to improve, so you resolved to have one more go at trying to fly your kite (something you had been attempting, and failing to do, for some time).

At school during the lunchbreak you sat alone – as you always do – eating peanut butter. Whilst you were eating, you spotted a beautiful redheaded girl that you had been attracted to for some time. Thinking that she could never be interested in someone like you, when she looked over in your direction you responded by covering your head in a paper bag so as to make yourself invisible. This left you feeling incredibly foolish, so you resolved once more to get your kite to fly in order to make yourself feel better.

After school, Lucy played an April Fool's trick on you by convincing you that the redheaded girl wanted to kiss you. Perhaps motivated by the feelings of embarrassment this provoked, you picked up your kite from your house and made your way to the nearby playing field. You have just arrived with an air of determination.

WHO ELSE IS THERE: You are alone.

WHO SHOULD YOU SING TO: Yourself. In audition, though, it is useful to address some of the thoughts to the panel, as if they are your inner-consciousness.

Textual Analysis

At the beginning of the music the imaginary kite should be in your hands. To make this clear, you should try to mime as if you are holding it and look down at the kite as if it is something that troubles you. During the first verse you are thinking about the lessons learned from your previous failed attempts to get it to fly. Your objective is: to remind yourself of the key points for successfully flying a kite. There is a moment at the end of this verse when you say 'whoops'. This indicates that at that moment that you suffer a minor setback, or accident. Try exploring physically what this might be. You might trip up on a bump in the ground, or fall because you stand on your shoelaces. Whatever choice you make needs to be thoroughly rehearsed so it is safe, clear and credible. It should also be funny. After this minor mishap your intention changes for the second verse. Your objective is now: to convince yourself to slow down and be more careful. You might mime some activity with the kite at this point, such as laying it cautiously on the floor.

In the bridge, try addressing the panel directly. Your objective in this section should be: to get the panel to agree that the bad luck you suffer is unfair. After this brief outburst, where you probably forget about the kite for a moment, you return to your main task. In the third verse your objective is: to remind yourself to stop talking and to get on with it. You might mime another activity at this point – like winding the string – to show you are back on track. During this verse you address the kite directly, you challenge it for refusing to fly. Towards the end of this section you should mime picking the kite up.

After you have said 'why not fly' the key event of the song occurs – where you launch the kite into the air and it begins to fly. After this takes place, your objective is: to convince yourself that the kite is really flying. You have failed so many times before that you think you might be hallucinating. Through the remainder of the song you need to mime the kite being airborne. To make this clear to the panel, try holding your hands about thirty centimetres apart, as if your right hand is on the spindle and the left is a little higher up on the string. Then look upwards to where the kite would be and imagine it being in the sky. Finally, after the kite catches the breeze, your objective is: to revel in your success.

KEY MOMENTS/TOP TIPS

1. As suggested, the kite-flying should to be mimed. To do this successfully you first need to gain a good understanding of the physical processes involved. If you have never flown a kite, there are videos you can watch on YouTube to help you get a sense of what occurs when you first get a kite to take off, and what happens when it is in the air.

2. The frenetic accompaniment of the verses is a clue to how you should shape your performance: Charlie is rushing the activities and making mistakes because of it. Work with a highly strung inner tempo, but still ensure your physical actions are defined – the panel must be clear what you are doing at all times.

3. As Charlie Brown was originally a comic-strip character, a heightened and exaggerated performance is stylistically appropriate.

4. In the show the kite crashes at the very end. This is very difficult to make clear, and not necessary in audition. It

also shows off your vocal abilities more successfully to sustain the last note instead, as you joyfully watch the kite soar into the air.

Vocal and Musical Analysis

WHO TO LISTEN TO: Anthony Rapp on the Broadway revival cast recording (1999).

VOCAL RANGE: B♭2 to E♭4 (with possible extension to G4).

ORIGINAL KEY: E♭ major.

ACCENT: General American.

STYLE OF MUSICAL: Contemporary musical (pop-based).

VOCAL SET-UP/MUSICAL TIPS

1. The introduction on the sheet music is too long for audition purposes. Cut the first four bars to leave a two-bar introduction.

2. The song should be delivered predominately in a Speech quality. To get the correct vocal style also add some twang to this set-up.

3. As a 'patter' song you need to work particularly hard on producing clear end consonants, so the text is communicated. On the suggested recording you can hear this being demonstrated on words such as 'tack' and 'slack'.

4. The point that Charlie thinks that he should wait a minute – and the kite first begins to fly – needs to be marked with a clear vocal change, as this is the event of the song. Try making these couple of lines much quieter, and perhaps use some aspirate onsets to create a sense of intensity. Once the kite catches the breeze, Charlie becomes exhilarated and this is reflected in the music. Sing the remainder of the song with simultaneous onsets and long, expansive legato phrases to mirror his joy.

5. In the score the last note on the word 'kite' is not notated, as in the show it is not intended to be sung at all. For audition purposes you should sing the word on a high E♭ for the last four bars. (This note is the one Rapp sings on the suggested recording.) If you wanted to show more range you could begin this last note on the E♭, hold it for two bars, then flip to the high G a third above it for the last two bars.

Sheet Music

The correct sheet music for this song is available at www.musicnotes.com.

'Use What You Got' from *The Life*

Music by Cy Coleman, lyrics by Ira Gasman

Choose this song if: you enjoy playing the charming, charismatic lowlife. The suggested version of the song sits mainly within the male speech register and is relatively easy vocally, so it suits the actor who sings.

Given Circumstances

WHO ARE YOU: Jojo (full name Joseph P. Morse), an opportunistic, manipulative pimp in his forties.

WHERE ARE YOU: A run-down side street near 42nd Street and 8th Avenue, next to the Port Authority Bus Terminal, New York City, USA. You are stood in a part of the street that was once a demolished structure, 'a missing tooth in the row of buildings'.

WHEN IS IT: 10.30 p.m., a busy, warm summer evening, 1980. (*Note*: The script denotes the scene as being set in the early morning, but this refers to the dialogue that precedes the song.)

WHAT HAS HAPPENED BEFORE: At the beginning of the show, on a grey morning in the late 1980s, you returned to this street for the first time in many years. As the narrator of the story you introduced yourself to the audience as the Vice President of Eros Entertainment, a company that makes erotic films. Although you are now wealthy and successful, you explained that once you were on the bottom rung of life's ladder. Remembering this time in your past, you began to take the audience back in time and explain what this area was like back during the night-time in the year 1980, when you were still a lowly street hustler. With your descriptive powers you began to conjure up the pimps, prostitutes and other denizens of the street who were a part of your world at the start of the decade.

After introducing the audience to your then business partner, Lou Pollack, you explained that you used to be a 'talent scout' for new prostitutes. You have just decided to give the audience a lesson about the life of a hustler.

WHO ELSE IS THERE: You are alone.

WHO SHOULD YOU SING TO: The audience (panel).

Textual Analysis

The introduction to the song is relatively long, but necessary, as it sets the musical tone of the piece. To make full use of this jaunty beginning you should play an objective during these opening four bars: to get the audience to gather round. Try starting at the back of the room, and then walk a few paces forward into the centre of the room, as this can give the song an arresting physical beginning.

The first unit of the song is a long one and comprises the first verse, first chorus and second verse. Your objective in this section is: to persuade the audience that in your profession you must grab your opportunities. You want them to comprehend that chances in life are fleeting, so they must be ruthless and make the most of any that come along.

You are a persuasive crook and take great pleasure in the mastery of your audience. During the second chorus your intention changes and your mood becomes darker. In this section your objective is: to convince the audience to be selfish and to use other people to get ahead, even if they are their friends. At this point you might use actions such as: I threaten, challenge and intimidate the audience to reveal this more sinister side of your personality. Having delivered what you believe to be a compelling case, in the final few lines, after you ask a rhetorical question about what a friend is for, your objective becomes: to convince the audience to follow your philosophy from now on. You want to recruit them.

1. In the cast recording there are sections for the ensemble which should be cut for audition purposes. The published vocal selections contain a solo version of the song (see below).

2. Jojo has a great deal of appeal and magnetism, despite his unsavoury lifestyle and point of view. Try using actions such as: I charm, amuse, attract, flatter, entertain, mesmerise and titillate in the long first unit.

3. In the first verse you refer to the audience as 'suckers'. This is a fun idea to play with: that you view them as gullible and foolish, and to be taken advantage of.

4. Low-status characters are often quite guarded and can sometimes have a shifty, twitchy physicality. In preparation for your performance, try observing real people who move in this manner and explore using aspects of their movements as a basis for a physical transformation. This will help your performance come across as authentic, and not too performative. Yes, Jojo is a charmer, but in the end he is of the street. Explore the idea that, underneath, his sense of self-worth is not as strong as it seems. Mix the physicality of the showman with that of the weasel.

Vocal and Musical Analysis

WHO TO LISTEN TO: Sam Harris on the original Broadway cast recording (1998).

VOCAL RANGE: $C3$ to $F\sharp4$.

ORIGINAL KEY: The original key is $C\sharp$ minor, though in this instance I would recommend performing the song in A minor, which is the key of the song in the published vocal selections from the show. This key is much easier to read and play for the audition pianists, and sits more comfortably within a baritone range. It also cuts out the ensemble sections. (The vocal range shown above is for the A minor version, which is four semitones higher in $C\sharp$ minor.)

ACCENT: New York.

STYLE OF MUSICAL: Contemporary musical (pop-based).

VOCAL SET-UP/MUSICAL TIPS

1. The song should primarily be delivered in a Speech quality. Try making the material as conversational as possible by half-speaking some words and making use of glottal and aspirates onsets at times for emphasis.

2. Cy Coleman's music is heavily influenced by jazz. To achieve this style you can afford to sing quartertones (notes that sit somewhere in between two notes on the piano), include pitch-glides up to notes, 'fall off' the pitch at the ends of notes, and include some jazz riffs. You can hear examples of all of the above in Sam Harris's performance.

3. Note that in the verses the majority of the notes at the ends of phrases are short. Ensure that you don't extend them unnecessarily, as this punchy phrasing helps give the lyric its bite.

4. Explore using legato phrasing as you progress through the key change. Allied with bending the pitch of some notes, this can help you sound like the smarmy manipulator.

5. When you sing the lyric about the clock of life ticking on, try half-whispering those words – as Harris does on the suggested recording – to help portray that this is a warning about how short life is.

6. On the higher notes the song moves into an Advanced-Speech position. Add some torso anchoring and a little thyroid tilt to help you achieve these notes safely.

7. As the published sheet music differs in places from the soundtrack it is strongly advised that you rehearse this particular song with a pianist before your audition.

Sheet Music

The correct sheet music for this song is available at
www.musicnotes.com.

CONTEMPORARY UP-TEMPO

'I Wanna Go Home'
from *Big The Musical*

Music by David Shire, lyrics by Richard Maltby Jr.

Choose this song if: you suit youthful, naive roles and have a flair for comedy. The song is relatively simple, both musically and vocally, so works well for an actor who sings.

Given Circumstances

WHO ARE YOU: Josh Baskin, a shy, introspective twelve-year-old boy who is struggling with his adolescent feelings, particularly how to relate to girls. You are slightly short for your age.

WHERE ARE YOU: In the Port Authority Bus Terminal (the largest bus station in the world), New York City, USA.

WHEN IS IT: Just after midnight, winter, 1987.

WHAT HAS HAPPENED BEFORE: Yesterday you were at your local hangout with your friend Billy. The pair of you were practising a hip-hop routine that you had copied off MTV when a group of girls came over. Amongst them was a thirteen-year-old called Cynthia Benson. For a reason you couldn't understand at the time (you were attracted to her), you found that you were speechless in her presence.

After the girls had left, Billy tried to convince you that Cynthia really liked you and gave you advice about how to chat to girls. That evening was the local carnival and Billy told you that Cynthia would be going alone. He encouraged you to attend and to ask Cynthia to be your girlfriend, but you were reluctant. Eventually, after your parents agreed to give Billy and yourself money for the Wild Thunder roller coaster, you decided to go.

At the carnival you were in the queue for the roller coaster when you noticed Cynthia standing just behind you. With

Billy encouraging you, you had just plucked up the courage to speak to her when a sixteen-year-old called Derek came over and put his arm around her. When you reached the front of the queue, you watched the pair going on the roller coaster together – whilst you were embarrassed at being turned away for being too short.

Feeling despondent, you began to wander the carnival alone until you happened upon a deserted, antique arcade. Inside was a strange and magical slot machine containing the head of a devil and with the writing 'Zoltar Speaks' written across the top. After you put a coin in the slot, the machine came to life and asked you to make a wish. In response you asked to be big. When you then saw that the machine wasn't plugged in, you realised something was very strange, became scared and ran home.

The next morning you woke to find that your wish had come true and you had been magically transformed into a thirty-five-year-old man, even though you still felt exactly like a child inside. In a state of panic you tried to avoid being caught by your mother, but she saw you and chased you from the house, thinking that you were a trespasser. After tracking down Billy, you managed to convince him of the reality of the situation. He suggested that the only solution was to go to New York City and find another carnival, where you would be able to locate a Zoltar machine and wish yourself back to normal (which is what eventually occurs).

About twenty minutes ago you both arrived in New York at the Port Authority Bus Terminal. An arcade manager told you that it would be three or four weeks before the next carnival. Billy said that he couldn't wait that long, but encouraged you to enjoy this opportunity, as it would be your chance to lead a grown-up life. He has just taken the bus back to New Jersey, leaving you alone in the bus terminal.

WHO ELSE IS THERE: You are in the bus shelter, so there are passers-by around (notably a man with a knife, and a woman with a beard), but you are far enough away from anyone else that no one can hear you.

COMEDY/CHARACTER

WHO SHOULD YOU SING TO: Sometimes you are singing to yourself, at other times you are addressing Fate.

Textual Analysis

During the introduction you are feeling very frightened, because you are alone in this huge, intimidating bus station. You immediately try to overcome your fears, so in the first verse your objective becomes: to convince yourself that being left alone is a positive experience. This is disrupted when you spot a man with a knife. This event changes your objective, so when you sing the title lyric you start appealing to Fate, rather than speaking to yourself. Your objective in this moment is: to get Fate to send you home. (This objective is repeated each time the title lyric is sung.)

The second verse follows a similar shape to the first. You begin by trying to convince yourself that you are on an exciting adventure, but when you spot a woman with a beard you immediately lose faith in this idea and implore Fate to send you back to New Jersey.

With your attempts to cheer yourself up failing, during the bridge you try to persuade Fate that you are blameless, that your adventure has already gone on quite long enough, and therefore couldn't you be allowed to return home now? Your objective in this section is therefore: to convince Fate that it is time to end your adventure.

Despite your best efforts, by this point Fate has not responded to your pleas, so you begin to talk to yourself once more at the start of the third verse. By pretending that you are in *Star Trek*, you try to convince yourself that what is happening is fun. Your objective is: to turn the situation into a game, in order to make it less frightening.

This attempt fails miserably, and you are left feeling upset and abandoned. So during the final section you once again try to get Fate to send you back. Your objective at this point is: to convince Fate how much you miss home.

KEY MOMENTS/TOP TIPS

1. In the first two verses you should make clear decisions about where the man with the knife and the girl with the beard are stood. Try placing them as if they are standing in opposite corners of the room, either side of the panel. If you look in their direction in a frightened manner as you sing about them, then turn your head sharply towards the panel on the note in the right hand of the piano that immediately precedes the next lyric, this can be very amusing. This technique of sharing a reaction as an aside to the audience is often seen in comedy, and can be fun to play with.

2. For the next two verses, try exploring positive actions, such as: I uplift, cheer, motivate, vitalise and brighten myself.

3. In the bridge, try appealing directly to the panel, as though they are Fate and therefore have the power to send you back to your family.

4. During the third verse, enjoy playing with an almost comic-book physicality and playfulness as you imagine being in *Star Trek*. You might pretend to hide, or aim your imaginary raygun, for example.

COMEDY/CHARACTER

Vocal and Musical Analysis

WHO TO LISTEN TO: Daniel H. Jenkins on the original Broadway cast recording (1996).

VOCAL RANGE: A♭2 to E4.

ORIGINAL KEY: C major.

ACCENT: General American.

STYLE OF MUSICAL: Contemporary musical (pop-based).

1. The introduction is slightly too long and repetitive for an audition. You should therefore cut the first couple of bars to leave a two-bar introduction.

2. The verses should be delivered in a Speech quality, but because the song is delivered in a General American accent, the back of the tongue should be raised, as it would be when speaking in that accent.

3. The bridge should be delivered in an oral Twang quality. Make this section more legato than the verses and run the vowels together.

4. The final section should be the quietest part of the song. Thin your vocal folds and raise the larynx to achieve this.

5. If possible, you should deliver the last note in a Cry quality, so it sounds sweet and vulnerable. If you find this difficult to achieve, explore doing this final note in a Falsetto quality. For this choice to be successful you need to make the preceding lines very quiet indeed, and really thin your vocal folds, so the transition between qualities isn't noticeable.

Sheet Music

The correct sheet music for this song is available at www.musicnotes.com.

'Larger Than Life'
from *My Favorite Year*

Music by Stephen Flaherty, lyrics by Lynn Ahrens

Choose this song if: you are a strong character actor with a
contemporary musical-theatre voice who enjoys narrative
songs and engaging directly with the panel.

Given Circumstances

WHO ARE YOU: Benjy Stone, an eager, idealistic, twenty-year-
old freshman sketch-writer, who writes for a television variety
show called *The King Kaiser Comedy Cavalcade.*

WHERE ARE YOU: The writers' office for *The King Kaiser
Comedy Cavalcade* in the RCA (Radio Corporation of
America) building, New York City, USA.

WHEN IS IT: 10.10 a.m., a Monday morning, autumn, 1954.

WHAT HAS HAPPENED BEFORE: Martha Raye, a famous
Hollywood comedy actress, had been booked to appear on this
week's show. This morning you and the other writers
gathered in the office to plan the programme. However, King
– the host of the show – came into the office a few minutes
ago and told you that her appearance had been cancelled. She
was to be replaced by Alan Swann, a swashbuckling
Hollywood icon of the 1940s. No longer the star he was,
recently Swann had developed a reputation for being
something of liability, because of his alcoholism and
inappropriate appetite for women. The reaction amongst the
other writers about Swann's impending appearance was one
of disappointment. You didn't feel this way at all. You were
thrilled he was going to be on the show, and asked if you could
write the sketch for his appearance. As you were considered to
be too junior and inexperienced for this last-minute
assignment, your request was denied. An argument about who

should write the sketch then broke out between your fellow writers, Alice, Herb and Sy. They have just left the office arguing, leaving you alone. You turned to the audience and began talking to them.

WHO ELSE IS THERE: You are alone.

WHO SHOULD YOU SING TO: The audience (in this situation, the panel).

Textual Analysis

The fundamental reason you sing this song is to explain why you are so passionate about writing a sketch for Alan Swann. In order to do this, you decide to tell the audience a story from your childhood. During the introductory section you lay out the background for this story. Your objective here is: to get the audience to understand how your love affair with cinema began. You explain that it started with your uncle Morty.

When the main melody begins you provide a detailed description of the RKO. Your objective in this section is: to get the audience to picture the inside of the grand old cinema. You want them to understand how excited it made you feel.

Having relived these memories, in the first dialogue section you now want the audience to appreciate the startling effect that the heroic Swann had on you when you first saw him on screen. Your objective during this dialogue, and in the second chorus, is: to get the audience to idolise Swann, just as you did.

In the bridge the song changes significantly, and it becomes melancholy as you divulge your feelings about childhood. You explain that the reason you came to admire Alan Swann, and daydream about living in the world of his movies, was because your own father walked out on you when you were a child.

After this disclosure you quickly choose to break the atmosphere, and in the second dialogue section you reveal that you had a childhood daydream that Alan Swann was your real father. Your objective here is: to convince the audience of the plausibility of your fantasy. In the final chorus your objective is: to encapsulate for the audience why Swann was important to you growing up, which was because, unlike your father, he never ran away and was a constant presence in your life – if only on the cinema screen. This final section is aimed at your father. Try playing the following objective here: to make my father take responsibility for abandoning me.

KEY MOMENTS/TOP TIPS

1. In *My Favorite Year*, Benjy often addresses the audience directly as the narrator of the story. Therefore it is useful to think of the audience, or in this case the audition panel, as your confidants. They are like your closest friends who you can share your secrets with.

2. During the song, Benjy remembers images of what it was like inside the RKO cinema. Before you practise the song, it is useful to create a list of all of these images: the blue lights, the star-covered ceiling, the cinema organ, etc. Ensure you can clearly visualise each of these 'memories'. In performance you need to be able to switch quickly between picturing what you are describing in your imagination and making eye contact with the panel as you narrate the story.

3. Benjy should be an engaging and entertaining storyteller. Try actions such as: I excite, mesmerise, intrigue, thrill, fascinate, entertain and amuse the panel.

4. When you recount the words of Uncle Morty, try creating a physicality and voice for him, as if you are doing an impression of your uncle.

5. I still vividly remember the first time I saw this song delivered when I was sat on a professional audition panel. That audition left a lasting impression on me, and the performance really captured the attention of those behind

the table. It is possible for you to make a real impact with this song if you are an actor who can talk directly to the panel, and entertain and engage them with Benjy's story.

Vocal and Musical Analysis

WHO TO LISTEN TO: Evan Pappas on the original Broadway cast recording (1992).

VOCAL RANGE: E♭3 to F4.

ORIGINAL KEY: E♭ major.

ACCENT: General American.

STYLE OF MUSICAL: Contemporary musical (pop-based).

VOCAL SET-UP/MUSICAL TIPS

1. The beginning of the song should be in Speech quality. To achieve the vocal difference between Benjy's natural voice and his impression of Uncle Morty, try lowering your larynx for the latter. This helps portray the difference in age.

2. When you sing 'RKO' for the first time this, should have a dreamy, romantic quality, so try to make this phrase as legato as possible.

3. The main section of the song should be predominately sung in a Speech quality with a hint of twang added. As the song is narrative-driven, the words are doubly important, so take particular care to clearly produce the consonants at the ends of words.

4. When you sing about the Great Wall of China and the red rugs in the cinema, take careful note of the phrase marks on the music; Flaherty wants you to sing through these moments as one long, legato phrase.

5. Try to match the voice you use for the singing with the spoken dialogue so you sound like one person.

6. When you talk about your father going out for cigarettes and not returning, the song should become more melancholic. Try delivering this section in a Cry quality to reflect that. (The last two lines also merit a similar set-up as they are dreamy and reflective.)

7. The word 'maiden' should be the loudest of the song, so add torso anchoring at this moment to help you achieve that.

Sheet Music

The correct sheet music for this song is available at www.musicnotes.com.

COMEDY/CHARACTER

'Miracle of Miracles'
from *Fiddler on the Roof*

Music by Jerry Bock, lyrics by Sheldon Harnick

Choose this song if: you are a character actor with a legit voice who enjoys playing warm-hearted, lovable characters.

Given Circumstances

WHO ARE YOU: Motel, a poor tailor from the small village of Anatevka in Russia. You are a shy, underconfident young man in your early twenties who is always nervous of being shouted at. You are sweet, kind and loyal.

WHERE ARE YOU: In the yard outside Tevye's house. (*Note*: In the film version the song takes place in the woods nearby instead.)

WHEN IS IT: 12.30 p.m., a Sunday, spring, 1904 – the year before the Russian Revolution of 1905.

WHAT HAS HAPPENED BEFORE: For over a year you have been engaged to your childhood friend Tzeitel, the eldest daughter of Tevye, the milkman. The engagement, which was decided secretly between yourself and Tzeitel, flies against the traditions of your faith as marriages are usually arranged by the village matchmaker, Yente.

Until today you had hesitated to ask Teyve for Tzeitel's hand in marriage. You had feared he would turn you down on account of you being so poor. To try and remedy this situation, you had been saving for a new sewing machine. You hoped that when you were able to buy the machine, it would impress Tevye and show him that you had the means to support a wife and a family. However, matters changed radically when Yente came to visit the house a few days ago. She told Golde, Tzeitel's mother, that she had arranged a match for Tzeitel with Lazar Wolf, the wealthy butcher. Upon hearing this terrible news, on Friday night Tzeitel tried to browbeat you into asking Tevye for your hand before the family ate for the Sabbath, but your courage failed you and the question went unasked.

Last night Tevye met with Lazar Wolf at the inn, and over the course of a drunken evening agreed to give his daughter away. A few minutes ago, having awoken late with a hangover, Teyve told Tzeitel that he had reached an agreement with Lazar. Distraught, Tzeitel begged her father to change his mind. He was just beginning to relent when you ran into the yard. Having heard the news about the arranged marriage, you had rushed over to Tevye's house. With your chance to marry the one you love about to slip away, you found the courage you needed to stand up to Tevye and tell him how much you love his daughter. You promised him that if he let you marry her, you would never let her starve. Impressed that you had thrown off your cloak of timidity, and feeling that he would rather break with the tradition of the matchmaker than see his daughter unhappy, Tevye agreed to let you marry. With both yourself and Tzeitel feeling deliriously happy, Tevye has just left, leaving the pair of you alone.

WHO ELSE IS THERE: Tzeitel.

WHO SHOULD YOU SING TO: Tzeitel.

Textual Analysis

When you begin the song you are incredulous; you truly believe a miracle has taken place. So during the musical introduction you are not simply excited, you are also trying to come to terms with an unbelievable change of fortune. You are in shock. When the first chorus begins, your objective is therefore: to convince Tzeitel that a miracle has taken place. Although you don't manage to convince your future wife, she takes enormous pleasure in your happiness. During the second half of the chorus, the objective changes, because you now want Tzeitel to understand how frightened you were before you spoke to Tevye. But this is still a very light moment and your objective here is: to amuse Tzeitel with your account.

During the first bridge section, when you talk about Moses and the Pharaoh, your objective is: to convince Tzeitel that being allowed to marry her was the greatest of all miracles. This moment should be endearing and heartwarming.

When the main melody returns, a second chorus begins. In this part of the song your objective is: to get Tzeitel to rejoice at the miracle that has occurred. Your joy and enthusiasm should be infectious at this point. From the beginning of the second bridge, when you speak about David and Goliath, through to the end of the song, your objective is once more: to convince Tzeitel that this was the greatest of all miracles. As the song builds to its conclusion there should be a palpable sense that this has been a life-changing experience – and this shy young tailor has now grown up to be a man.

KEY MOMENTS/TOP TIPS

1. The key to this song is that Tzeitel, whilst overjoyed and surprised by Tevye's decision, does not believe that what occurred was one of God's miracles. By seeking to change her mind, and convince her that something miraculous has taken place, it will stop your acting through song straying into a generalised emotional state of joyous excitement.

2. In this song Motel is like an excitable jack-in-the-box. Allow your physicality to be very free and playful; don't be afraid to be bold in your use of the space – Motel can hardly stand still.

3. Motel is thinking very quickly during the song. In order to portray this successfully, you need to change action frequently. Your range of actions should be incredibly positive and uplifting, so try choices such as: I excite, animate, thrill, amuse, awaken, captivate, enliven and fascinate you.

4. Motel has spent his entire life being shy and on the back foot. He has been forced to constantly internalise his feelings, rather than speak out. As a consequence, this moment should be an exuberant discovery of a newfound self-confidence.

Vocal and Musical Analysis

WHO TO LISTEN TO: Leonard Frey on the film soundtrack (1971).

VOCAL RANGE: E3 to F♯4.

ORIGINAL KEY: D major.

ACCENT: Russian/Yiddish. In many productions, Motel is performed with a General American accent – including on the suggested recording – though of course there is no logical reason for this, beyond the fact that the musical was written by Americans. If you are struggling with the Russian/Yiddish accent you could copy this choice.

VOCAL SET-UP/MUSICAL TIPS

1. The first chorus should be delivered in a breathy Speech quality. The lyric is quite fast, so using aspirate onsets would give the start of the song a hushed, excited quality and also help to ensure the lyric is clearly comprehensible.

2. On the line about the lion's den you should affect a crescendo before returning to the breathy Speech quality on the next line. Achieve the crescendo by switching into a simultaneous onset for that line and removing your thyroid tilt.

3. The first bridge section should be broader, and more legato. Make more use of simultaneous onsets at this point and look to run the vowels together.

4. At the end of the first bridge – when you sing about all of God's miracles through to and including the line about

being like a lump of clay – you should sing in a Cry quality to make this moment more tender and reflective. During the last line of the section, when you sing about becoming a man today, you should then gradually remove the thyroid tilt to thicken your vocal folds and finish in a loud, rich Speech quality.

5. The second chorus should be in Speech quality. This time remove the aspirate onsets to make the sound fuller. This will help portray Motel's burgeoning self-confidence.

6. The second bridge should be sung in a similar manner to the first, but with legato phrasing. You should shout the word 'yes!' when singing about David and Goliath.

7. The penultimate line, when you tell Tzeitel that you thought your love could never be, should be sung as quietly as possible in Cry. Lift your larynx as high as you can at this point and really thin your vocal folds. During the final line remove all of your thyroid tilt, lower the larynx to a neutral position, and anchor your torso to end in a full, rich sound.

Sheet Music

The correct sheet music for this song is available at www.musicnotes.com.

'Premature'
from *A Slice of Saturday Night*

Music and lyrics by The Heather Brothers

Choose this song if: you are good at comedic roles and enjoy
playing the cocky, jack-the-lad teenager. The song is relatively
easy vocally and musically, so is suitable for an actor who
sings, yet still contains a relatively easy-to-achieve, but
impressive-sounding, Belt.

Given Circumstances

WHO ARE YOU: Gary, the alpha male of a group of young lads
in their late teens. You are a self-confident ladies' man who is
prone to delivering a cheesy chat-up line, and can be a bit of a
love rat.

WHERE ARE YOU: The Club-a-Go-Go, a run-of-the-mill club
in a small town somewhere in the commuter belt around
London.

WHEN IS IT: About 11.00 p.m., a Saturday night, summer,
1964.

WHAT HAS HAPPENED BEFORE: Shortly after 7.00 p.m. you
arrived at the club for your regular Saturday night out with
the lads, Ricky and Eddie. You have been dating a girl called
Sue, who is much put-upon, and who worries that she is not
skinny like the famous fashion model of the time, Twiggy.

As soon as you arrived, you started trying to chat up two
other girls named Penny and Bridget. Despite your cockiness
and self-confidence, you were unsuccessful in your
seductions. Ricky and Eddie were equally fruitless in their
efforts to pull any of the girls. Seeing all of this, Eric 'Rubber-
Legs' De Vene – the fatherly owner of the club – offered you
his advice on how to succeed with women.

COMEDY/CHARACTER

An hour or so ago, you secretly 'copped off' with a girl nicknamed Bang-Bang Bertha. Having discovered this, Sue finally found the courage to stand up to you and humiliated you in front of the rest of the girls. In response, you got hideously drunk with Eric, which resulted in you being sick in the toilets.

Fifteen minutes ago you managed to make up with Sue, when she fell for your ludicrous lie that, rather than kissing Bertha, you were in fact giving her mouth-to-mouth resuscitation. Taking the opportunity of this reconciliation, you managed to get Sue to agree to come outside to have sex with you. In your excitement you have just ejaculated in your pants before you could undo your trousers.

WHO ELSE IS THERE: Sue has just left, so you are alone.

WHO SHOULD YOU SING TO: The audience, so in this situation, the audition panel. Think of the audience being your best friends and confidants.

Textual Analysis

During the opening section of the song you are appealing to the panel. Your objective is: to get them to pity you. You want them to appreciate how hard you have tried to conquer your problem with premature ejaculation.

When the main tempo kicks in, you decide that, if you are to get the audience to sympathise with you, you need to tell them the full story. Your objective in this moment is: to get them to understand how difficult it is to avoid a premature ejaculation when a good-looking girl dances with you and then agrees to have sex. In telling this tale you should be a witty, entertaining and engaging storyteller. For example, when you talk about first meeting a girl and dancing with her, try acting out this encounter in a comedic way (by doing an impression of the girl and then dancing in a silly manner).

From the chorus onwards until the end of the song you publicly confess your feelings of despair and humiliation.

Although you can still address some thoughts to the panel, it should feel like you are appealing to Fate at this point. Your objective here is: to get Fate to take pity on you.

KEY MOMENTS/TOP TIPS

1. If the panel have never heard this song, then there is a good chance they will laugh when you sing the title lyric. To avoid giving away the joke in advance, introduce your song as its abbreviated title 'PE' when they ask you what you are going to sing.

2. One of the funniest moments is during the riff on the words 'oh no', as this is when the panel first realises what has happened to Gary. As you descend in pitch at the end of that phrase, try slowly looking down towards your crotch in despair. When you relive the embarrassment of this moment, it is the event of the song.

3. The song is, of course, comedic, but works best when the stakes are really high. The more Gary is in despair about his predicament, the funnier the material becomes.

4. Play around with the idea that your interactions with the panel are influenced by the gender of those behind the table, exactly as Gary would. For example, you could try flirting – in a very light and jovial manner – with the women, and confiding in any male panel members as though they are one of your gang of friends.

COMEDY/CHARACTER

Vocal and Musical Analysis

WHO TO LISTEN TO: David Easter on the original London cast recording (1990).

VOCAL RANGE: E3 to F4 (in the score the word 'slow' extends to G4, but this line is usually spoken rather than sung).

ORIGINAL KEY: F major.

356

ACCENT: General London/Estuary.

STYLE OF MUSICAL: Contemporary musical (pop-based).

VOCAL SET-UP/MUSICAL TIPS

1. The accent is really important in this song. The delivery should sound like an extension of the spoken voice, so allow the tongue position to be the same as if you were speaking in the accent, i.e. the back of the tongue moves up and down with the vowel shapes.

2. When you first say 'oh no', the music is a parody of a 1960s, Elvis-style riff. Enjoy playing around with the comedy of this.

3. The vocal line of this song benefits from interpretation, so don't feel you need to adhere rigidly to the rhythms notated in the score. As Easter does on the recording, let the delivery be informed by the rhythms you would use if you were speaking the lyric.

4. The last two words should be belted. There is a feeling that Gary is sharing his despair with the universe at this point. Use this to help you find the physical set-up for the Belt quality of lifting your chin and anchoring the torso, perhaps by using a strong gesture with your arms open wide.

Sheet Music

The correct sheet music for this song is available at www.scribd.com.

'The Phone Call'
from *Lucky Stiff*

Music by Stephen Flaherty, lyrics by Lynn Ahrens

Choose this song if: you enjoy playing highly strung, nervous, put-upon characters. The song requires a command of physical comedy and gives you the opportunity to show off a good vocal range.

Given Circumstances

WHO ARE YOU: Vincent (Vinnie) Di Ruzzio, an optometrist from Atlantic City, New Jersey, USA. You are a little uptight and like your life to be calm, orderly and within your own control. You don't respond well to dangerous or chaotic situations, as they cause you to panic, become irrational and lose your temper.

WHERE ARE YOU: At a telephone booth in Nice Airport, France.

WHEN IS IT: 9.30 p.m., a Friday evening, some time in the early 1990s, before mobile phones became commonplace.

WHAT HAS HAPPENED BEFORE: Your sister, Rita La Porta, came to visit you earlier this morning at your office in Atlantic City. She confessed that she had been having an affair with Tony Hendon, the manager of her husband Nicky's casino. She revealed that Tony and herself had embezzled six million dollars in diamonds from Nicky and were planning to elope to Europe. The previous night Rita had gone to visit Tony at his house and saw a woman leaving in the early hours of the morning. In a jealous temper she went into the house to confront Tony. The house was dark, and Rita – who is legally blind and who was not wearing her glasses – accidently shot dead a man whom she believed to be Tony Hendon. (Later in the show we find out she actually shot Luigi Gaudi, a friend

COMEDY/CHARACTER

358

of Tony's, and that the whole scheme had been an elaborate plot by Tony, who is actually alive and well.) Later, after reading an article in the Atlantic City newspaper, Rita discovered that 'Tony' had willed the six million dollars to his English nephew, Harry Witherspoon, on the strict condition that Harry take Tony's corpse (it is really Luigi's corpse) on one last holiday to Monte Carlo. Harry agreed to this unusual request and set off for Monte Carlo.

Rita then told you that Nicky had discovered that money had been disappearing from the casino, and that she had blamed this on you, saying that you lost the money gambling. Subsequently Nicky has a contract out on your life. On hearing this news, you reluctantly agreed to accompany Rita to Monte Carlo to track down Harry and the diamonds. Having jumped straight on a plane, with no time to pack, you have just arrived at Nice Airport, still in a state of shock, and have decided you need to call your wife to let her know where you are and what has happened.

WHO ELSE IS THERE: In the show, Rita is using the phone booth directly opposite. For the purposes of the audition you can perform the song as if you are alone, though it can be helpful to imagine that at times you are in earshot of either your sister or other people in the airport.

WHO SHOULD YOU SING TO: Your wife Mary-Alice, who is on the other end of the telephone.

Textual Analysis

When Mary-Alice first answers the phone you are very relieved, as you have been trying to get through to her for some time and are glad to finally hear her voice. As the phone connection is poor, your objective in the first couple of lines is: to check whether Mary-Alice can hear you. Once you realise that she can, your mood quickly turns into one of nervous apprehension, as you know Mary-Alice will not be at all pleased to hear that you won't be home for dinner. Your objective at this point is: to prepare Mary-Alice for bad news.

After you have told Mary-Alice that you won't be home for dinner, she starts to shout at you down the phone. The dynamic of your interactions at this stage should suggest that you are scared of your wife and are used to being yelled at whenever you displease her. Annoyed that you are not getting the sympathy that you deserve, your objective in the remainder of the first verse becomes: to get Mary-Alice to empathise with your plight. You are unsuccessful in this objective, as your wife simply laughs at you.

You are not at all happy that she is finding your predicament funny, so in the first chorus your objective becomes: to instruct Mary-Alice to cancel both dinner and all of the events in your diary, such as your work appointments. You should do this in a very melodramatic, attention-seeking manner.

During the four-bar instrumental, your wife reacts to your attempt to take control with a long tirade where she shouts at you once more. In response, at the start of the second verse, your objective becomes: to mock Mary-Alice for her outburst. She then begins to cry. At this point your anxiety grows as you slowly realise that, not only have you forgotten that today is her birthday, but that it is her fortieth. Your objective thus becomes: to apologise for missing her birthday. Despite this, as the number builds towards its climax, your exasperation grows as Mary-Alice fails to show any sympathy at all about your life being threatened. In the last four lines you completely lose your temper and experience a feeling of triumph when you once again assert that you won't be home for dinner. Your objective here is: to show Mary-Alice that you are the boss. This intention is completely undercut in the last line when Mary-Alice hangs up – leaving you feeling very foolish indeed.

KEY MOMENTS/TOP TIPS

1. This song is one of the rare occasions where I suggest you use a prop. I wouldn't advise you to inform the panel you

intend to do this, just have your mobile phone in your pocket and take it out just as you are about to sing. It is also a good idea to make sure it is switched off!

2. There is no introduction on the published sheet music, so you will need to ask the pianist to play a 'bell note' for you. The note you need to ask for is an A.

3. As discussed, at the beginning of the song there appears to be a bad connection. You should convey that you are struggling to hear Mary-Alice in the first two lines.

4. There is a lot of fun to be found by playing Vinnie's reactions to what Mary-Alice is saying on the other end of the line. You might become indignant when you realise she is laughing at you, for example. During the instrumental gaps there is comedy to be had from holding the phone away your ear (as if Mary-Alice's shouting is hurting your eardrums) before returning to the phone to ask if she has finished.

5. As the phone call takes place in a public place, you can at times play that you don't want the details of the conversation to be overheard. As Rita is in neighbouring telephone booth when you call her 'crazy', you may want to deliver this under your breath so as not to provoke her.

Vocal and Musical Analysis

WHO TO LISTEN TO: Stuart Zagnit on the York Theatre Company cast recording (2004).

VOCAL RANGE: D3 to F♯5.

ORIGINAL KEY: D major.

ACCENT: General American.

STYLE: Contemporary musical (pop-based).

VOCAL SET-UP/MUSICAL TIPS

1. This song should be delivered almost entirely in a Speech quality. You should modify this set-up by raising the back of the tongue and adding a little twang, to enable you to also realise the General American accent.

2. Towards the end of the song – on the higher notes that occur on the words 'answer', 'Mary-Alice' and 'won't' – you should add some torso anchoring. This helps support the voice as you move higher than is usual in a Speech quality.

3. The choruses are notable musically because they suddenly release into a bright march. Relish this musical flourish, as it marries with Vinnie's melodramatic behaviour.

4. The final time you assert that you won't be home for dinner you are extremely frustrated. To convey this, you may want to add some 'growl' to your voice. You can do this by adding a little false vocal-fold constriction.

Sheet Music

The correct sheet music for this song is available at www.musicnotes.com.

COMEDY/CHARACTER

www.nickhernbooks.co.uk

facebook.com/nickhernbooks

twitter.com/nickhernbooks